The Globalization of Nothing

To Sue, who is really something.

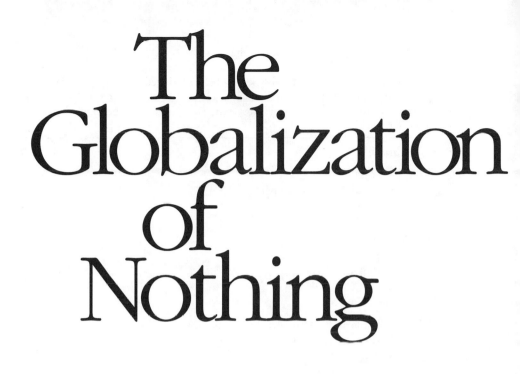

The
Globalization
of
Nothing

GEORGE
RITZER

University of Maryland

PINE FORGE PRESS
An Imprint of Sage Publications, Inc.
Thousand Oaks • London • New Delhi

For information:

 Pine Forge Press
A Sage Publications Company
2455 Teller Road
Thousand Oaks, California 91320
www.pineforge.com

Sage Publications Ltd.
6 Bonhill Street
London EC2A 4PU
United Kingdom

Sage Publications India Pvt. Ltd.
B-42, Panchsheel Enclave
Post Box 4109
New Delhi 110 017 India

Printed in the United States of America

Library of Congress Cataloging-in-Publication Data

Ritzer, George.
The globalization of nothing / George Ritzer.
    p. cm.
Includes bibliographical references and index.
ISBN 0–7619–8806–8 (cloth)—ISBN 0–7619–8807–6 (pbk.)
    1. Globalization. 2. Nothing (Philosophy) I. Title.
JZ1318 .R58 2003
303.48′2′01—dc21

                                        2003007016

03   04   05   06   10   9   8   7   6   5   4   3   2   1

Acquisitions Editor:	Jerry Westby
Editorial Assistant:	Vonessa Vondera
Production Editor:	Melanie Birdsall
Copy Editor:	Toni Williams
Typesetter:	C&M Digitals (P) Ltd.
Proofreader:	Kristin Bergstad
Indexer:	Kathy Paparchontis
Cover Designer:	Ravi Balasuriya
Production Artist:	Sandra Sauvajot

Contents

Preface

The main issue to be addressed in this book is, as the title indicates, the globalization of nothing. However, it is only part of a broader set of concerns that involves two types of globalization (and three subtypes of one of them) and their relationship not only to nothing, but also to something. In addition, four basic types of nothing and something are delineated, as are five continua to differentiate among and between them. A title that covered all of these complex relationships would have more accurately conveyed a sense of what this book is about, but its main point would have been obscured or lost. Thus, while our main concern is with the globalization of nothing, it must be remembered that this issue is only one aspect of a much larger set of dialectical relationships and concerns.

This book's main theses will greatly challenge the reader's thinking on a number of issues since many of its arguments are counterintuitive, counterfactual, and in some cases deeply troubling. We can start with the difficulties posed by the book's two central concepts—*globalization* and *nothing*.

First, everyone knows at least a few things about globalization and likely has strong feelings about it. The unique and challenging position articulated here on globalization is likely to upset at least part of this book's readership.

Second, although all readers know a bit about nothing (if, from nowhere else, *Seinfeld,* the television show famously about . . . nothing), devoting a large portion of a book to nothing must sound odd, if not reprehensible, in an era with so many pressing social and political problems. In fact, we will go to great lengths to demonstrate that nothing (as it is to be used in this book; see below) is far from nothing (as that term is conventionally used), that it is of great importance, and that it is, in some ways, an important social issue. Furthermore, as we will see, especially in the Appendix, there is a large and diverse literature on nothing and some of the greatest thinkers in the history of the world have thought, and written, about it.

Third, the combination of the two central terms—the *globalization of nothing*—also must be jarring and seem counterintuitive. After all, everything one reads these days indicates that globalization is something of great importance. However, as we will see, the basic argument to be made here is that the globalization of nothing is, indeed, important and its development and spread should be of great interest, significance, and concern to readers.

My focal interest in these pages is in the globalization of nothing within the realm of consumption, itself proliferating throughout the globe at a breathtaking rate. For example, supermarkets, chain stores of all sorts, shopping malls, and airports (sites that make possible the consumption of flights and in which, by the way, one increasingly finds shopping malls dominated by chain stores), among many other phenomena (for example, credit cards, Gap jeans, Gucci bags, ATMs, clerks at chain stores and their scripted ways of interacting with customers), can all be thought of as nothing in the way that concept will be used here, as obviously centrally involved in contemporary consumption and as being globalized extensively.

Consumption is clearly playing a growing role in the lives of people in developed countries and, to the extent that they can afford it, in less developed countries as well (although they are more likely to be producers of nothing than its consumers). To the degree that consumption is increasingly dominated by nothing, peoples' lives are similarly involved with nothing and to an increasing degree.

While this focus on consumption seems highly delimited, the fact is that many aspects of the social world usually not thought of in this way can be viewed as arenas of consumption. For example, although there is undoubtedly much more to hospitals, physicians, pharmaceuticals, and biotechnology, it is the case that patients can be seen as consumers of all of them. Similarly, education is not reducible to consumption, but students can be looked at as consumers of that which is provided by schools and educators. Thus, while this book adopts a limited focus on consumption, its reach is quite long because many areas of the social world can be examined, at least in part, through this lens. This means that it is not just everyday shopping that is increasingly dominated by nothing, but so, to at least some degree, is the consumption of things like health care and education. Specific assertions such as these, like this book's more general arguments, are likely to seem challenging, if not objectionable, to many readers. After all, to take one example, isn't modern medicine characterized by increasingly remarkable advances? Yes, but from the perspective of this book, it is *also* taking on more of the characteristics of nothing, sometimes *because* of such advances.

This book, at least its first three chapters and a good portion of the Appendix, can be seen as an effort to introduce the concept of nothing (and its globalization) to a broad readership. That idea actually has a long lineage in philosophy (in the work of such classic and more contemporary thinkers as Kant, Hegel, Heidegger, and Sartre) and in many other fields (literature, physics, mathematics), but the way nothing is used in those literatures is much different from the way it is used here.

While there are many different definitions of the concept of nothing, it will be employed here to mean *generally centrally conceived and controlled social forms that are comparatively devoid of distinctive substantive content*. Thus, for example, in the realm of consumption, the Mills corporation (and others like it) create and control shopping malls (e.g., Potomac Mills in Virginia, Sawgrass Mills in Florida, and Ontario Mills in California) as forms, as structures that, in themselves, have little, if any, distinctive content; the content of any given mall depends on what (particular shops, goods, restaurants, employees, customers, and so on) happens to be in it. A mall in one part of the world (say, London or Hong Kong) may be structured much like that in another location (Chicago or Mexico City, for example), but there will be innumerable differences in their specific contents. More important, people use the mall in innumerable ways, many of which may not have been anticipated by the mall designers and owners, and their behaviors will vary greatly in different parts of the globe.

With that meaning and example in mind, it will be argued that the United States, and the world more generally, are increasingly characterized by such forms, by nothing. While such an assertion sounds like a criticism, forms that are largely empty of social content are *not necessarily problematic*. Indeed, they have many advantages (e.g., convenience, efficiency) that are central to understanding why they have proliferated.

Four types of nothing are dealt with here: non-places, non-things, non-people, and non-services. Thus, people around the world are spending more time in *non-places* (the shopping mall, the Las Vegas casino) and with *non-things* (Old Navy T-shirts, Dolce and Gabbana dresses), *non-people* (the counter-people at Burger King, telemarketers), and *non-services* (those provided by ATMs, Amazon.com).

All of this acquires greater clarity when we realize that there is both a general something–nothing continuum and more specific subcontinua: places–non-places, things–non-things, people–non-people, services–non-services. Clearly, nothing in general, as well as the specific aspects of nothing of concern here, only make sense when they are seen as part of these continua and in relationship to something and its various forms. This means, of course, that something and nothing are relative concepts and one has no meaning without a sense of the other. Further complicating matters is that what is judged to be something (or nothing) will vary in terms of time and place. This book's analysis is embedded in a particular time (the early 21st century) and place (the developed world, especially the United States) and cannot easily be generalized to other times and places.

If, within the confines of this analysis, the shopping mall is an example of nothing, then we can think of a local farmers' market as something (flea markets, craft fairs, and co-ops are other examples). To this day, a farmers' market is created anew each time the farmers, who happen at that particular time to have produce to sell, arrive at the appointed place. There is no preset structure into which farmers must fit, although they may, by custom, sell particular things in particular spots. Which farmers are there, and what they offer for sale, will vary greatly from one time (especially season) to another. Most important, once the market has ended for the day, whatever structure has been created may be dismantled and then created again, perhaps somewhat differently, the next market day. And the farmers' market is no mere throwback to an earlier time period; it remains viable not only in many areas of the United States, but even more commonly in most other parts of the world, including the highly developed countries of western Europe.

While there is a dispassionate character to the analysis that follows in the body of this book—an effort to describe nothing and its relationship to something as objectively as possible—it is recognized from the outset that not only are there problems with such a modern (see below) disinterested approach, but that it is peoples' subjective definitions of the phenomena of concern here that are of greatest importance. Whether or not places, things, people, and services are characterized as nothing (or something), what ultimately matters is how people define them. Many of the phenomena that are seen from the point of view of this book as falling toward the nothing end of the continuum are, in fact, viewed by many people as something. We will need to address the nature of, and reasons for, this disparity.

However, this is not just, or even mainly, a book about nothing, but also nothing's proliferation around the world—the *globalization* of nothing. The basic argument is that globalization and nothing (at least in the sense of centrally conceived and controlled forms that are substantively largely empty) go hand in hand. By definition, it is easier to globalize that which is centrally conceived and controlled. Conversely, it is much more difficult to globalize that which is locally conceived and controlled. In addition, it is far easier to globalize largely empty forms than those that are loaded with content (although these days virtually everything is globalized, at least to some degree). The main reason is that that which has much content also offers much that has the potential not to fit into, even to conflict with, aspects of other cultures around the world; the more the content, the greater the chance that some phenomenon will not fit or be accepted. Ironically, however, we will see that empty forms have problems of their own in gaining and maintaining acceptance. Most important, cultures loaded with their own substantive content (and cultures always are) sometimes (perhaps depending on the nature of their content) have trouble accepting forms—malls, for example—that are empty. It may appear to many in such cultures that emptiness is threatening not only local content, but content that has been part of long-term cultural traditions. In spite of this, it is still far easier (and much more profitable) to export nothing (in its multitudinous forms) and to have it accepted, hence our focal concern with the globalization of nothing.

This book will also cast new light on globalization itself. For one thing, we will see that the concept of globalization is too broad for our purposes since it combines what will be seen here as two subprocesses that are, at least to some degree, contradictory. The first is the well-known process of *glocalization* whereby the interaction of the global and the local produces something new—the glocal. However, this ignores global processes that tend to overwhelm the local. To parallel the notion of glocalization, a new term will be coined here—*grobalization*—to describe the process in which *grow*th imperatives (e.g., the need to increase sales and profits from one year to the next in order to keep stock prices high and growing) push organizations and nations to expand globally and to impose themselves on the local. As a result, globalization is seen here as involving two major subprocesses that, while they both can be seen as global, are also at great odds with one another. Thus, globalization involves a profound struggle between the grobal and the glocal.

One of the key derivatives of this view is the idea that fewer and fewer areas and phenomena throughout the world are unaffected by globalization. Among other things, this means that the purely local is fast disappearing. More and more of the local is affected by the grobal; in other words, it is transformed into the glocal. Thus, while supporters of glocalization theory see a basic conflict between the global and the local and its resolution in the glocal, this analysis foresees the *death of the local* and the emerging essential worldwide struggle as that between the grobal and the glocal. This means, among other things, that while there are important differences and conflicts within it, globalization will reign supreme throughout much of the world. After all, whatever their differences, the grobal and the glocal are *both* part of the global. To put this another way, the most basic struggle will occur *within* the global rather than between the global and the local.

Yet another key issue that emerges from this is that of the triumph of the global: where are tomorrow's cultural innovations (there are other types of innovations—for example, technical and scientific—and these may well stem more from the grobal than from the glocal) to come from? This question stems from the belief that in the past cultural innovations have tended to come from the local. If the local is dead or dying, what then? Clearly, there is much to the argument that the death of the local threatens cultural innovation, although it could be that it will be out of the glocal, and the interaction among various glocalities, that future innovations will come. However, this is by no means assured and it is possible that, at least culturally, this will become a less creative, and therefore a less diverse, world.

While it is not my intention, there is something to offend virtually everyone, or at least catch their attention, in this book. For example, many of the things that large numbers of people throughout the United States, and the world, are drawn to and like a great deal, even love, are dealt with here under the heading of nothing. If most of them turn out to be not quite nothing, they at least fall toward that end of the something–nothing continuum. Among the many likely to be offended by this analysis are devotees of the Gap, shopping malls, jeans, *USAToday,* ATMs, virtually anything related to or with the Disney name (except, perhaps, some of the early, full-length cartoon movies), Whoppers, massive cruise ships, those who staff drive-through windows of any kind (and the windows themselves), almost all movie sequels, airports, tract housing developments, *Newsweek,* Amazon.com, and on and on. Clearly, virtually everyone reading this Preface has consumed (or has consumed in) at least one, if not many (most, all), of these at one time or another. Thus, many readers are likely to be offended by the inclusion of these things in this "honor roll of nothing." Furthermore, this list will be extended significantly as this book progresses.

To assuage at least a few hurt feelings, I hasten to add, once again, that nothing is *not* used in a pejorative sense in these pages. Centrally conceived and controlled forms largely devoid of distinctive content are not necessarily "bad," and those that are rich in distinctive content (something) are not inevitably "good."

However, there is a more critical aspect to the argument to be made in this book and it involves the idea of *loss amidst monumental abundance.* Accompanying the ascendancy of nothing is an age of unprecedented plenty, but its rise also carries with it a tendency toward the loss of something—of that which is locally conceived and controlled and is distinctive in content. It is this loss that is at the center of the critical argument made here. Thus, for example, the rise of the fast food restaurant has made a wide variety of inexpensively priced foods available to large numbers of people, but tending to be lost in the process is what Ray Oldenburg calls "great good places" like local cafes and the sense of community that was often associated with them.

This leads immediately to the paradox that will concern us below and later in this book: If settings like the shopping mall are nothing and tend to involve a loss, why is it that so many people seem unaware and unconcerned about these issues, flock to such settings, and seem to be having so much fun in them?

The main reason lies in the fact that the loss to be described here exists in a structural sense (for example, organizational, interpersonal differences between shopping malls and farmers' markets), but it is not necessarily subjectively felt as a loss by the people who are so attracted to nothing. For one thing, they may have few, if any, encounters with what is defined here as something, with the result that they cannot possibly be aware of a loss in their contacts with nothing. For another, they may be aware of the loss, but feel that it is of little significance in comparison to the advantages of nothing.

After considerable thought, I have chosen to highlight the concept of nothing here because it is so eye-catching and is unlikely to escape the prospective reader's attention (I don't want the book to be seen as nothing, in either a descriptive or a pejorative sense). And since this is to be a work, in part, of social criticism, it is natural that there be some emphasis on the negative side of nothing. Nearly everywhere else, much time, money, and energy are devoted to extolling the virtues of the various types of nothing discussed in these pages with the result that their positive side is well known and widely accepted. Surely, there is a place for a book that deals, at least in small part, with the negative side of nothing!

In spite of the emphasis here on the loss associated with nothing, not only does nothing mean a great deal to many, but people are often able to take all of the forms of nothing discussed here and to transform them into something. In spite of these efforts, sometimes quite heroic, this book addresses at several points the tension between the need of producers to create nothing and the efforts of consumers to turn nothing into something. Given this fact, we also address the issue of why producers are so hell-bent on the production and global dissemination of nothing.

In addition to those who have a positive view of what is defined here as nothing, a second group likely to be offended by this book is those who are advocates, supporters, and beneficiaries of globalization. As in the previous point, the main goal here is simply to describe *one aspect* of that which is proliferating as a result of globalization. However, it is because of the attention given to the negative side of the globalization of nothing (for example, the death of the local and the decline of cultural innovation, the loss associated with the spread of nothing) that supporters of globalization are likely to take offense at the ensuing argument. This is the case even though one of the major goals here is to make a distinctive contribution to the literature on globalization and to the understanding of that deeply important process.

Finally, a number of scholars are likely to be offended by this book's preference for a modern mode of analysis in an era in which the modern, especially its methodology, is under assault from many directions. Thus, a variety of well-known modern concepts (for example, globalization, rationalization) will be employed here, and several new concepts will be developed (the use of nothing as a sociological concept, for example) and, in the modern manner, carefully defined and differentiated from one another. Furthermore, dualities lie at the base of this analysis (e.g., something–nothing, place–nonplace) and those dualities form the poles of the overriding continuum (something–nothing) as well as a variety of subcontinua (unique–generic, to take one example). (Dualities and continua are seen by some as not only gross oversimplifications but as epitomes of a modern way of thinking.) The overall position of a given phenomenon (say, Gap jeans) on the something–nothing continuum will be a summation (although it is not simply additive) of its position on the various subcontinua. In addition, a modern *grand narrative*—a long-term trend in the direction of the increasing proliferation of nothing especially through the process of globalization—lies at the core of this analysis.

Overall, modern concepts, methods, and approaches are at the base of this work (although the author is acutely sensitive to the postmodern and feminist positions and their critiques of the modern orientation) and are likely to offend those who believe that a modern orientation has been rendered obsolete and indefensible as a result of decades of criticisms. However, while this book adopts a decidedly modern approach, it is one that is informed by, and modified as a result of, these critiques. Even so it reaffirms the need, following Zygmunt Bauman, to do a more rational sociology of (post)modernity than a highly irrational postmodern sociology.

The first three chapters of this book will be devoted to a detailed presentation of what is meant here by nothing. Chapter 4 will focus on the equally important concept of globalization and a series of its subdimensions—glocalization and grobalization (including capitalism, McDonaldization, and Americanization)—that are central to understanding this book's main argument. That argument is not made, at least in detail, until Chapter 5, in which the relationship (and it is a complex one) between the book's two central concepts—nothing and globalization—is discussed. In the sixth chapter, what is perhaps the ultimate example of the globalization of nothing—large-scale Internet sites devoted to consumption (e.g., Amazon.com)—will be dealt with in depth. Chapter 7 deals with a range of other issues that relate to nothing and it is in that chapter that the issue of loss amidst monumental abundance is explored. Chapter 8 deals with a series of issues relating to globalization (and nothing), including what can be done by those concerned about the problematic aspects of the globalization of nothing. Finally, some of the methodological issues raised by this analysis—especially its modern approach—will be discussed in the Appendix, which, among other things, will also deal with prior work, especially in philosophy, on nothing.

Finally, brief mention needs to made of the relationship between this book and my three previous books of this genre—*The McDonaldization of*

Society (1993, 1996, 2000, forthcoming), *Expressing America: A Critique of the Global Credit Card Society* (1995), and *Enchanting a Disenchanted World: Revolutionizing the Means of Consumption* (1999, forthcoming). First, all of the substantive concerns in those books—fast food restaurants, credit cards, and means of consumption such as superstores (e.g., Toys R Us)—play a central role in this book and are major examples of nothing (although many other examples are added to this base). Second, the concern in all three books with the ways in which these phenomena (and others) are being aggressively exported to the rest of the world (largely from the United States) reappears here, but now as part of the larger process of grobalization. Third, and related, two of the major processes dealt with in those earlier books—McDonaldization and Americanization—play a central role in this analysis as subtypes under the broader heading of grobalization.

However, while this book builds on its predecessors in several ways, it goes far beyond them in an effort to develop a novel approach to what has become one of the central topics in the social world and a central concern in the academic world: globalization. It does so by not only distinguishing between grobalization and glocalization, but by relating both to two topics—something and nothing—that, while they have been of concern in other fields, have drawn little or no attention from social scientists. In addition, capitalism is accorded a more central role here than in my previous books. Thus, this book has roots in my earlier work, but goes far beyond it and strikes out in what I think are some dramatic new directions.

Acknowledgments

There are a large number of people to thank for their help in the writing of this book. First, I would like to thank an extraordinary group of graduate students, especially Mike Ryan, Jeff Stepnisky, and Todd Stillman, for their many insights and ideas. An undergraduate (but soon-to-be graduate student), Nicholas Wilson, was not only a valued research assistant, but contributed many useful ideas, especially to the discussion of the Internet. Dr. Kornelia Hahn, a visiting professor from Lueneburg University, Germany, contributed much to the development of this book. In addition, my colleague Len Pearlin offered some excellent insights into an early version of this book. I was allowed to solicit reviews from a number of notable scholars and friends from around the world and they contributed greatly to the development of this manuscript: Alan Bryman, Loughborough University (England); Daina Stukuls Eglitis, George Washington University (U.S.): Eva Illouz, Hebrew University of Jerusalem (Israel); Douglas Kellner, University of California, Los Angeles (U.S.); Chris Rojek, Nottingham Trent (U.K.); Hermann Strasser, University of Duisburg (Germany); Hernan Vera, University of Florida (U.S.); and Jonathan Turner, University of California, Riverside (U.S.). In addition, Pine Forge Press solicited a number of additional reviews and they, too, proved very helpful in completing this book. Those reviewers are Doug Constance, Sam Houston State University; Celestino Fernandez, University of Arizona; Eric Mielants, Western Kentucky University; Ken Mietus, Western Illinois University; Chris T. Papaleonadros, Ohio State University; Victor N. Shaw, California State University, Northridge; and Steve Zehr, University of Southern Indiana. Finally, I would like to thank the people at Pine Forge, especially my editor— Jerry Westby—who has been a constant source of support and encouragement. It has been a real pleasure working with him and I look forward to working with him on many other projects in the future.

Chapter One

Nothing

A Brief (No Need to Be Lengthy) Introduction

Vast, fully-enclosed shopping malls. Lots of glass, light, stainless steel, chrome, and granite. Hundreds of shops along lengthy corridors that criss-cross at various points. Most of the shops are outlets of large chains; that is made clear by their well-known signs and logos. Large numbers of people traipsing through familiar structures, along well-traveled corridors, and past shops with names well known to them. Some are just strolling, others window-shopping, while still others dart in and out of shops to make purchases, usually using credit cards. These malls, corridors, consumers, and shops could be almost anywhere—Los Angeles, Singapore, Moscow, Rio de Janeiro, or Johannesburg.

Whether or not they shop in malls, consumers throughout the world are increasingly drawn to more-or-less mass-produced and -distributed products and brands: Ikea sofas, L.L. Bean shorts, Sharper Image "boy toys", Victoria's Secret lingerie, Nike athletic shoes, Mickey Mouse ears, Dolce and Gabbana frocks, Gap jeans, and Hard Rock Cafe T-shirts.

1

In purchasing these things, in logo-ed shops, in or out of malls, consumers around the globe encounter employees who are less and less likely to be knowledgeable about what they sell and increasingly likely to interact with them in an impersonal, even highly scripted, manner. The shops are increasingly also on the Internet, where consumers are more likely to encounter "shop-bots" than people.

Anywhere they go in the world (or on the Net), consumers are increasingly unlikely to receive much in the way of service from such employees and, in fact, are likely to serve themselves or to interact with technologies like the Web site of an online retailer, the ATM, the self-service gasoline pump, or the "speedpass" booth on the toll road.

These four vignettes exemplify the major forms of nothing to be discussed in this book and the fact that nothing is becoming an increasingly global phenomenon. To argue that such phenomena are nothing (lacking in distinctive substance) is clearly counterintuitive and controversial if for no other reason than the fact that, judging by their thoughts and actions, most people seem to feel very differently—that all of this is quite something. At least as controversial and counter to the prevailing belief is the association, indicated in this book's title, between globalization and nothing. However, it is *not* being argued here that globalization *is* nothing, merely that we are witnessing the globalization *of* nothing (for example, malls, Gap jeans, scripted employees, and ATMs). Certainly, as will be made clear, a great deal of that which is of great substance—*something*—is also being created and dispersed throughout the globe (art, crafts, sports like soccer and American-style football, etc.). In other words, there is a simultaneous process of the "globalization of something," although that will concern us far less in these pages because the objective here is not only to critique globalization, but to do so from a somewhat different perspective than is ordinarily the case.[1]* *Although the focus of this book is on nothing (and its globalization), it should be borne in mind that this should always be seen as part of the ongoing[2] relationship between something and nothing.*

This book clearly takes some controversial positions, but the bulk of this chapter, as well as of the ensuing two chapters, is devoted to a discussion of

---

*Citations may be found at the back of the book beginning on page 217.

the idea of nothing (and something—one cannot be discussed without the other). Indeed, we will not get to a discussion of globalization until Chapter 4 and it will not be until Chapter 5 that we connect the two focal concerns in a discussion of the globalization of nothing. There are two basic reasons for this imbalance in the discussion. On the one hand, the ideas about nothing to be presented here are quite unique and often counterintuitive. A significant amount of space is required to clarify the idea and to lay out its various ramifications for this analysis. Interestingly, there is a surprisingly large literature on nothing; we could even conceive of a field called "nothingology."[3] In fact, some of our greatest thinkers—Immanuel Kant, Georg Hegel, Martin Heidegger, Jean-Paul Sartre, Jerry Seinfeld(!)—have made important contributions to our understanding of nothing, but as we will see in the Appendix, the way nothing is used here has little relationship to their use of the concept.

While there is a surprising amount of work on nothing, it pales in comparison, especially in recent years, to that devoted to globalization. It is likely that no topic has received more attention in recent years from scholars and lay people alike than that of globalization. While there are complexities and difficulties in the way this idea is used, as we will see in Chapter 4, the reader is, in the main, generally familiar with globalization, at least its main outlines and implications. Hence a discussion of it can be deferred, but there is no postponing a discussion of nothing.

Nothing

The social world, particularly in the realm of consumption, is increasingly characterized by nothing. In this case, "nothing" refers to a *social form that is generally[4] centrally conceived, controlled, and comparatively devoid of distinctive substantive content.* This definition carries with it *no judgment* about the desirability or undesirability of such a social form or about its increasing prevalence.[5]

Let us use the credit card as an example of both this form and its expansion, specifically the steps involved in obtaining a credit card.[6] At the extreme, literally nothing is involved, at least in terms of the nature of the offer extended to the consumer. This is clearest when an unsolicited offer for a credit card, usually with a predefined credit limit, arrives in the mail. In terms of the definition offered above, this is nothing because it was conceived and is controlled centrally and there is no distinctive content involved in this invitation—thousands, hundreds of thousands, perhaps millions of potential cardholders receive exactly the same invitation in the mail. Even if potential credit card holders are grouped into categories based on their credit ratings, those in each group receive the same invitation with the same credit limit.

Somewhat more is involved in a telephone call offering one a credit card. The call requires more complexity since the telemarketer may need to respond to some idiosyncratic questions from the potential cardholder. However, there are often centrally conceived scripts for responding to all but the most unusual questions and, of course, the basic approach is highly scripted and great control is exerted by supervisors over those employing those scripts. So even here the process of offering a credit card is (largely) nothing since everyone who is solicited in this way will hear much the same centrally controlled and conceived pitch with little room for individual variation.

Furthermore, the nature of the offer, especially the all-important credit limit associated with the card, is determined by a computer program that bases its decisions on a set of objective criteria. All potential cardholders who fall within certain parameters will receive the same credit limit.

More generally, a credit card can be seen, in this context, as a relatively empty form. That is, in itself it is little or nothing—a small rectangular piece of plastic with a few names, numbers, dates, words, a logo, and maybe a hologram. There is little of distinctive substance inherent in the card itself (except for the cardholder's name and number)—little to distinguish one card from any others.[7] And, of course, the nature and design of the card is a product of the central offices of a credit card bank, as is control over how the card is used.

In terms of expansion, the modern credit card, and therefore the methods discussed above to solicit new cardholders, was invented in the mid-20th century in the United States and since then the number in use has boomed not only here but in many other countries around the world. In the case of the United States, the number of major credit (bank) cards (e.g., Visa, MasterCard) in use increased from 213 million in 1990 to 419 million in 1999 and is projected to rise to 502 million by 2005. The amount of high-interest bank card debt owed by American consumers grew from $2.7 billion in 1969 to $154 billion in 1990, $430 billion in 1998, and is projected to be $615 billion by 2005. Finally, bank credit card spending rose from $213 billion in 1990 to $839 billion in 1998 and is projected to be $1,457 billion by 2005.[8] Comparatively affluent Americans (and those from many other countries) are traveling abroad more often and they are very likely to use their credit cards to pay for expenses incurred on such trips. Thus, the global expansion of this relatively empty form—one that gains much of its substance in actual use—exemplifies the first of this book's arguments.

This contention involves what the postmodernists call a "grand narrative,"[9] a story of a large swath of human history, asserting that we are witnessing a general historical trend in the direction of more and more nothing. That is, there is historical movement toward that which is centrally controlled and conceived and increasingly devoid of distinctive substance (as well as, as we will see, of uniqueness and individuality, among other things). Most of these nullities (the preapproved offer of a credit card is one example) were developed in the modern West, especially the United States. Today, this development that is most obvious here has spread throughout the developed world, but becomes far less clear and commonplace the less developed the nation in question. There is little effort and inducement, as yet, to export these nullities, at least in large numbers, to the least developed areas of the world. In addition, those areas are unlikely, at least thus far, to have developed many of their own versions of these nullities. Nonetheless, there are dynamics pushing in the direction of the ever-greater global proliferation of nothing. Some of those dynamics are based in the nation (a nation's, and its corporations', desire to export or import the latest developments in nothing in order to enhance power, profits, prestige, and so on), while others are a result of processes largely independent of any nation (for example, the global financial network).[10] As a result of these dynamics (and many others), nothing is finding its way into an ever-increasing portion of the world.

While it would be tempting to overgeneralize, this grand narrative (as well as the rest of this book's main arguments) is best restricted to the realm of consumption. It is there that we are most clearly witnessing the proliferation of largely empty social forms such as the credit card and the ways in which it is offered to potential cardholders. However, that does not mean that arguments could not be mounted that would allow us to extend this narrative to even the most unlikely of domains. For example, a reasonable argument could be made in support of another counterintuitive view—a grand narrative of the proliferation of nothing in the medical domain (education would be yet another).[11] We could think of modern hospital chains and the way they are run, the latest pharmaceuticals, the most up-to-date biotechnology, and so on as nothing in the sense that they are centrally conceived and controlled forms that are largely empty of distinctive content and spreading to many different places throughout the world. A particularly good example of this is the chains of so-called "docs-in-a-box" that have sprouted up throughout the United States (and one would anticipate similar global expansion in the near future). These are limited service, drive-in medical facilities that offer fast, but circumscribed, services on the model of the fast-food restaurant. Docs-in-a-box are largely empty shells, replicated in many different geographic settings, that are given substance by the way they are used by patients and by what the medical personnel who staff them do (another side of this argument will be presented below). They are designed and managed by the main office of the chain.

This reminds us of the fact that the grand narrative being developed here is merely *descriptive*—what is being pointed to here is a trend in the world as a whole in the direction of nothing. It is in this descriptive sense that this book's grand narrative can be extended from consumption to medicine, indeed to many domains of the social world. However, as is implicit in much of this discussion, and will be made explicit in Chapter 7, this book goes beyond description to *evaluation*. While many domains may be moving in the same direction, it is far easier to be positive or critical of that development in some domains than in others. While there is a mixed bag of benefits and liabilities associated with the movement toward nothing in all domains, the relative mix varies from one to another. Thus, while the benefits of the increase in nothing in medicine (e.g., greater availability of consistent, more effective, and affordable care) clearly outweigh the costs, the same may not be the case in areas that we more closely associate with consumption such as shopping or tourism. More specifically, while the proliferation of nothing may save lives and prevent disease in the medical domain, in tourism it might lead to boredom as an ever-increasing portion of the world comes to be characterized by the same empty forms (indoor shopping malls, hotel chains, and the like). The latter example is related to the major critical argument in this book that focuses on the *loss* of something (in this case, tourist attractions true to local traditions) in the face of the massive expansion of nothing (hotel chains with no ties to the local area).

By the way, the central focus of this book—the globalization of nothing—is a derivative, although by no means of secondary importance, of this first argument about the increasing proliferation of nothing. That is, one of the most important and dramatic aspects of this proliferation is its spread beyond the confines of the United States to much of the rest of the world. As we will see, the United States is the point of origin and center of much that is described in these pages as nothing (the modern credit card was, as we have seen, an American invention). However, in recent years many forms of nothing (including credit cards) have been aggressively exported to many corners of the rest of the world, which, in the main, are quite eager to receive them. Furthermore, many other nations are now much more actively engaged in the production of nothing and exporting it throughout the world, including back to the United States. For example, another American invention, the fast-food restaurant chain, now finds itself competing with foreign chains that are invading the United States at an increasing rate (Pret A Manger from England, Pollo Campero from Guatemala, and others[12]). We will not say more about globalization at this point; it will assume center stage in Chapters 4 and 5.

It should be made clear that in spite of the negative connotations generally associated with the word *nothing,* the phenomena to be discussed under that heading are, in fact, viewed very positively, if not worshiped, by many people throughout the world. Thus, for example, while we may be critical of credit cards, the ways in which they are offered and obtained, the indebtedness that many find themselves in because of them, and the world of hyperconsumption that they play such a huge role in creating, there are clearly innumerable consumers who love their credit cards and delight in the advantages (convenience, ability to consume without cash on hand or in the bank, etc.) offered by them. Similarly, as is clear in one of the vignettes that opened this chapter, name brands are generally associated with the trend toward the increase in nothing, and will come under critical scrutiny at various points in this analysis, but many people feel very strongly about their favorite brands—Coke, Nike, Rolex, Dolce and Gabbana, and so on. Later in this chapter we will need to return to this seeming contradiction between this analysis of brands (and other forms of nothing) and many people's love affair with their favorite brands.

Given such complexities, we need powerful analytical tools to analyze nothing as clearly as possible, study its expansion, and eventually render judgments with more balance and greater nuance about the implications of its increase. In fact, Chapters 2 and 3 will be devoted to the development and use of a variety of conceptual and methodological tools that will allow us to grapple better with the substantive, and potentially value-laden, issues of concern here.

Getting a stronger grasp on what has been discussed to this point, and more important the balance of this book, depends on the creation of a better sense, and definition, of *nothing*. However, in order to define that term better, we also need a definition of *something*, as well as the ways in which it can be distinguished from nothing. In fact, neither nothing nor something exists independently of the other; *each makes sense only when paired with, and contrasted to, the other.* We will devote much attention to defining these terms, and iterating and elucidating their subdimensions, but it is necessary at this point to offer a preliminary, orienting definition of something as *a social form that is generally*[13] *indigenously conceived, controlled, and comparatively rich in distinctive substantive content; a form that is to a large degree substantively* unique. While presented as a dichotomy,[14] this implies a *continuum* from something to nothing and that is precisely the way the concepts will be employed here—as the two poles of that continuum.

Phenomena that exist toward the nothing end of the continuum can also be thought of as largely devoid of individuality. This means, of course, that those entities found on the something end of the continuum are likely to be highly individualized. However, I hasten to add that *no* phenomenon is either totally individualized or completely devoid of individuality.[15] Thus, the phenomena of focal concern in this book exist at or near the nothing end of the continuum; all phenomena exist somewhere between the extremes of the nothing–something poles of the continuum. Much more on this to come!

Having looked, albeit briefly, at the nothing end of the continuum, in part through the example of the credit card, it is incumbent on us at this point to offer a brief parallel discussion of the something end of that continuum. If the credit card loan is a largely empty form through which what are in effect lines of credit are extended to consumers, then a line of credit negotiated personally between banker and customer would be the parallel within the realm of something. Such a line of credit is, of course, a form (of lending money), but it is a form that is much more likely to be locally conceived and controlled and to be rich in distinctive substance. For example, a long-term relationship may develop between lender and borrower that may inform decisions on the need to borrow and the willingness to lend. Lenders are apt to have deep and personal knowledge of borrowers and that knowledge has a profound effect on their decisions. In the course of a single negotiation, or better in a number of such negotiations over a lifetime, a great deal of distinctive substance develops in this relationship. In this case, it is the richness of a personal relationship between customer and banker—its high degree of individualization—that helps make the personal line of credit something, at least in comparison to the credit card loan.

The historical trend of interest here is the long-term movement away from such highly personal and locally controlled lines of credit (and, more generally, something) to the centrally controlled offer (e.g., through bulk mailings) of credit cards with specific limits, and the periodic increase in credit limits associated with those cards, without any personal interaction between loan officer and credit card holder (and, more generally, nothing).[16]

However, we must not assume that such a method of obtaining personal lines of credit and such a personal relationship is necessarily good. Personally negotiated lines of credit had (and still do, where they continue to exist) a number of advantages. Great care was taken in granting lines of credit, and bad decisions were less likely because loan officers knew their customers personally. If a loan came due and the debtor was unable to pay as a result of any number of unforeseen circumstances, the banker could consider these exigencies in the context of a long-term and personal relationship with the debtor and on that basis could choose to extend the deadline or even extend additional credit. Ultimately, of course, both borrower and lender could derive personal meaning from their relationship.

Of course, there were liabilities associated with such relationships and such a method of extending credit. Among other things, it was time-consuming, cumbersome, and expensive. Most important, as we have seen, the fact that lenders employed personal considerations in making their decisions meant that they were quite likely to discriminate in favor of some borrowers and against others.[17]

A relationship is not necessarily a good one simply because it is local, rich in distinctive substance, and individualized. The converse is also true. A relationship is not necessarily bad because it lacks much in the way of unique substance. For example, the likelihood of obtaining today's credit card loan is not affected by the personal feelings of loan officers (indeed, it is unlikely that a loan officer will be involved at all). The more general point, of course, is that just because an entity lies toward the nothing end of the continuum, we must not assume that it is necessarily bad; that the disadvantages outweigh the advantages. Conversely, that which exists toward the something end of that continuum is not necessarily good; that there are more advantages than disadvantages.

The social world, in particular the world of consumption, involves some combination of nothing and something wherever on the globe it may exist. Nothing may predominate in some times and places, while something is pre-eminent at other times and places. Furthermore, nothing and something are not static categories; they are not cast in stone. Entrepreneurs are constantly trying to transform something into nothing in order to produce and sell more over greater expanses of time and place. Conversely, others, usually consumers, are often actively engaged in the process of seeking to transform nothing into something. Indeed, as pointed out previously, there is always a dialectic between something and nothing. However, at this point in world history, nothing fits far better than something with the imperatives of both the capitalist economic system and the current phase of globalization[18] with the result that it is nothing that is more likely to find its way into every corner of consumer society and to the far extremities of the globe. Furthermore, in many cases, the spread of nothing (e.g., credit card loans) involves the displacement, even reduction and elimination, of something (e.g., personal loans). By the way, the addition of the notion of something adds greater clarity to this book's grand narrative. It is now clear that what is involved is a general historical trend *away* from something and *toward* nothing.[19]

The same tools to be developed here to help us analyze nothing should be equally useful in working the something end of the continuum, as well as everything in between. Indeed, it is hoped that this will be one of the great strengths of the concepts and continua developed here. Thus, more specifically, we should be able to use the concepts and continua to be developed below to think about *both* credit card loans and personal lines of credit. Those tools should allow us to pinpoint the essential differences between them, as well as the many other forms that exist on the continuum from something to nothing as it relates to credit (and everything else in the realm of consumption).

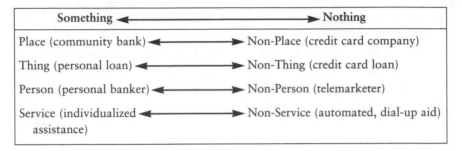

Something ←————————————————→ Nothing

Place (community bank) ←————→ Non-Place (credit card company)

Thing (personal loan) ←————→ Non-Thing (credit card loan)

Person (personal banker) ←————→ Non-Person (telemarketer)

Service (individualized ←————→ Non-Service (automated, dial-up aid)
assistance)

Figure 1.1   The Four Major Subtypes of the Something–Nothing Continuum
(with Examples)

Again, while these two polar concepts are of equal importance conceptually, my primary concern is with nothing and the nothing end of the continuum, as well as a description of the historical trend in the direction of nothing. A major source of my interest in nothing, especially conceptually, is the work in social geography by the anthropologist Marc Augé on the concept of *non-places*.[20] To Augé, non-places are "the real measure of our time."[21] I would generalize this to say that nothing is, in many ways, the true measure of our time!

In this book I seek to extend the idea of non-places to *non-things, non-people,* and *non-services.* If a credit card is a non-thing, then a contemporary credit card company—one that may be little more than a telephone center—is a non-place,[22] the highly programmed and scripted individuals who work there are non-people, and the often automated functions can be thought of as non-services.

Of course, as with something and nothing, each of these concepts implies a continuum with *places, things, people,* and *services* as the opposing, *something* poles (see Figure 1.1). To be on the "non" end of any of the four continua, phenomena must tend to be centrally conceived and controlled forms lacking in distinctive substance. Those entities that are to be found at the other end of each continuum are locally conceived and controlled forms that are rich in distinctive substance. Continuing with our example, if a thing is a traditional personal loan, then a place is the community bank to which people can still go to deal with other people—bank employees—in person and obtain from them individualized services.

An Illustrative Excursion to the Movies

A powerful illustration of the various types of nothing is to be found in the recent movie, *One Hour Photo* (2002). Robin Williams plays Si Parrish, the operator of a one-hour photo lab within the confines of a fictitious "big-box" store named Sav-Mart (a thinly disguised send-up of Wal-Mart). The Sav-Mart store is clearly depicted in the movie as nothing. It is certainly part of a great chain that has been constructed on the basis of a model that was created by a central office that also manages what goes on there on a day-to-day basis. Like the chains on which it is modeled, it is likely that one Sav-Mart looks much like every other one. There are great long aisles with endless shelves loaded with products lacking in distinctive substance. There is a pervasive coldness in the store atmosphere (and in the attitude and behavior of the store manager) that is abetted by the abundance of white and icy blue colors. In case anyone misses the point, there is a dream sequence in which Parrish envisions himself standing alone in one of the store's great aisles amidst a sea of totally empty shells. The red of the blood that begins to stream from his eyes is sharply distinguished from the whiteness that surrounds him. The pain in his face is in stark contrast to the coldness that envelops him. Sav-Mart is clearly a non-place, as is the photo lab housed within it.

Employees who operate the one-hour photo stand (and Sav-Mart more generally) are expected to be non-persons. The make-up, the nondescript clothes, the shoes that squeak when Si walks the store aisles, and his unassertive and affect-less demeanor all combine to make it seem as if Si Parrish is the ideal non-person required of his position. Si has worked at the photo stand for a long time; he is virtually a fixture there. Indeed, like store fixtures, he acts, and is to be treated, as if he is not there. He is expected to interact with his customers rapidly and impersonally. This is made abundantly clear in the uncomfortable reactions of customers when Si deviates from being the ideal non-person by attempting to interact with them in a more personal manner.

The photo lab is offering a non-thing—rapidly and automatically developed photographs. Those who oversee the development of the film and then hand over the photographs are not supposed to take a personal interest in them or to take a role in the process by which they are developed. This is clear when Si calls in a technician because the Agfa photo machine is producing pictures that are slightly off and the technician becomes enraged for being called in on such a minor matter. The technician knows that few employees, let alone customers, recognize, or care about, minor variations in the quality of photos from such a non-place as the photo lab at Sav-Mart.

Finally, Si is supposed to provide a non-service. That is, he is expected simply to accept, in a very routine fashion, rolls of film handed him by customers, to have them developed as quickly and efficiently as possible, and to hand them back to customers in exchange for payment. However, Si cares about the photos and their quality, at least as much as the automated technology will allow. He wants to provide the best possible service, especially to his favorite customers. Of course, he is not supposed to have favorites (that would be something) and this is where the movie grows interesting, because Si, for his own personal reasons, has sought to turn nothing into something. Indeed, the movie can be seen as a cautionary tale on what happens when efforts are made to transform the nothing that pervades our everyday lives into something.

Si is quite taken with one particular family that he regards as ideal (Si's personal life is totally empty; indeed, he buys a photo of a woman at a street market and later shows it off claiming that it is of his mother). When the mother and son of that family come in with some film to be developed, it is clear that he is fond of them and he acts like, and wants to be treated by them as, a person. He also treats them as people and, even though it is late in the day, he agrees to have the photos developed before the close of business. In other words, he offers them personalized service! Furthermore, when he learns that it is the boy's birthday, he gives him a free instant camera claiming (falsely) that it is store policy to give children such gifts on their birthdays. In acting like a person (he also demonstrates personal knowledge of the family and asks personal questions), Si is seeking to turn these non-places (one hour photo, Sav-Mart) into places. And the non-things that he works with—automatically developed photos—are obviously transformed into things by Si.

It turns out that Si has an unnatural interest in this family and is routinely making an extra copy of every photo he has had developed for them. Further, he is papering his otherwise desolate apartment with these photographs. When another woman brings in a roll of film to be developed (he inappropriately—for a non-place and from a non-person—asks if he knows her from somewhere), he remembers her from one of his favorite family's photos on his wall. It turns out that she works with the husband of that family and when, late at night, he examines her developed photos, he discovers that the two are having an affair. Enraged, Si sets out to end the affair, first by "accidentally" putting a photo of the lovers in with a set of photos developed from the camera he gave the child. When, after viewing that photo, the wife does not seem to react in the desired way by confronting the husband and throwing him out (Si spies on the family that night and witnesses a normal dinner free of confrontation), Si follows the lovers to a hotel (also depicted as a non-place) where he has a confrontation with them using his camera as a "weapon." While Si ends up being arrested, the affair seems at an end and it is at least possible that the "ideal" family will be restored to its "proper" state. One lesson seems to be that "somethingness" lurks beneath the nothing that pervades our lives. Another is that the norm in our society and in our lives is pervasive nothing and those who violate it are at least slightly abnormal and do so at great risk to themselves.

Nothing (and Something): Further Clarification

While there is obviously an evaluative element involved in the selection, for illustrative purposes, of the movie *One Hour Photo,* and the nature of that critical position will become clear in Chapter 7, the term *nothing* is used here and throughout the ensuing five chapters in the analytical sense of centrally conceived and controlled forms largely empty of distinctive content. In this sense, nothing, as well as something, are ideal types that offer no evaluative judgment about the social world, but rather are methodological tools to be used in thinking about and studying the social world.[23] As was pointed out earlier, a major objective here is to develop a series of analytic tools to allow us to do a better job of theorizing about and empirically studying nothing (and something).

While it sometimes will seem as if that is precisely what we are doing, we cannot really discuss these phenomena apart from their relationship to human beings. People and services obviously involve consideration of human relationships and their relative presence or absence. However, even a discussion of places and things requires that we analyze the human relationships (or their relative absence) that serve to make them something, nothing, or everything in between. Thus, settings become places or non-places (or somewhere in between) because of the thoughts and actions of the people who create, control, work in, and are served by them. Objects are turned into things or non-things by those who manufacture, market, sell, purchase, and use them. And even human beings (and their services) become people or non-people (and non-services) as a result of the demands and expectations of those with whom they come into contact. To put this more generally and theoretically, nothing and something (and everywhere in between) are *social constructions.*[24] In other words, being something or nothing is not inherent in any place, thing, person, or service.[25] The latter are transformed into something or nothing by what people do in, or in relationship to, them. And, whatever is done in, or in relationship to, them can be defined as something, nothing, and all points in between. It is for this reason, as we will see, that there will often be a discrepancy between what will be defined in these pages as nothing and the definitions of those involved in, or with, them who are likely to define them as something.

However, while there are no characteristics inherent in any phenomenon that make it necessarily something or nothing, there are clearly some phenomena that are easier to transform into something while others lend themselves more easily to being transformed into nothing. Thus, one could turn a personal line of credit into nothing, but the personal relationship involved makes that difficult. On the other side, one's relationship to one's credit card company could be transformed into something, but the distant, preconceived, controlled, and impersonal nature of that relationship makes that problematic. Thus, still another way of putting the grand narrative of concern here is to argue that we have witnessed a transformation from phenomena that lend themselves more easily to becoming something to phenomena that are more easily transformed into nothing.[26]

Nothing Is Nothing

While much of this first chapter has been devoted to the idea of nothing and its significance, it is time to make it clear that *nothing is nothing* (and, relatedly, that something always has its elements of nothing).[27] What does this seeming double-talk mean?

First, no phenomena exist at the furthest extreme of the nothing end of the something–nothing continuum. That is, all phenomena have at least a touch, a tad, of something. (Even a physical vacuum is not completely empty![28]) As alluded to above, this also means that no phenomena exist at the extreme something end of the continuum; all have at least some degree of nothing (i.e., some elements that are strictly formal) associated with them.

Second, there are always at least some people who find meaning in phenomena that are relegated by this analysis to the farthest reaches of nothing. In fact, as has already been mentioned, and will be discussed later, much of what is regarded here as nothing is of great importance to large numbers of people. And, again on the other side, that which appears to virtually everyone to be quite something will, to at least some, seem to be nothing, or at least pretty close to it.

Third, some people (Si Parrish, for example) struggle mightily to transform that which seems like nothing into something and it is possible that their efforts will succeed, at least in their minds, to some degree. Conversely, there are those who, in their dealings with something, work equally hard to turn it into nothing.

For these and other reasons, while we will discuss nothing throughout this book, the paradoxical point should be borne in mind that *nothing is truly nothing!* In fact, that should be obvious from the fact that an entire book is being devoted to . . . nothing. If nothing was truly and completely nothing, this book would be simply a series of blank pages.[29] It is clear to this author, at least, that phenomena at the farthest reaches of the nothing end of the continuum have at least a bit of something; that the most empty forms of nothing can be transformed into something; that nothing and its proliferation are of great importance; and that the long-term trend from something to nothing is a development that everyone should be aware of, think about, and perhaps, if they are so disposed, even do something about.

In Defense of Nothing

The arguments to this point have been mainly descriptive, but the critical aspect of this analysis has been anticipated and underscored in the discussion of the movie, *One Hour Photo*. We will also deal with the positive side of nothing, especially in Chapter 7. The flavor of that argument has recently been anticipated by a journalist who makes a strong case *for* nothing in an article titled "Quaint's Nice, But Sprawl Makes Me Weak at the Knees."[30] David Lindley grew up in England, spent most of the past 20 years in the United States, and has become an American citizen. He recently spent a year and a half in England doing research for a book and he arrived there with "deeply etched images of my native country: thatched cottages, neat rose gardens, narrow country lanes and gruff jolly yokels in the pub, ooh-arr-ing engagingly."[31] At first, his romanticized images of something were reaffirmed: "There I was living on the edge of the Cotswolds. Hills dotted with sheep, secluded hamlets at the end of twisting roads, ancient stone walls, a cock crowing every morning, rabbits and pheasants darting across the lanes and fields. Deer, too, but dainty ones with spindly legs."[32]

However, Lindley soon found himself attracted to the English town of Milton Keynes, a centrally planned community with neat houses looking very similar to, if not identical to, one another. In the terms of this book's primary definition of nothing, Milton Keynes falls toward the nothing end of the continuum (a non-place) and is regarded in this way by many in Britain who use it as the butt of many jokes and see it as "the very definition of *soulless modernity* and suburban *aridity*."[33] Yet, Lindley liked the fact that

> On either side of the roads smartly trimmed grassy areas ran down to neatly planted trees, which partly conceal the residential areas. At the intersections there were shopping areas, with enormous stores where you could buy all the sneakers and kitchen appliances you might need. There appeared to be plenty of parking. Elsewhere there were industrial areas, of the modern, sanitized kind. . . . In the land of ancient villages and ivy-clad walls, I found myself daydreaming about shopping plazas and suburban sprawl, about strip malls and parking garages."[34]

In other words, the journalist daydreamed about nothing (especially the forms of nothing associated with, and pioneered in, the United States), but he was also put off by the something of old England: "As I was living so close to Oxford, I thought it would be easy to dash into the city for books or exotic foods from the city's covered market, to visit museums or just stroll around and act the tourist. . . . But a couple of times I tried driving into Oxford, only to chug around slowly for half an hour, fail to find a parking place, then give up and go home."[35] As a result, he came to the realization that while the quaintness of old England was okay for vacation, he wanted to live in the modern. England, or at least the area around Oxford, was seen as trapped in the "dead weight of historical tradition" and he found that he preferred the transience of the United States and its strip malls and shopping plazas. He concludes, "I'd rather live in urban America than in any Cotswold village."[36]

Thus, while this book has a critical edge, especially in Chapter 7, we must not conclude that there are not problems associated with something or that there are not people today, perhaps a majority, who prefer nothing to something and who have good reasons for that preference.

The Production of Nothing

As was pointed out several times, and should be abundantly obvious by now, this book focuses on consumption. It does so for many reasons, not the least of which is the tendency for many scholars and lay people to focus on issues relating to production (work, factories, unemployment, and so on). There is a wide-scale "productivist bias" that this book seeks to counter by focusing on consumption. As a result, we will have little to say about the production of nothing, but that does not mean that it is an unimportant issue.

Much of the nothing to be discussed throughout this book has little to do with what a very large portion of the world consumes. This is especially the case for most of Asia and Africa, where people are having a hard enough time simply surviving, let alone being knowledgeable about, or able to afford, Cartier watches or even a Whopper. Indeed, as powerful as the globalization of nothing is, it has made few inroads into some parts of the world. This is the case not because of an inability to do so on the part of globalizing forces, but because there are simply few if any profits to be derived from incursions into these areas. Nonetheless, it is likely that those forces will colonize more and more of these areas as their economies develop and the possibility of profits increases.

Thus, this is largely a book about consumption in the developed world. It is there that large numbers of people are able to worry about whether to buy Coke or Pepsi, or whether they can really afford yet another Valentino frock. Nevertheless, globalization knows no bounds and it constantly seeks to expand into new areas. Furthermore, its influence is felt long before it actually enters a new market. Those in less developed nations may not yet be able to afford Nike sneakers, but it is not unusual to see them wearing more affordable caps or T-shirts emblazoned with the famous Swoosh.[37]

However, when we turn from the consumption to the production of nothing, we find a very different situation. That is, while those who inhabit the least developed portions of the world can afford to purchase little, if any, of the various forms of nothing, and in any case have little or no access to many of them, it is they who are increasingly likely to *produce* the wide array of nothing sold primarily in the world's more developed countries. Thus, the various forms of nothing are increasingly less likely to be produced in high-wage, developed countries when all of this nothingness can be produced in much the same way, but far more cheaply, in less developed parts of the world.

For example, over 100,000 Indonesians are involved in producing Nike shoes.[38] Their wages are a fraction of those paid comparable workers in the United States and not enough to support a family. In addition, workdays can be extraordinarily long (as much as 15 hours per day, 6–7 days per week); the factory is likely to be hot, noisy, and smelly; on the glue line there is the danger of inhaling toxic chemicals; on the shoe-press machine it is not unusual for workers to lose parts of their fingers; and sexual abuse and favors are not unknown.

The problems of third-world workers in such factories (and in many other settings) are well documented. However, this analysis points to yet another problem that relates to poverty surrounded by unprecedented affluence. As their workday proceeds, third-world producers of nothing (say, Nike sneakers) may find themselves surrounded by mountains of it and, in this, they are much like the consumers in wealthy countries. However, *unlike* those consumers, these workers cannot, and likely will never be able to, afford to consume the non-things (Nike sneakers cost about the same in Indonesia as they do in the United States, while income in Indonesia is a fraction of that in the U.S.) that are quickly packaged and shipped off to developed nations where there are large numbers of people who can afford them.

Not only are the problems of those in less developed countries well known, but so are the ways in which those problems have been exacerbated by globalization.[39] Most generally, the argument is made that instead of bringing untold benefits, globalization has made the situation worse in the less developed world.[40]

This discussion points to yet another problem—the *double affliction* that confronts those who do such work in those countries. That is, they are both forced to produce much of the developed world's various forms of nothingness *and* they are unable to afford to buy most, if not all, of them, even though they are surrounded by them during their (usually long) workdays and are involved with their production on a daily basis. It must be abundantly obvious that they are producing, at low wages, that which is to be enjoyed by those of much greater wealth in the developed world. To at least some of these workers, this must be frustrating, galling, and the cause of enormous hostility and aggression. Of course, the abject poverty and the many other hardships that accompany all of this are far greater problems, but this poverty surrounded by an abundance of nothing can only serve to make everything seem that much worse.

The point is that while we will focus on consumption in the chapters that follow, there are many issues relating to production that are also worth thinking about and pursuing. While we have been discussing the problems of workers in less developed countries in this section, many workers in developed countries face many of the same problems. While they may be able to afford Nike caps, expensive forms of nothing like Gucci bags (unless they are cheap knock-offs) remain out of reach for large numbers of these workers.

Chapter Two

Conceptualizing Nothing (and Something)

The preceding chapter proposed a continuum ranging from *something* to *nothing* as a tool to analyze the various phenomena of concern in this book.[1] This is obviously a crude distinction. These polar notions, as well as everything that stands between them, are far from being very clear-cut or refined. Furthermore, there is certainly *no* social phenomenon that can unequivocally be classified as either something or nothing. As pointed out in Chapter 1, all such phenomena have elements of *both* something and nothing.[2] To put it another way, all social phenomena can be positioned somewhere between the poles of this continuum. Of course, that is not to say that placement on the continuum is easy, precise, or uncontroversial. Furthermore, as we will see in the Appendix, the whole idea of the continuum itself, as well as the binary opposition (something–nothing) that lies at its base, is highly controversial.

It should be noted that the development of the polar types of nothing and something is part of a long tradition of such work in sociology. The most famous precursor is Ferdinand Toennies's *gemeinschaft* (family, neighborhood, and friendship relationships) and *gesellschaft* (urban, national, and cosmopolitan relationships).[3] Other famous typologies of this kind include status and contract (Maine), militant and industrial (Spencer), mechanical and organic (Durkheim), folk and urban (Redfield), sacred and secular (Becker), and so on.[4] However, none of these offers a perspective that resembles that of nothing–something. Furthermore, all of them seek to differentiate between broad types of societies while the concern here is much narrower in the effort to distinguish between places–non-places,

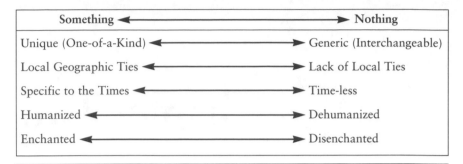

Figure 2.1   The Something–Nothing Continuum and Its Five Subcontinua

things–non-things, people–non-people, and services–non-services in the realm of consumption. However, there are common elements as well, such as the desire to use these typologies as heuristic tools to look at the social world and a sense that there is a long-term trend from one to the other.

While this entire chapter will, in a sense, be devoted to defining nothing, as well as something and the nothing–something continuum, in greater detail, it is worth reiterating the initial definitions in order to orient the ensuing discussion: Nothing is defined as that which is generally centrally conceived and controlled and largely lacking in distinctive substance, while something is defined as that which is generally indigenously conceived and controlled and possesses much in the way of distinctive substance.

These are obviously highly abstract definitions, so this chapter will provide much more depth, detail, and concreteness by developing each end of the continuum, and the continuum itself, through a multitude of subdimensions and subcontinua. What follows is an iteration and brief discussion of the five subcontinua that will be employed to help us differentiate between nothing and something. The position of any given phenomenon on the broad something–nothing continuum is a composite of its positions on each of the subcontinua developed below.[5] Bear in mind that these are *all* continua and that any given empirical reality will fall somewhere between the two poles of *each,* as well as the more general something–nothing continuum. Note that in each of the following subcontinua, the first idea(s) relates to the something end of the continuum while the second relates to its nothing pole[6] (see Figure 2.1).[7]

Unique–Generic, One-of-a-Kind–Interchangeable

This subcontinuum is premised on the idea that something is closely associated with uniqueness (being one-of-a-kind), while nothing is linked to a lack of uniqueness, to that which is generic (interchangeable).[8] That which is unique is highly likely to be indigenously created and controlled and to be rich in distinctive substance. That which is generic is likely to be centrally created and controlled and to be lacking in much, or even any, distinctive substance. A unique phenomenon is, by definition, different from every other one of its ilk.[9] That is, it has no like or equal. In order to be unique, something must have substance that differentiates it from all others. While something could, at least theoretically, be unique because it is totally devoid of substance, or because it has one or a small number of elements that distinguish it from all others, the view here is that unique phenomena almost always either have far more distinctive substance than generic phenomena or at least possess a number of distinctive substantive characteristics that set them apart from that which has few, if any, such characteristics.

Thus, a wealth of distinctive components or elements will tend to make something unique, while a (relative) dearth of the same is associated with the generic. The greater the number of distinctive components, the richer and the more complex the phenomena. And richer and more complex phenomena have a greater likelihood of being unique by dint of the fact that this diversity produces a phenomenon that is much more difficult to duplicate, let alone transform into a generic product. By contrast, phenomena with little in the way of distinctive substance are far more likely to be generic or to be transformed into generic phenomena.

Let us take as our examples a gourmet meal prepared by a highly skilled cook[10] (unique) and a pre-prepared meal in a microwaveable package (generic) made in the factory of a large corporation. In this, we follow the usual pattern of discussing polar opposites, but the fact is that here (and throughout this chapter) we are discussing continua with the result that most phenomena fall somewhere in the middle. For example, a home-cooked meal prepared by an unskilled cook would be in that realm (although toward the something end of the continuum), as would a microwave meal to which is added a few additional ingredients before serving (although this would be more toward the nothing end of the continuum).

A specific example of a microwaveable, prepackaged meal is Tyson Foods' Chicken 2 Go (there are many others), which includes chicken nuggets (a simulation of McDonald's highly successful Chicken McNuggets), French fries, and ketchup (in snack packs). The food is neatly packaged in a microwavable tray with a clear lid. Each tray is designed to be a single meal and to be heated at work, at home, or elsewhere.

The gourmet meal is unique because it is created on the spot by the cook who controls every facet of its preparation and it is composed of a complex array of distinctive ingredients and elements. This includes, but is not limited to, the selection, array, and quantity of raw ingredients and seasonings that go into the meal. It also includes the innumerable judgments made by the chef, the cooking utensils employed, the nature of the pots and pans, the degree and type (gas, electric, etc.) of heat used, the way the food is arranged on the plate, and the manner in which it is served. There are many options open to the gourmet cook and the specific choices made make each meal unique.

The microwaveable meal is cooked centrally and its later preparation is controlled by instructions printed on the package. It may have a similar (or even greater) number of seasonings and ingredients as in a unique meal,[11] but it lacks the other components—there are no options and no judgments are required of the "cook" (and, of course, virtually no skills are needed; it is even difficult to think of one who prepares a microwave meal as a cook), no tools other than the container that holds the food and the microwave are used, the temperature to be employed is predefined and only a microwave oven can be used, the food is prearranged in the container, and it is generally served in that container. Thus, there is simply much more of distinctive substance associated with a gourmet than a microwave meal with the result that much more variation is possible in the former than in the latter. Thus, no two versions of veal parmigiana prepared by different skilled cooks (or even the same cook) are likely to be the same, while every package of microwaveable veal parmigiana is likely to be much like every other one. As a result, any given gourmet meal is likely to be unique, but even the idea, let alone the reality, of a unique microwave meal is laughable.

In addition to simply having much more distinctive substance, that which is unique may have one (or a few) overriding characteristic that sets it apart from the generic. In the case of the gourmet meal, it is the skill and ability of the chef that is the primary factor distinguishing it from the microwave meal in which virtually no skill is required to "cook" the meal. Another defining characteristic might be the use of fresh and natural ingredients in gourmet meals, while microwave meals rely on pre-prepared, often unnatural, ingredients. Then there might be the use of unique, even exotic, spices in gourmet meals, while the prosaic salt predominates in microwave meals. Microwave meals, and more generally that which is generic, tend to eschew anything that smacks of being exotic.

This overlaps with the related distinction between the one-of-a-kind and the interchangeable. The gourmet meal created by the skilled cook is a one-of-a kind event. Even if the cook tried to replicate the meal exactly at a different time or in a different place (and a truly skilled cook would probably not even try), it would never be quite the same due to variations in the mood of the chef, differences in the ingredients, a tad more or less of this or that seasoning, slight variations in the way the food is cooked and served, and so on. On the other hand, microwave meals of the same type are pretty much interchangeable; one meal is prepared just like every other one of that type and they all look and taste pretty much the same no matter when or where they are "cooked."

In a rather interesting twist on this, there are now cookbooks available—for example, *Top Secret Recipes: Creating Kitchen Clones of America's Favorite Brand-Name Foods*[12]—that allow at-home preparation of the same kinds of foods to be found in microwave packages or at the local fast-food restaurant. On the latter, one can consult Gloria Pitzer's (given the substance of her book, the similarities in our last names are too close for comfort) *Secret Fast Food Recipes: The Fast Food Cookbook*[13] if one is inclined to prepare such things as one's own Big Mac at home. Needless to say, closely following a recipe for such generic food products is highly unlikely, to put it mildly, to lead to the creation of unique meals.

In sum, no two gourmet meals composed of the same dishes, even if they are prepared by the same skilled cook, will ever be exactly the same, but every microwave meal, no matter who prepares it (or when they prepare it), will be just about the same. Thus, the gourmet meal can be placed on or near the unique end of this subcontinuum, while the microwaveable meal can be found toward the generic end of that continuum.

More generally, the unique—in this case the gourmet meal—falls toward the something end of our most general continuum and the generic—here the microwave meal—is found near the nothing end of that continuum. Furthermore, this means the following:

1. Not only does the unique gourmet meal tend to be a form rich in distinctive substance and the generic microwave meal tend to be a form largely devoid of such substance, but there is a long-term trend toward the ascendancy of the microwave meal and the gourmet meal is in decline (at least relative to the increase in the microwave meal). Of course, the microwave meal is but one example of the generic in this realm. Others include predecessors like Campbell's soup, boxes of Kraft Macaroni and Cheese, and Swanson's frozen TV dinners, as well as more recent innovations like snack packs and Lunchables (another Kraft product, although a subdivision—Oscar Mayer—is listed on the package).

Lunchables may look like microwaveable food, but unlike the latter they require no "cooking" (or refrigeration); they can be eaten, as is, directly from the package. The typical Lunchable includes a few slices of some meat (for example, ham or turkey), cheese, and a few crackers neatly arranged in the three compartments of a sealed container. Schoolchildren (the main clientele for Lunchables) no longer need to put up with the surprises associated with a unique[14] lunch to be found in the brown bag brought from home. Instead, they can look forward to a generic Lunchable in which the only surprise is likely to be which meat or cheese is to be found in the appropriate compartment of that day's container.

The key point is that the Lunchable is yet another step in the direction of the progressive replacement of the unique by the generic in the domain of food. Not only are we likely to see further strides in this direction in the future, but the same general trend is occurring in virtually every other domain in the world of consumption.

2. There are advantages to both the unique (in this case the pleasures involved in eating a gourmet meal) and the generic (e.g., the low cost, efficiency, predictability, and so on of a microwave meal or a Lunchable).

3. There are disadvantages associated with both the unique (high cost, availability of gourmet meals mainly to societal elites or to those with the time to cook them) and the generic (mediocre quality of microwave meals). While this is generally true, it is also the case that home-cooked meals can be quite low in cost and the seemingly inexpensive microwaveable meals, Lunchables, and the like are usually quite costly when one carefully calculates what one is really getting in those containers. The consumer pays for the expensive packaging, and there is a lot of it—plastic container, plastic wrap, sauce packets, labels, and so on—some of it may not even be biodegradable. The minuscule portions of meat and cheese could be purchased far more cheaply on their own than as part of the Lunchable package. As is always the case, there is a high cost associated with prepackaged food (and many other things) in contrast to what the cost would be if one packaged it oneself.

4. As with something–nothing in general, the unique–generic continuum can be analyzed using all of the conceptual tools being developed in this chapter. For example, anticipating the next section (and conceptual tool), that which is unique—the gourmet meal—tends to have local roots (e.g., use of fresh, local ingredients; the skills of individual cooks in their own kitchens) while that which is generic—the microwave meal—tends to lack such roots; it tends to be from anywhere and everywhere (e.g., ingredients from many different areas; skills built into instructions on the package and accessible to everyone, everywhere).

Local Geographic Ties–Lack of Local Ties

Phenomena that are found at or near the something end of the continuum are likely to have strong ties to local geographic areas while those at the nothing end of the spectrum have few, if any, such ties.[15] As we have seen, this is linked, albeit imperfectly, to the unique–generic continuum with phenomena that have local ties more likely to be unique (they will be different from similar phenomena with ties to other localities) and those lacking in such ties more likely to be generic (sharing characteristics with other, perhaps many other, phenomena of the same type in many different locations). Thus, it is argued that phenomena with local ties are more likely to internalize the rich complexity and the distinctive substance of the local environment. Conversely, those without such ties are likely to be lacking in such complexity and distinctive substance.[16] This, of course, is closely related to the issue of the presence or absence of centralized conception and control. That which is local tends to lack such centralization, while that in which local ties are absent tends to be centralized.

Our examples in this case are a piece of handmade pottery from, let's say, a small town in Mexico and pottery mass-manufactured in a variety of geographic areas for a world market. The piece of handmade pottery is, at least in part, something for the reason discussed above—it is unique, one of a kind. In contrast, any given piece of mass-manufactured pottery is nothing because it is generic and each piece of a given type is interchangeable with every other piece. Beyond that, however, the handmade piece is something because it reflects many characteristics of the local area from which it emanates. For example, the clay may be a very distinctive local variety, it may be fired in particular ways, the ovens and even the fuel may be idiosyncratic, the pottery may reflect designs indigenous to a very particular area of Mexico (or even to a specific craftsperson), which differ from designs developed only a short distance away (or by a different craftsperson), and it may depend on a series of skills that are specific to the artisans of that area or even to a single artisan.

In this section we focus on the local pottery of the Oaxaca area of Mexico.[17] Some years ago an American was an apprentice there and he described the highly local nature of its pottery (note how well it illustrates several of the preceding points):

> So I work in Coyotepec—no throwing wheels or gas/electric kilns used here. And the clay comes from up the hill in baskets on burros.
>
> I've also got some potter friends in Atzompa—another nearby pueblo. Almost every house there has a stone kiln in the yard. They make a distinct type of pottery there (from Coyotepec) and use wholly different techniques and different clay—two villages probably 20 miles apart.[18]

While some of the pottery skills employed in these pueblos might be derived from general sources such as books, courses, seminars, and the like, even then they are likely to be modified greatly by the procedures of a local group of artisans or even the individual potter. The following is a good description of some of the procedures employed in producing Oaxaca's local pottery:

> From clay, fire, and hands full of knowledge passed from mother to daughter in an unbroken lineage that fades into the days of another age comes to life the pot. It is formed without a wheel and shaped with simple tools: a piece of gourd, a strip of leather, and the deep experience of patient time. It is warmed in the morning sun and fired in an open bonfire. What emerges from the flame is the creation of simple perfection and grace, the work of masters.[19]

The mass-manufactured pottery is likely to be lacking in all these respects.[20] It is centrally conceived and controlled and may be produced in exactly the same way in several, even many, different factories in various parts of the world. A very common clay is likely to be used or it may even be the case that many different clays from different areas will be used depending on available supplies. Clays might even be mixed to create varieties that lack distinctive ties to any geographic area.[21] A single firing technique (e.g., one that is the most efficient, least expensive) is developed and it is used over and over. The designs are likely to be generic and even when they are derived from local, unique designs, they are likely to become generic as a result of being used over and over in many geographic locations. Further, original unique designs are likely to be modified, usually simplified, so that overly complex elements (much of the substance) are removed, as are components with only local meaning or that might be considered bothersome or even offensive by some potential consumers elsewhere in the world. The skills involved are likely to be a series of well-known and simplified steps that can be used in many different production facilities in many different locales; the skills have no ties to any specific geographic area or to the people indigenous to such a locale. Unskilled or semi-skilled workers are likely to predominate with few, if any, artisans in evidence.

Of course this distinction can be applied, as well, to the preceding example of the gourmet–microwaveable meal. The gourmet meal is likely to be linked to a specific geographic area where, for example, some of the ingredients might be local and obtainable, at least fresh, only there (e.g., the use of locally gathered truffles in a Parisian gourmet restaurant or, in a less elite example, of herbs raised in a window-box in a Bronx apartment). While we tend to think of generic Mexican food, especially fast-food tacos (typical of the Mexican food sold in the United States and bearing little resemblance to the tacos sold on the streets throughout Mexico), the fact is that there is great regional diversity in gourmet Mexican food. In fact, Oaxacan cooking is especially fashionable these days. Said a cook featured on PBS, "I had taught Mexican cooking, and when I came to Oaxaca I had to re-learn everything I knew. . . . Most ingredients are toasted, roasted or fried before cooking."[22] In contrast, the microwaveable Mexican meal has no ties to any specific area, it can be bought and cooked anywhere that electricity and microwave ovens are available and affordable, and it is likely to be composed of ingredients from many different places and to follow a generic recipe designed to appeal to the broadest possible range of consumers.

We now return to the four issues discussed in the previous section:

1. That which has local ties tends to be a form rich in distinctive substance, especially that which is specific to and defines that area (e.g., the piece of Atzompa or Coyotepec pottery), and that which lacks such ties is more likely to be a form largely lacking in substance (e.g., mass-produced pottery). There is, of course, a long-term trend away from the predominance of the local (e.g., all types of crafts) and in the direction of that which has few, if any, such ties (e.g., all types of mass-manufactured products). A sense of this change in made clear by the potters of Oaxaca:

> In the waning days of this century the pottery of Oaxaca is disappearing. Tin, plastic, and aluminum are impatiently filling the place of clay. Today the potters still work, the pottery lives. But the question arises, how many more mothers will be able to pass the ways of clay, fire, and hands down to their daughters?[23]

2. There are advantages associated with local pottery (e.g., maintenance of traditions, sustaining local crafts), but the eradication of local ties in mass-manufactured pottery also has its advantages (e.g., a more general appeal, greater availability, lower prices).

3. There are disadvantages associated with both local pottery (e.g., limited availability) and mass-made pottery that lacks local ties (e.g., an absence of touches and nuance that can come only from a craftsperson).

4. As with all the others, this continuum can be analyzed using the other tools outlined in this chapter. For example, once again anticipating the next section, local pottery tends to be linked to a specific time period while mass-manufactured pottery tends to be time-less in the sense that term is used here (see below). Thus, as is made clear in one of the preceding quotations, the pottery of Oaxaca has a specific historical lineage, while the mass-produced pottery cannot be tied to any such period of time.[24]

Specific-to-the-Times–Relatively Time-less

We can differentiate not only among phenomena that are, or are not, specific to a given locale, but also specific to a given time period. Those that are specific to a time period would tend to be distinctive (and more likely to be something), while those that are more time-less would tend to lack distinctiveness (and more likely to be nothing). (I hyphenate *time-less* here to distinguish it from *timeless,* which has a different meaning—everlasting—than the one I intend here—*that which cannot easily be tied to a given time period.* In fact, timeless, as the word is usually used, is associated with that which is specific to the times.) Those phenomena that are particular to a time period (and, as we saw in the case of Oaxaca pottery, that time period can be quite long) would tend to be loaded with the substance of the slice of time in question, while those that are relatively time-less would tend to lack such substance. In fact, the need to seem time-less requires that virtually all substance that might have related to any particular timeframe be removed or at least muted.

That which is locally conceived and controlled (e.g., Oaxacan pottery) tends to be specific to the times, while that which is centrally conceived and controlled tends to be time-less. Local producers naturally reflect the time in which they live or a longer sweep of time of which they are part and are only the most recent reflection. Centralized producers are more likely, because of their desire to maximize sales and profits, to be motivated to produce that which is time-less since such entities are likely to appeal to the widest possible audience. However, as we will see in the following example, even centralized producers can, either purposely or inadvertently, produce products that come to be seen as embedded in a particular time period.

Certain automobile styles have become timeless (not time-less) classics and one of the reasons that they have achieved that status is that at least some people have come to define them, consciously or more likely unconsciously, as reflections of the era in which they were manufactured.[25] Take the American muscle car,[26] for example, the 1969 Pontiac Firebird. Muscle cars, of course, are big, powerful cars that are especially noted for motors with a great deal of horsepower. To aficionados they have come to be seen as products of an era in which the United States was astride the world both economically and militarily and the continued interest in classic cars of this period, as well as in more contemporary versions of such cars, reflects the fact that the United States continues to occupy such a position in the world.[27] I hasten to add that the 1969 Pontiac Firebird, and indeed all muscle cars, were mass-manufactured to be time-less. It was only later that fans of the cars came to define them as something, in part because they were such good reflections of a particular epoch.[28]

Another example is the original Volkswagen (VW) Beetle (it was Adolph Hitler who believed that the car should be modeled after a beetle), which was a product of Nazi and Hitlerian ambitions to conquer the world. The Volkswagen, first produced in 1938, was to be the simple, low-cost, mass-manufactured automobile for the masses that would soon and had already come under the sway of Nazism. WWII prevented this goal from being achieved, but after the close of the war Beetle sales began to take off. By 1972, approximately 15 million Beetles had been manufactured. After ceasing production of the original Beetle in most of the world in 1975 (it continues to be produced in Mexico), a new version of the Volkswagen "Bug" appeared in 1998.[29] However, the earlier models, based on the original and highly distinctive style, remain classics and very attractive to collectors and enthusiasts.

The continuing appeal of old and new Beetles makes it clear that the specific time period being referred to here can, in fact, be quite long. The new Beetle was clearly launched with the idea of being part of a longer tradition. While it was modernized in many ways, its ties to the original Beetle (sans its Hitlerian associations) were very clear. Similarly, Ford's reintroduction of the retro-designed Thunderbird (some even call it the retro-bird[30]) was designed to tie it not only to early versions of that car—the first ones were manufactured in 1954—but even earlier road cars. Says Ford: "It's a truly modern rendering of the original American Dream Car."[31] More generally, some of the appeal of the convertible stems from the fact that it is a self-conscious descendant of early horse-drawn carriages since, "In the beginning, all cars were open."[32] A more recent source of today's convertibles is the open touring cars of the roaring 1920s (important new convertibles were introduced in the late 1920s). However, sales of convertibles in the United States declined and in 1976 Cadillac announced that it was building the last American convertible (European manufacturers continued to produce convertibles). But, in 1982, the American convertible reappeared as the Chrysler LeBaron and since then several American (and international) convertible brands have been produced. Their current popularity is traceable, at least in part, to the historical lineage of which they are only the latest manifestation.

These examples make it clear that while most automobiles are manufactured to be time-less, some (muscle cars, the original Beetle) come to be defined as timeless at least in part because fans see them as having ties to a particular time period. However, these examples also make it clear that manufacturers can self-consciously create automobile models—the new Beetle, the retro-Thunderbird—that are linked explicitly to a particular period of time, a longer tradition of which they are part.

There are innumerable examples of classic automobiles and, among other things, they tend to be cars that reflect something important about a given time period. One could say much the same about classics in many other realms. Such perennials would fall toward the something end of the continuum, while those things that are not intimately associated with a particular time period—those things that are relatively time-less—are more likely to be found at the nothing end of that continuum. Thus, a relatively generic car—one that has little to distinguish itself and that takes little, if anything, distinctive in terms of character and styling from the era in which it is built—will be highly unlikely to become a classic, to become something. Examples today would be many of today's low-end cars such as those produced by the Korean manufacturers Hyundai and its subsidiary Kia. Low-end cars of American manufacturers—say the Dodge Neon—are in a similar position.[33] Such cars are generic machines with generic designs that, among other things, take little from and say little about the era in which they were built. Thus, while the Web page for the Thunderbird embeds the car in a historical tradition, Kia's offers no such vision, but instead focuses on pragmatic issues such as price, warranty, and special offers. History is strewn with long-forgotten brands of generic automobiles, but the truly unique ones, those that said, and perhaps still say, something about a given time period, continue to be of interest and even to have books written about, and clubs devoted to, them.

It is safe to predict that some of today's cars—even some of today's relatively inexpensive cars—will become the classics of tomorrow and one of the reasons they will achieve that position is that they say, or will come to be seen as saying, something about the early years of the 21st century. Another way of putting this is that these cars—like the muscle cars, the VW Beetle, and the Thunderbird described above—are likely to become cultural icons. The Beetle has clearly attained the status of such an icon[34] and as a result a number of books have been written about it (it is unlikely that even one book will be written about the Kia or the Dodge Neon).[35] There was even a Disney Movie—*The Love Bug* (1969)—that featured Herbie, a VW Beetle. Again, it is difficult to envision a film featuring Howie the Dodge Neon!

Of course, while we have focused on centrally conceived and produced products in this discussion, it is the indigenous products that are far more likely to reflect a specific time period and to do so to a much greater degree. Such products are quite simply deeply embedded in specific periods of time (and places) and must reflect them, at least to a large degree. On the other hand, those involved in the centralized conception and control of products often seek, quite consciously and usually successfully, to extract them from identifiable periods of time (and places). However, at times, even they are interested in trying to produce things that are portrayed as being enmeshed in a given time period.

Once again we look at the four issues that concern us for each contin-uum, this time the specific to the times–time-less dimension:

1. That which is specific to a given time period (e.g., the muscle car) tends to be a form rich in distinctive substance (especially the reflection of a particular era), and that which is time-less (e.g., today's Kia) is more likely to be a form largely lacking in distinctive substance. Once again, there is a long-term trend from the predominance of that which is specific to a given time period (e.g., a classic in any one of many domains) to that which is time-less (e.g., the vast majority of mass-manufactured[36] products and, after all, virtually everything is made that way these days). In the case of automobiles, there are various niche cars—the VW Beetle, the Ford Thunderbird, the convertible—that have a measure of success, but the vast majority of cars sold, and the best-selling models, all are rather time-less products. Indeed, it could be argued that broad success requires time-lessness. Linkage to any specific time period may attract some buyers, but the unique characteristics associated with it are likely to be unattractive to, or even repel, most potential buyers. Thus, the vast majority of manufacturers feel impelled to emphasize the production of the most innocuous, time-less automobiles (and other products) since it is in that direction that the greatest sales potential lies.

2. There are advantages associated with that which is time-bound (those who identify with the time period represent a ready clientele), but the time-less have advantages as well (appeal to a far wider and larger audience with no particular allegiance to any time period).

3. There are disadvantages associated with both that which is specific to a given timeframe (limited interest) and that which lacks such specificity (an absence of "soul," of content that is a reflection of a particular time period).

4. Needless to say, the specific-to-the-times–relatively time-less continuum can also be analyzed using the other tools outlined in this chapter. As has become the pattern, anticipating the next section, the Volkswagen Bug has a very personal human imprint. Unfortunately the name most often associated with it is that of Adolph Hitler (today, Volkswagen executives shrink at the mention of that association[37]). However, the Volkswagen was more the product of Ferdinand Porsche, whose name was later to be associated with expensive, high-performance automobiles. Similarly, the Chrysler LeBaron convertible, and before that another iconic car—the Ford Mustang—were very much the products of a giant of the era in the automobile industry, Lee Iacocca.[38] These automobiles are more the product of human beings and human relationships than they are of dehumanized bureaucracies and bureaucrats (more likely the source of automobiles like the Kia and the Neon). Of course, this is even more true of the specific to the times products that emanate from local communities.

Humanized–Dehumanized

That which is something tends to be associated with deep and highly meaningful human relationships, while nothing is linked to the relative absence of such human relationships: to dehumanized relationships.[39] Those things that are enmeshed in strong human relations are likely to have a great deal that is substantively distinctive associated with such relationships (e.g., the detailed interpersonal histories associated with them). On the other hand, dehumanized phenomena are far less likely to permit the development of substantial personal relationships among those involved. Overall, that which is characterized by human relationships is more likely to be something, while that which is lacking in such relationships is more likely to be nothing.

The exemplary contrast here might be the small teaching college and the Internet university.[40] The small teaching college is a largely American phenomenon characterized by relatively small classes and professors whose prime responsibility is teaching and not research (the reverse is the case in large state and elite universities such as the University of Michigan and Yale University). The Internet university (University of Phoenix is a major example[41]) offers the possibility of obtaining a degree wholly, or in large part, online.

The Internet university is, by its very nature, centrally conceived and controlled. In contrast, a small teaching college is characterized by largely local conception and control. Such a college is, almost by definition, characterized by close, even intimate relationships among the people involved (although online contacts of various types are increasing in these settings). This is likely to be true not only of relationships between professors and students but also among the students (and professors) themselves. It is these highly personal relationships that are likely to place the small teaching college toward the something end of the continuum. Furthermore, it is likely to have many of the other characteristics of something discussed above. It is more likely to be a setting with which people identify strongly and, in some cases (especially the faculty), remain associated with for a long time. Even though students are likely to stay for only four or five years, they are more likely than students of Internet universities to identify strongly with the college during the time that they are there. Furthermore, they are more likely to retain that identity and therefore to return for class reunions, be involved in alumni associations, and so on. (Can an Internet university even have something resembling a reunion or an alumni association? After all, a reunion implies the personal relationships that the Internet university never had in the first place.) They are also likely to be strongly tied to a place (for example, the small teaching colleges of New England such as Amherst or Smith) and a particular time period (there are likely to be efforts to retain historic architecture and longstanding and sometimes seemingly outmoded traditions). And, of course, each teaching college is likely to be quite unique.

The online university is almost diametrically opposed to the small teaching college and stands, therefore, toward the nothing end of the continuum. Almost by definition, it will be impossible to develop personal relationships in such universities either between teachers and students or among the students. As an Internet site, it is by definition a place of flows—information, students, and professors logging on and off, and so on—and highly unlikely to become a locale in which such flows slow down and even stop for a time (see Chapter 3 for a discussion of the relationship between locales and flows). Educational sites on the Internet are likely to appear and disappear with great rapidity. Furthermore, those who visit these sites are apt to have the most ephemeral of contacts as they dip in and out at a rapid rate. Internet universities certainly have, and offer, no sense of place, unless it is their specific Internet addresses. And, they have no historical ties (at least as yet), unless it is to the general era of the arrival of the personal computer and the Internet. Internet universities are likely to closely resemble one another with the result that not one of them can have much in the way of uniqueness.

We now return to the issues that concern us in each of these sections:

1. The forms that involve deep human relations tend to be rich in distinctive substance (for example, a small teaching college and the innumerable interpersonal relationships that develop while one is a student there) and those that are dehumanized and dehumanizing tend to be forms largely devoid of such substance (for example, the Internet university in which it is literally impossible to develop such relationships). Furthermore, there is a long-term trend away from that which involves humanized relationships to that which is dehumanized. More specifically, while there will continue to be a place for the small teaching college (especially for elites who can afford it), it is likely that an increasing number of students will be educated in, and obtain degrees from, Internet universities. In addition, even those students who remain in traditional colleges and universities will get a lot more of their education over the Internet. Indeed, at least some of those colleges and universities will become increasingly involved in making their educational resources available (for a [high] price) on the Internet.

2. There are advantages to both the forms with deep human relationships (for example, the satisfactions of relating to people one knows well in a small teaching college, the greater learning possibilities that exist in face-to-face relationships among teachers and students) and the dehumanized

forms (for example, the freedom and the efficiencies associated with lack of personal involvement with others in the Internet university).

3. There are disadvantages associated with both that which has strong human relationships (for example, entanglements with people one might rather avoid at a small college, the hostility of particular professors) and that which is dehumanized (for example, an absence of meaning or soul at Internet U).

4. Again, the humanized–dehumanized continuum can be analyzed using the various tools being developed here. For example, anticipating the next section once again, small teaching colleges tend to be quite enchanted, while Internet universities are apt to be highly disenchanted. For many, being a student in a small teaching college can be something approaching a magical experience, but little in the way of enchantment is likely to be involved in a student's relationship with an Internet university that, because of its very nature, must be highly rationalized and therefore, by definition, disenchanted.

Enchanted–Disenchanted

This final continuum tends to bring together all of that which has come before. That which is something tends to have an enchanted, magical quality, while that which is nothing is more likely to be disenchanted, to lack mystery or magic. Thus, the foods delivered to us from Domino's, in the Lunchables our youngsters devour, and in the microwaveable package we open for dinner are unlikely to have much in the way of enchantment associated with them. Think of that wonderfully rationalized Lunchable package with its neat compartments and its uniform slices of meat and cheese, to say nothing of those little packets of ketchup. It is hard to think of any food more rationalized, and less enchanted, than this. And, of course, to most observers, its taste is in line with its packaging. Indeed, some may prefer to eat the package than the food inside it.

On the other hand, homemade gourmet meals may well have an enchanted quality about them. Taking a wide range of ingredients and seeing them transformed into a gourmet meal is likely to seem quite magical. The novel *Like Water for Chocolate* offers wonderful examples of the enchantment associated with food preparation and the consumption of lovingly made home-cooked meals. (Similarly, the movie *Chocolat* features handmade candies that have similarly enchanting qualities.) At one level, there is the magic associated with the various steps involved in the preparation of food including "peeling the garlic, cleaning the chiles, and grinding the spices"[42] and then seeing that come together in the creation of homemade sausage.

At another, there is food like chilies in walnut sauce acting as an aphrodisiac, creating "heat in her limbs, the tickling sensations in the center of her body, the naughty thoughts."[43] In contrast, one does not experience the magic of creating a Domino's pizza and it is hard to imagine eating one of those pizzas having an impact like that of those chilies in walnut sauce or, more to the point, anyone writing a novel depicting such a pizza as an aphrodisiac. Even if it was to be written, a novel titled *Like Water for Lunchables* is unlikely to attract much of a readership.

Once again, we can see the way in which all of the preceding continua relate to this, perhaps culminating in an overarching, enchantment–disenchantment continuum. The unique—as in the home-cooked sausages described above—is much more likely to seem enchanted than the generic—yet another Domino's pizza—which clearly seems to be associated with, and has many of the characteristics of, disenchantment. This is directly linked to the fact that foods like homemade sausage are local products and such sausages are likely to vary greatly from one locale to another. It is the local nature of the ingredients and the particular way in which they are combined in a given locale that gives such foods much of their magic. Needless to say, Domino's pizza has no such local ties; it is exactly the same wherever it is produced and eaten and this contributes to its disenchanted character.

A similar point can be made about the issue of time. Using ingredients that are specific to a given time period is more likely to produce enchanted products than using those that are time-less. For example, the use of ingredients that are seasonal—for example, summer fruits and vegetables—is more likely to produce enchanted dishes than is the case with using ingredients available year-round. A medley of summer fruits or a salad made up of summer vegetables is more likely to seem magical than salads made with apples available year-round (and often stored for long periods and deteriorating over time) or a medley of potatoes, onions, and other vegetables available throughout the year. Similarly, a fresh summer fruit salad is likely to seem more enchanted than one served during the winter and made with frozen or canned fruits.

It is human beings who are likely to create magical phenomena of all types; it takes a creative cook to create a magical dish. Similarly, disenchanted dishes are likely to be the result of dehumanized processes (e.g., following instructions and heating up meals in the microwave). A similar point applies to the consumption of food. Eating an enchanted meal at home or in a gourmet restaurant can be a very human experience, whereas eating in a fast-food restaurant, or worse in an automobile after one has obtained one's food at a drive-through window, is likely to be a dehumanized and dehumanizing experience.

Of course, that which is conceived in some centralized setting and which is tightly controlled (a Lunchable is a perfect example) is highly unlikely to be enchanted; indeed, it is almost by definition disenchanted. And that which is conceived and controlled locally (and the chilies with walnut sauce dish discussed above is an excellent example of that) is far more likely to have at least some enchanted qualities.

We now return for a final look at the four key issues:

1. Those enchanted chilies with walnut sauce are loaded with distinctive substance, while that disenchanted Domino's pizza is lacking much of the way of distinctive substance. There is a long-term trend away from meals characterized by enchanted foods to those composed entirely of disenchanted foods like microwave meals and Domino's pizza. The decline in meals made (especially from scratch) and eaten at home and the corresponding rise in premade dishes brought home from the local market, home delivery of pizza, and meals eaten out in fast-food (and other chain) restaurants are all indicators of this dramatic change in our eating habits.

2. Enchanted foods have their advantages (a magical dining experience), but so too do disenchanted foods (the ease of obtaining that pizza).

3. And both have their disadvantages. Homemade chilies with walnut sauce are available to only a few. Home-delivered pizzas are available to many, but they could hardly be seen as offering the kind of magnificent dining experience associated with those chilies.

4. Finally, and returning to the first of our continua since no new ones follow, the enchanted tends to be unique (homemade sausages vary from area to area, time to time, and even family to family), whereas the disenchanted tends to be generic (Domino's pizza is the same from one time and place to another).

How Does This Relate to Globalization?

While we have not said much about globalization to this point, and will not deal with it in detail until Chapter 4, we need at least to touch on this issue here. The central point is that those phenomena that stand toward the nothing end of the general nothing–something continuum, as well as that end of each of the specific subcontinua discussed in this chapter, are far more likely to be globalized than those that stand at the something end of both the five subcontinua and the nothing–something continuum. Thus, returning to the specific examples discussed above, the microwave meal (and the Lunchable), mass-produced Mexican pottery, generic automobiles, higher education on the Internet, and fast-food pizzas are all important global phenomena. The parallel examples in the realm of something—the gourmet meal, handmade Mexican pottery, muscle cars, small teaching colleges, and those exotic chili dishes—do not have nearly the global presence of their counterparts in the realm of nothing. Nonetheless, it is a reflection of the power of globalization that even the various forms of something have a global reach. In some cases—such as the Volkswagen Beetle—that global reach is quite extensive.[44] It is clear that it is the various forms of nothing that are, and by a wide margin, the more significant players and forces in the global marketplace. We will deal with this, and why it is the case, later in this book.

Objective, or Are They?

The conceptual arsenal laid out in this chapter seems quite straightforward and very neat. Presented here are five very clear sets of concepts (and the overarching nothing–something continuum), as well as five continua on which one of the paired concepts represents one pole and the other the opposite pole. Although a few wrinkles have arisen here and there in the discussion, there would seem to be little difficulty in using these seemingly objective tools to arrive at a quite unbiased conclusion about where any given phenomenon lies on each of these continua and by combining those positions in some way on the overall something–nothing continuum.

While this is *one* of the ways in which the ideas developed in this chapter are intended to be used, it is just not that simple. Not only has the social world changed, especially from the point of view of this book in the increase in nothing (and its globalization), but the intellectual world has as well. Interestingly, in some ways the changes that have taken place in the social and intellectual worlds are diametrically opposed to one another. While nothing has become increasingly common in the social world, in a way it has become less and less possible to offer nothing in the intellectual world, at least in the social sciences and humanities. That is, it is harder to offer abstract concepts, devoid of content, that purport to be accurate descriptions of the social world or that claim to be scientific tools that can be used in an objective, value-free analysis of that world. Scholars are increasingly questioning whether the objective creation and utilization of such substantively empty concepts is either possible or desirable. In addition, it is argued that it is illusory to think that scholars can do what others cannot do—be completely objective about their world and its activities. Instead, it is argued that it may be that highly subjective analyses, that is, those using concepts that are saturated with the realities of the social world rather than being abstracted from that world, are not only inevitable but also preferable.

In the Appendix we will discuss the problems involved in conceptualizing nothing (and something, as well as the various subcontinua) created by the development of new ways of looking at the social world. We will see that, at best, the kind of objective, "scientific" approach presented in, and implied by, this chapter is only one of several possibilities. Whatever the complexities of contemporary social science and its critics, the fact remains that at the minimum the tools developed here and elsewhere in this book are designed mainly to help the reader get a better sense of nothing (and something). While they may not yield an objective, scientific sense of nothing, or even necessarily help the reader be more objective (although I think they will) about this issue, they do offer much that enriches our understanding of nothing (and something).

Chapter Three

Meet the Nullities

In this chapter we examine the four major forms of nothing—non-places, non-things, non-people, and non-services—and their relationship to the corresponding forms of something—places, things, people, and services. In so doing we use the five subcontinua developed in Chapter 2 and, more generally, the something–nothing continuum and, as usual, we focus on consumption.

Non-Places (and Places)

The idea of a non-place is rooted in cultural geography[1] and the distinction between a space and a place. In fact, as pointed out in Chapter 1, it is the thinking on non-places that is a major source of this book's concern with nothing in general and, more specifically, with the extension of the idea to non-things, -people, and -services.

A useful place to begin is with the work of Edward Relph, who, in a number of books, most notably *Place and Placelessness*,[2] developed a series of ideas on the issue of the relationship of place to placelessness. To Relph, places are loaded with distinctive substance: "Places . . . are full with meanings, with real objects, and with ongoing activities. They are important sources of individual and communal identity, and are often profound centres of human existence to which people have deep emotional and psychological ties."[3] Placelessness, then, is "an environment without significant places and the underlying attitude which does not acknowledge significance in places. It reaches back into the deepest levels of place, cutting roots, eroding symbols, replacing diversity with uniformity."[4] Relph sees a dangerous and powerful long-term trend away from place and in the direction of placelessness, from that which is rich in distinctive substance to that which is lacking in such substance, from something to nothing. He urges people to transcend placelessness in an effort to halt, what is to him, a worrisome trend.

While a non-place would be another way of describing what Relph conceives of as placelesness, of far greater and more direct use to our analysis of such settings, as well as their polar opposites[5]—places (and the other nullities of concern here)—is the work of the French anthropologist Marc Augé, especially *Non-Places: Introduction to an Anthropology of Supermodernity*. In turn, a major intellectual source of Augé's thinking on non-places is the work of one of the most important classical anthropologists, Marcel Mauss, and that of other ethnologists on *place*, or "a culture localized in time and space."[6] It is worth underscoring the fact that Mauss is seen as using, at least by implication, several of the dimensions—time (especially specific-to-the-times–relatively time-less) and space (especially local geographic ties–lack of local ties)—used in this book to distinguish between something and nothing. However, Augé goes beyond this ethnological view to argue that a place has three other characteristics—relations, history, and identity—and these, too, are either related to continua employed here—humanized–dehumanized—or to issues such as aura of permanency-ephemeral and identity–lack of identity that will concern us later in this book. These characteristics lead Augé to the definition of a non-place as "a space which cannot be defined as relational, or historical, or concerned with identity."[7] Augé is clearly anticipating many of the dimensions employed in this analysis either as the continua that lie at the base of this work or as factors that enter the analysis at various points as we proceed; indeed his work is an important source of many of them.

While Augé describes places as involving fantasy and myth, he clearly is more positively inclined to them than non-places and the historical trend in their direction. For example, he seems to prefer the organically social character of places to the contractual solidarity of non-places. Furthermore, many of the terms he uses to describe non-places—solitary, fleeting, similitude, anonymity, lacking in history, and so on—communicate a critical attitude toward non-places. (We will discuss our own critique of nothing in Chapter 7.)

The distinction between places and non-places is closely related to Manuel Castells's[8] view that we are moving from a world characterized by "spaces of places" to one dominated by "spaces of flows."[9] Spaces of places tend to be unique settings characterized by rich geographic ties and an array of characteristics with deep ties to specific points in the locale's history, while areas defined by flows tend to be generic, to lack geographic ties, and to have a time-less quality. More generally, there is a high, but not perfect, correlation between spaces of places and something and spaces of flows and nothing. Given their constant and ubiquitous fluidity, it is very difficult for spaces of flows to become something. Spaces of places are more likely to be something because they have the stability to develop a distinctive substantive base, but flows lack such stability and therefore tend to be relatively devoid of such substance.

We can take as an example of spaces of places a well-established local residential community in which each house has been built to the owner's specifications and is therefore different from every other house. That is, the array of houses is not centrally planned or controlled by developers and builders. Those who live in such communities are more likely to have lived there for long periods of time and to have deep ties to them. These communities are likely to be integral parts of the larger geographic settings in which they exist and to have an organic relationship with their environments. They are also likely to be products of a specific time period and to continue to have deep ties to it. Given all these characteristics, such communities are likely to be quite unique and, most generally, to be positioned close to the something end of the something–nothing continuum.

The contrast—that is, those communities that can be considered spaces of flows—are the myriad tract house and planned communities that followed in the wake of the construction of the paradigmatic Levittown[10] in the post-WWII era (see also the discussion of the English planned village of Milton Keynes in Chapter 1). The houses in such communities are built according to a limited number of designs so that many houses are identical to many others. The entire community is conceived by a central source (usually a developer) and once in existence is subjected to centralized control (especially today's gated communities). In the main, these communities have not been created to last and the houses built in them are constructed of inexpensive materials so that they are unlikely to survive nearly as long as the houses built in more traditional communities. Not only do the communities and the houses in them come and go, but more importantly so do the residents, and at a much more rapid rate than they do in more traditional communities. That is, residents move in and out of these communities rapidly and rarely settle in for long periods of time. Thus, there is an ephemeral quality to these communities, as well as to the houses and people in them. Much the same setting, style, and configuration of housing are likely to be repeated in many different places with the result that it seems hard to differentiate among such communities. In addition, they often seem to be imposed on the local geographic area rather than being an organic part of it. Finally, the communities and houses are purposely rather time-less[11]; they seem to lack ties to a specific time period (or a given geographic location). Such settings can be thought of as "nowhere," as models of what concerned James Howard Kuntsler in *The Geography of Nowhere*.[12]

Given this general background, let us turn now to a discussion of each of the continua as they relate to places–non-places. However, instead of discussing the continua in general terms, in each case we will focus on a specific example of a non-place[13] and contrast it to a place (we will do the same and focus on specific examples in ensuing discussions of non-things, non-people, and non-services). In the case of places–non-places the specific contrast will be between a diner[14] (more likely to be a place) and a fast-food restaurant[15] (more likely to be a non-place).

A Brief Excursus on Great Good Places and McDonaldized Non-Places

Before getting to that discussion, we need to introduce the ideas of a great good place and McDonaldization, which, as the reader will see, neatly complement one another and inform our discussion of diners and fast-food restaurants and, more generally, places and non-places.

A diner can be seen, in most cases, as a specific type of what Ray Oldenburg calls a "great good place"[16] or a "third place" (in contrast to first [home] and second [work] places). Oldenburg's examples of great good places include German beer gardens, English pubs, French cafés, American taverns, coffeehouses, book shops, and so on. Also included under this heading are settings that have largely disappeared from the American scene such as "soda fountains, malt shops, candy stores, and cigar stores."[17] Interestingly, Oldenburg does not explicitly include a diner under the heading of a great good place, but it will be our example because of the ways in which it fits the category as well as the interesting and revealing ways in which it does not, the fact that while it still exists it may be going the way of the malt shop, and because the diner has been the subject of a large amount of research and writing.

To Oldenburg, great good places are "informal gathering places."[18] As such, they are "the core settings of informal public life . . . [and] host the regular, voluntary, informal and happily anticipated gatherings of individuals beyond the realms of home and work."[19] There are a variety of characteristics that make for a great good place, including the fact that it is a neutral ground for all, it is a leveler in that virtually everyone is welcome because of the absence of formal criteria for either admission or exclusion, it is easily accessible and readily available, the setting is unpretentious, the mood is playful, there are many regulars, and conversation is the main activity within these settings. One study of an African American tavern (Trena's) identifies a number of regulars and contends, "Much of the time the regulars spend in Trena's is spent talking about a variety of topics."[20] Great good places may be seen as homes away from home giving us roots, a sense of possession and control, an environment where we can be regenerated and restored, a place where we have great freedom, and a setting of great warmth. One regular at Trena's says the following: "If you can't reach me at Trena's, then try calling me at home. But you're more likely to catch me here."[21]

Ann Sather, a local Chicago restaurant, is another good example of a great good place:

> Regulars make up about one-third of the customers at Ann Sather, Tunney [the current owner] said. "I spend a lot of time in the front-of-the-house and try to remember names." That goes a long way. "We train our servers to be that way, too," he added.
>
> "We have so many regulars that they have developed friendships just by being there at the same time," he added. "It's a warm and friendly atmosphere where they feel comfortable eating alone, too."

Being a visible, hands-on owner makes it easier for Tunney to create that sought-after sense of community. "That's the personal touch for which there really is no substitute," he said.[22]

While a fast-food restaurant *could* become a great good place, there are major impediments (see below for a discussion of some of them) to it taking on the basic characteristics of such a place. Nonetheless, there are certainly times when every fast-food restaurant does, at least for short periods of time, function much like a great good place. Furthermore, this may be regularized when, for example, seniors are allowed to use the restaurant one morning a week for their bingo games. And, there is evidence that in other cultures, fast-food restaurants are much more likely to function like great good places than they do in the United States. As James Watson puts it, "East Asian consumers have quietly, and in some cases stubbornly, transformed their neighborhood McDonald's into local institutions."[23] Specifically, in Hong Kong, teenagers turn the fast-food restaurant into a great good place for at least a few hours a day after school by transforming it, with the owner's permission and even encouragement, into a setting in which to socialize with friends.[24]

While fast-food restaurants *can* be transformed into great good places, it is difficult to do so and, as a result, rarely occurs. The reason relates to the basic structure of such restaurants and the fundamental principles that lie at their base: the principles of McDonaldization.[25] Fast-food restaurants are structured in a way that generally prevents them from becoming great good places. Think, for example, of the increasingly popular drive-through windows that are designed to keep people out of the restaurant and to prevent informal groups, especially of regulars engaged in lively and playful conversation, from developing in it. Then, there are the famous chairs that are designed to be so uncomfortable that people want to leave soon after they sit down. The bright colors grow ever-more off-putting the longer people remain in the restaurant. Or, there is the spartan, even antiseptic, environment that is hardly conducive to staying long enough to create a great good place.

These structures, as well as much else about the fast-food restaurant, stem from the basic principles of McDonaldization that informs all of them. One of those principles is *efficiency,* or the discovery of the optimum means to whatever end is chosen. The drive-through window is, of course, a highly efficient mechanism for allowing people to obtain their food. More generally, everything that transpires in the fast-food restaurant is designed for maximum efficiency. Structures and environments that emphasize efficiency are, by their very nature, antithetical to the emergence of a great good place. Interaction and conversation, the core of such a place, do not thrive and are not encouraged in a domain committed to, and characterized by, great efficiency.

Similarly, *predictability,* or the effort to ensure that products and services are the same from one time or place to another, militates against a great good place. People are simply not going to want to congregate for long, or very many times, in a setting that is numbingly predictable. The good conversation and the playfulness of great good places thrive more in settings that are unpredictable and encourage unpredictability.

Then there is the emphasis in McDonaldized settings on *calculability,* on quantity rather than quality. Among other things, this means that fast-food restaurants want the experience of their customers to be fast and cheap. Furthermore, they do not care much about the quality of the experience customers have in the restaurant and they are not interested in doing much to make that experience better, more meaningful.[26] On the other hand, great good places like Trena's and Ann Sather care deeply about just such things and do what they can to enhance the quality of their customers' experiences.

McDonaldized systems also seek to exercise great control over customers and workers through the use of *non-human technology.* The drive-through window and the uncomfortable chairs are examples as far as customers are concerned, while numerous technologies (automatic French fry machines, soft-drink machines with sensors that shut off the flow when the glass is full, and so on) control employees' actions. Most generally, control is inimical to the freedom, even playfulness, of great good places. More specifically, these control mechanisms are used to prevent the development of characteristics of great good places. For example, employees are encouraged to limit their interaction with customers and to rely on preset scripts instead of engaging in conversation freely and creatively. The result is that the conversation between employee and customer is greatly limited, stymieing the possibility of the emergence of a great good place. In contrast, in the latter it is often the case that personal relationships develop between customers and workers (and sometimes owners) and this is a key component of a great good place.

Finally, McDonaldized systems are characterized by the *irrationality of rationality,* one of which is *dehumanization.* Great good places are based on human relationships, just the kind of relationships that are actively discouraged in fast-food restaurants. Thus, at Trena's bartenders and regulars often have deeply human relationships based on their detailed personal knowledge of one another. In a fast-food restaurant, counter people and customers are unlikely to know one another well, if at all. Their interaction is not only superficial, but dominated by scripts that counter people must follow in relating to customers. For these reasons, and others, relationships in fast-food restaurants tend to be less human, to be dehumanized.

Thus, it is clear that there are major differences between great good places and McDonaldized settings. To put it in the terms of this chapter, the former are places while the latter are non-places. With this as background, we turn to a more detailed discussion of our two specific examples: the diner (a place) and the fast-food restaurant (a non-place).

Analyzing Places–Non-Places

The nothingness of non-places like fast-food restaurants is manifest first in the fact that they are generic rather than unique and interchangeable rather than one-of-a-kind. In contrast, virtually every diner is different, often in quite profound ways, from every other one. This is the case even though for many years, and especially in the two decades after the end of WWII, large numbers of diners were prefabricated by a relatively small number of manufacturers and many were identical to one another in both external design (often shaped something like a railroad or trolley car) and interior structure.[27] However, most owners seek at least superficial structural differences in order to distinguish their diner from competitors. There are many common elements in almost all diners—the counter, the griddle, the cashier station, and so on—but these are all likely to be arranged slightly differently and to include elements that are likely to be found in few, if any, other diners.

However, while there are strong physical similarities among many diners, they are not nearly as similar as the exterior structure and interior design of fast-food restaurants, especially in their early years. Furthermore, there is no parallel in diners to the golden arches of McDonald's or the statue of the Big Boy in front of the chain of restaurants bearing that name. But what is truly unique about the diner is the ambiance created by owner and employees and the interaction between them and customers, as well as that between customers, especially the regulars. Furthermore, as chains of fast-food restaurants grew and became powerful competition to diners, the latter had to respond, if they hoped to survive, by taking on more of the characteristics of a great good place.

One indicator of the profound difference between these phenomena is the fact that while fast-food restaurants have proven to be ideal for the development of chains of generic, interchangeable units, diners have proven far less amenable to such a business structure with the result that efforts to form chains of diners have been notably unsuccessful. Diners lie toward the unique, one-of-a kind end of the continuum and the failure of efforts to create chains is an important factor keeping them there. Furthermore, basic to the whole idea of a franchise is the centralized conceptualization of the chain as whole, as well as of every unit in it. In addition, chains, at least since the creation of McDonald's, are based on centralized control. Prior to McDonald's, chains had foundered because the central office had little interest in a unit once a basic initial fee had been paid; it had little or no continuing control over its units. McDonald's originally asked a very small initial fee for a franchise, but continued to receive a substantial percentage of its profits. This gave the company's central headquarters a continuing interest in, and oversight and control over, its franchises. Furthermore, McDonald's used (and continues to use) inspectors to ensure that franchises live up to its standards and guidelines. Thus, McDonald's and other contemporary chains of fast-food restaurants are characterized by comparatively high levels of central control. In contrast, since they are usually individual, stand-alone operations, diners are subjected to neither centralized conceptualization nor control.

One exception to the failure to produce chains is Silver Diner, a small chain of twelve diners in the Washington, D.C., area. While such a chain is not without significance, this is a far cry from the 30,000 or so McDonald's restaurants, to say nothing of the hundreds of thousands of other fast-food restaurants that are parts of chains. Furthermore, while many chains of fast-food restaurants have generated huge revenues and profits, the small chain of Silver Diners has, as I write, lost money for the past five years straight.

There are undoubtedly many reasons why fast-food restaurants succeed so well and diners are such abysmal failures as chains. One that immediately comes to mind is that a diner seems like a throwback to an earlier time in our history while a fast-food restaurant, even though some of the early ones go back to the 1920s (A&W Root Beer stands), seems much more time-less. The boom in fast-food restaurants began with the first of the

McDonald's chain in 1955, while the heyday of the diner, which had begun several decades earlier, was beginning to wane at that point, in part because of the rise of the fast-food restaurant.[28] While some of the big fast-food chains, especially McDonald's, have recently experienced problems in terms of growth[29] and profitability (even experiencing some recent losses), it is likely that we have yet to see the peak of their development.[30] Thus, fast-food chains seem on the ascent, with new ones frequently coming to the fore, while the diner seems at best stagnant, and more likely in decline, if not on the verge of disappearance. In this context, it is difficult to see new efforts to form chains of diners succeeding.

In addition, diners, perhaps because they are reminiscent of an earlier time, seem to have an image in peoples' minds of being highly idiosyncratic. When they want to go to a diner, people tend to want to experience one that has its own distinctive characteristics. Even if they want to imbibe the generic in the fast-food restaurant, they do not want that in the diner. Thus, the patrons who are drawn to diners are more likely to prefer those that are idiosyncratic, perhaps the more idiosyncratic the better, and to shun those that are, or seem to be, part of chains. Furthermore, they may well be the kind of relatively unusual people whose presence serves to make diners even more idiosyncratic; more like great good places. Of course, it is also likely that there are some who enjoy going to generic fast-food restaurants on some occasions and idiosyncratic diners on others.

Then, there are generational differences between those who patronize these two types of restaurants. Fast-food restaurants are attractive mainly to younger people, while the diner tends to attract customers at the other end of the spectrum in terms of age. Diners were already well into their decline before today's youth were even born. Young people have little experience with diners and certainly did not experience them during their heyday. Thus, they are not likely to seek out such experiences, especially the uniqueness associated with them. In contrast, older patrons, especially those who had such experiences when they were younger, are likely to want to replicate them in their later years. Even if they have romanticized what diners were, and even are, they are still apt to crave the experience.

Yet, there is nothing inherent in the diner, or anything else for that matter, that makes it impossible to create a chain of diners. Indeed, as we have seen, there have been efforts to create chains of diners, some successful to some degree. In fact, McDonald's, itself, has dabbled in the diner business and would endeavor to create a large chain of such diners if it thought it could be successful. The basic elements of a successful diner could be isolated, predefined, and prefabricated, and replicated in many different settings. One could even envision a time in the future when society goes through a "retro" craze and a chain of diners becomes a huge success. In fact, there are currently chains of restaurants like Applebee's ("Neighborhood grill and bar,"[31] "Everything a neighbor ought to be") that try to present themselves as some sort of throwback to an earlier period of time when the neighborhood bar and grill (like the diner, a "great, good place") thrived. However, Applebee's can be found in almost, 1,500 "neighborhoods" in 49 states and in other nations.[32] Further, most of its so-called neighborhoods are on well-traveled roads and highways where the only "neighbors" are likely to be other chains and the people who eat in these places are likely to have arrived by car, perhaps to have driven quite some distance, and are very unlikely to know any of the other diners in the restaurant. It is highly unlikely that any of them are their neighbors in the traditional sense that term is used. In spite of its efforts to convince us otherwise, it is hard to think of, or treat, an Applebee's restaurant as a great good place.

The central point here is that diners tend to remain unique, despite their prefabricated structures and some effort to create chains of them, while the outlets that are the elements of a chain of fast-food restaurants are, with some (usually minor) exceptions, generic and interchangeable.

The first continuum (unique–generic) is closely related to the second, dealing with the presence or absence of local geographic ties. And this, in turn, is linked to at least part of the ethnologists' interest in places as cultures localized in space (we will deal with time next). The non-places of concern here—for example, fast-food restaurants—tend, of course, *not* to have local geographic ties and *not* to be localized in place (or time). In contrast, a great good place like a diner is likely to be deeply embedded in the local geography. As the founder of the Silver Diner said, "People think of the diner not as a chain, but as a *neighborhood* restaurant."[33]

This dimension is closely related to one of the basic characteristics of McDonaldization—predictability. In terms of settings, this means that chains must be more or less the same from one place (and time) to another. If McDonaldized settings were to vary greatly from one locale to another and to blend into the local environment, those who are searching them out would find it difficult, or impossible, to find them. Furthermore, even when they found them, the settings would not, if they had become highly localized, offer the experiences that consumers had come to expect. There is some evidence that non-places do change to some degree over time, and do adapt somewhat to local realities, but the fact is that they must retain a high level of predictability to survive, and localization in terms of place (and time) tends to reduce such predictability. Thus, McDonaldized settings have a vested interest in *not* having local ties,[34] or at least not very many of them, and in order to survive must avoid being pushed in the direction of becoming too enmeshed in any given locality.

In contrast, the local diner is not expected to have this level of predictability. In fact, it is expected to be unpredictable. Of course, some predictability is required—certain types of food, availability of all meals and snacks during the day, comparatively low prices, a train- or trolley-car-like structure, and so on—but it need not have near the degree of predictability of a chain restaurant. Indeed, patrons are often attracted, and look forward, to some distinctive characteristics and are apt to prize one diner over another (and certainly over a fast-food restaurant) for its distinctiveness. Of course, that distinctiveness works only when it is part of a setting with the requisite predictable elements. This points to the issue of the proper mix of predictable and unpredictable elements as it applies not only to diners but also to chain restaurants. The diner must mix some predictable elements into an otherwise unpredictable setting, while a chain restaurant must mix some unpredictability into a highly predictable setting. If either goes too far in one direction or the other, it likely creates problems for itself.

Of course, the unpredictability of the diner is only relative to the predictability of the chain restaurant. To those who work or eat there, a diner would be highly predictable. However, that predictability is *locally produced* while the predictability of a chain restaurant is, at least in part, centrally produced in accord with a corporate blueprint. Thus, the short order cook at a diner may prepare scrambled eggs the same way every time, but the method chosen and its repetition is produced by that particular cook or the manager-owner of the diner. In contrast, the griddle person at a chain restaurant may also cook scrambled eggs the same way every time, but that is a product of corporate training, guidelines, guidebooks, and close surveillance and supervision.

Since a diner is usually the idiosyncratic product of a local businessperson, it is likely that it will grow out of, and reflect, the nature of the local environment. Although it has ties, if only informal ones, to the larger culture of diners, each diner springs, in the main, from a local community and is likely in many ways to reflect that environment. For example, one might expect a diner in the northwestern United States to reflect something of the character of that area (say, for example, having its walls covered with the kind of wood paneling found in a lodge, or pictures of animals, fish, or greenery indigenous to the area). It would differ from those in the southwest (where kokopellis[35] might be a common decoration), Texas (with lots of cowboy pictures and paraphernalia), or the southeast (with reminders, perhaps, of Miss Pittypat's porch[36] from *Gone With the Wind* [1939]). While much of the food—waffles, scrambled eggs, burgers—would be the same, there would also be regional variations such as more salmon in the

Northwest, huevos de rancho more likely in the Southwest, and grits more common in the South. And the manner of dealing with customers (southern hospitality or a more no-nonsense approach in the Northwest) would reflect similar regional differences. This list of local geographic ties could obviously be extended in many different directions.

Any given fast-food restaurant is far less likely to reflect the local environment and far more likely to reflect the structural demands and expectations of the corporate entity of which it is part. While local contractors are likely to be used, they will operate in accord with blueprints, templates, and dictates from central headquarters. Furthermore, many of the components of the restaurant—signs, marquee, counter, and so on—are likely to be prefabricated components that are identical to the components of many other outlets. In the end, there will be little to distinguish a McDonald's in the Northwest from one in the Southwest or the Southeast. If there are differences, they are more likely to spring from the increasing demands from central office for some diversity than they are from local realities. In fact, burned by the critics of their architectural homogeneity and their imposition of a uniform style on widely divergent localities, some fast-food chains have been endeavoring to build more architectural diversity into their systems. It is certainly the case that some franchise outlets seek to give themselves a local flavor, but this is largely due to a self-conscious desire to do something about the criticisms of the cookie-cutter image of such outlets. Thus, while a diner is more likely to grow organically out of a local environment, a franchise outlet is more likely to internalize self-consciously some local elements. There is a huge difference between creating a local diner out of elements derived from the locale and strategically using a few local elements to give a chain restaurant the feel of the area. While the latter may defuse opposition and allow the chain restaurant to seem to fit better into the local community, it falls far short of making it a genuine part of that community. In any case, the chain restaurant cannot go too far in the direction of the local community or, as we have seen, it would begin to lose the sameness that is the hallmark of a chain and a key source of its success. In contrast, a diner can totally immerse itself in the local realities and the deeper it dives into the local community, the more likely it is to be successful.

Specific-to-the-times–relatively time-less, too, is related to the issue of predictability, although it plays itself out very differently in this case. Both the diner and the chain restaurant require a measure of predictability as far as time is concerned. However, the diner should have at least some elements that indicate that it is a predictable throwback to an early part of the 20th century, while a chain restaurant should be predictably time-less.[37] Reflecting the fact that diners tend to be tied to a particular historical epoch, a recent visitor to one Silver Diner reacted somewhat negatively:

"This feels a bit more like a chain. . . . If you think of the old diners from 1950s and 1960s, they're sort of family run operations."[38] However, every diner is likely to reflect its historical roots in different ways and to varying degrees, while every chain restaurant will manifest its time-lessness in more-or-less the same way in accord with corporate dictates.

The diner was very much a product of not only its place, but also its time (roughly the 1920s through the 1960s). It grew out of a specific epoch and remains wedded to it. Over time, because it changed little, it became increasingly anachronistic and, as a result, many diners were forced to close their doors. The dilemma for the diner is that if it had changed dramatically and become more contemporary, it would have lost that which defines a diner in peoples' eyes, especially those who are likely to frequent it. For example, if the diner surrendered the traditional look of an early 20th century railroad or trolley car and took on the appearance of, say, a 21st century rocket ship, it would be very difficult for most people, especially devotees, to think of such a setting as a diner.

Similarly, a diner is associated with the era of made-to-order food. Thus, patrons expect to order their food and have it prepared specifically for them, perhaps even watching from the counter as the short-order cook whips up some scrambled eggs or waffles. They would likely be repelled by a diner that sought to modernize by offering pre-prepared food in shrink-wrapped, Styrofoam containers. Consumers would also expect to be served, usually by a waitress, either at the counter or at a table. And, they would expect to have someone clean up after them.

In contrast, as a paradigmatic non-place and purposely constructed in that way, a McDonaldized chain restaurant is designed not only not to be space-specific, but also non-time-specific: time-less.[39] True, there is something vaguely modern about such settings. In fact, however, this was more true of the early versions of, say, McDonald's where the abundance of glass, steel, and so on gave one the feeling of something related to the then-new era of supersonic planes or even space travel. However, over the years much of that has been lost as McDonald's and other fast-food chains have sought to adapt to different locales (or have been forced to by zoning laws) with more muted and diverse architectural styles. A given McDonald's might include some very local and traditional elements, some brick to suggest the past and some stainless steel to suggest the future. In other words, in the main they are designed to be time-less, abstract enough to last well into the future without seeming to be old-fashioned.

Closely related to the issue of time–time-lessness is that of permanency–impermanency. In contrast to the aura of permanency surrounding places, there is a kind of ephemerality associated with non-places. Of course, they all are in a real sense ephemeral—they are all destined to disappear at some point—but there is a difference more in the way they present themselves and are experienced than in their actual longevity. Given the short lifespan of most small businesses, most great good places, including diners, are not likely to survive very long (there are notable exceptions), and they may well be outlived by non-places such as McDonaldized chains. However, at least some great good places seek to surround themselves with an aura of permanency, with the image that they have been there for a long time and will continue to be there for the foreseeable future. For example, business at the Silver Diner increased recently when the chain reintroduced low-priced "blue-plate specials," associated nostalgically with the early history of the diner. Of course, chains of non-places seek to create such images as well. Thus, McDonald's, approaching its 50th anniversary, increasingly presents itself as a tradition and Johnny Rockets wants to be seen as a reincarnation of a 1940s hamburger and malt shop. Nonetheless, any given McDonald's (or Johnny Rockets) restaurant, and more generally any non-place, feels more ephemeral than the typical diner, or great good place.

The idea that non-places tend to be characterized more by flows while places are more concrete geographic settings is not unrelated to many of the dimensions discussed above. A great good place like a diner is much more substantial than a McDonaldized setting. That is, the former is a distinctive place to which customers are not only expected to go, but to linger for a time. The physical setting is designed to welcome them, to make them comfortable, even embrace them. Thus, diners are seen as "homey meeting places" where customers are "welcome to come in and drink bottomless cups of coffee."[40] It is clear that customers will be expected to leave eventually, but while they are there, the physical setting is designed to make them feel welcome. A diner's customers are in transit, but the feeling is that they have paused in their movements, at least briefly, so that they can enjoy a particular setting and what it has to offer. To put it another way, a great good place is designed to be a safe haven, which offers a respite from the ever-present flows within which people increasingly find themselves.

In contrast, a non-place is an integral part of the larger space of flows where visitors rarely, if ever, feel as if they have arrived anywhere (at least for any length of time). Furthermore, it is itself a set of flows that meshes seamlessly with larger flows both into and out of them. There are many good examples of this. In McDonald's, people flow through the restaurant, rarely staying for very long. Of course, the drive-through lane is a good example of this as people and their cars flow through them barely stopping long enough to pay for, and obtain, their food. And this, in turn, is part of a larger flow of people from, for example, work to home, one leisure setting to another, and so on.

Places like diners are more likely to be characterized by human relationships while non-places are more likely to be dehumanized. All of the characteristics of places discussed above—their unique, one-of-a-kind character; their ties to a specific place and time—serve to make it more likely that deeper and more personal human relationships will develop in places such as diners. Being in a unique setting is likely to lead people to want to linger longer and to return. The same is true of settings that are place and time specific. This rootedness gives visitors the comforting feeling that this is a place to go, because they can anticipate returning over and over. And there is a well-defined physical space in these settings, a space where one at least gets the feeling that one is welcome and able to pause, if only for a time, before moving on. And all these things are conducive to the development of human relationships with those who work in these settings as well as with other customers.

In contrast, dehumanized relationships are more likely to occur in generic, interchangeable non-places like fast-food restaurants characterized by their lack of ties to specific geographic locales and time periods, and the sense that one is simply flowing through them. This is traceable largely to the fact that their fluidity makes it difficult or impossible to develop genuinely human relationships with others. One Silver Diner customer makes the differences between diners and fast-food restaurants on this dimension clear: "It's [Silver Diner] an easy place to tell people to meet you. The food is good, and the people are nice. . . . I'll kid with them, and they kid with me. It's an easy place to drop in and chat. If they go in a McDonald's, you don't get a chance to know the wait staff."[41]

Similarly, social relationships may develop and be repeated over and over in a chain restaurant, but if they occur, it is usually in spite of efforts to discourage or even prevent them. In contrast, a diner is likely to encourage such relationships because they are likely to lead to repeat business.

Closely related to the preceding point is the fact that people are far more likely to identify with their diner than with their fast-food restaurant(s). In fact, while people might think of their favorite diner as "their" diner, it is hard to imagine very many people thinking of a given fast-food restaurant as "theirs." They are likely to identify with the diner itself, as well as with many of those who frequent, and work in, it. In contrast, those who eat in a particular fast-food restaurant are unlikely to identify with it. They might develop some identity with the chain as a whole (e.g., Pizza Hut), but not likely with any particular outlet which, after all, is hard to differentiate from any other. Similarly, those who dine at fast-food restaurants rarely have enough contact with other diners or workers to identify with them.

Finally, the diner is much more likely to seem enchanted than the fast-food restaurant, which, after all, is the paradigm of rationalization and therefore disenchantment.[42] In a way, all the preceding continua serve to enchant diners and disenchant fast-food restaurants. Unique settings like diners are far more likely to seem magical than are generic settings like fast-food restaurants, which are highly rationalized. Diners are more likely to internalize elements of a specific place and time, as well as the magic of being embedded in such contexts. In contrast, the place-lessness and time-lessness of fast-food restaurants serve to contribute to their rationalized character lacking in much, if any, magic. Because of their aura of permanency, diners are better able to make themselves seem enchanted, whereas the ephemerality of fast-food restaurants militates against enchantment. The same is true of the ideas of locales–flows. That is, as more substantial locales, diners have the base on which to build enchantment, whereas the constant movement associated with fast-food restaurants makes it nearly impossible to create any sense of magic. Almost all enchantment flows out of human relationships, and their greater likelihood in diners makes diners more likely to seem magical than fast-food restaurants. Along the same lines, people are much more likely to feel that that with which they identify (diners, in this case) is more likely to seem magical than that with which they do not identify (fast-food restaurants).

There is little question that diners, and more generally places, tend to seem more enchanted than fast-food restaurants and, more generally, non-places. One need look no farther than the way the two have been treated in the movies. The setting for the movie *Diner* (1982) is a place to which the characters return over and over. It clearly has an enchanted, nearly religious quality as far as they are concerned. On the other extreme, in *Falling Down* (1993) the fast-food restaurant is a metaphor for a cold, unfeeling world, and the gun-toting "hero" (portrayed by Michael Douglas) is depicted as venting his rage against such a disenchanted world on the restaurant and its employees.

However, the movies also provide examples of the ways in which some of the earlier forms anticipated problems that were exacerbated in later forms. For example, in *Five Easy Pieces* (1970), Dupea—a character played by Jack Nicholson—attempts to order toast in a diner.

Dupea: I'd like a plain omelette, no potatoes, tomatoes instead, a cup of coffee, and wheat toast.

Waitress: (She points to the menu) No substitutions.

Dupea: What do you mean? You don't have any tomatoes?

Waitress: *Only* what's on the menu. You can have a number two—a plain omelette. It comes with cottage fries and rolls.

Dupea: Yeah, I know what it comes with. But it's not what I want.

Waitress: Well, I'll come back when you make up your mind.

Dupea: Wait a minute. I have made up my mind. I'd like a plain omelette, no potatoes on the plate, a cup of coffee, and a side order of wheat toast.

Waitress: I'm sorry, we don't have any side orders of toast . . . an English muffin or a coffee roll.

Dupea: What do you mean you don't make side orders of toast? You make sandwiches, don't you?

Waitress: Would you like to talk to the manager?

Dupea: . . . You've got bread and a toaster of some kind?

Waitress: I don't make the rules.

Dupea: OK, I'll make it as easy for you as I can. I'd like an omelette, plain, and a chicken salad sandwich on wheat toast, no mayonnaise, no butter, no lettuce. And a cup of coffee.

Waitress: A number two, chicken sal san, hold the butter, the lettuce and the mayonnaise. And a cup of coffee. Anything else?

Dupea: Yeah. Now all you have to do is hold the chicken, bring me the toast, give me a check for the chicken salad sandwich, and you haven't broken any rules.

Waitress: (spitefully) You want me to *hold* the chicken, huh?

Dupea: I want you to hold it between your knees.

Waitress: (turning and telling him to look at the sign that says, "No Substitutions") Do you see that sign, sir? Yes, you'll all have to leave. I'm not taking any more of your smartness and sarcasm.

Dupea: You see this sign? (He sweeps all the water glasses and menus off the table.)

Thus, diners had aspects of a non-place and those who reacted with hostility to such characteristics were not unknown. However, the reaction of the Jack Nicholson character (Dupea) to the diner pales in comparison to that of the character played by Michael Douglas in *Falling Down*. This is reflective of the fact that the diner falls closer to the place, and the fast-food restaurant the non-place, end of the continuum discussed in this section.

Non-Things (and Things)

It is clear that one can make a strong case that we are witnessing the proliferation of non-places, but what of the non-things that are usually offered in them? Following our general definition of nothing, a non-thing is centrally created and controlled and is lacking in distinctive substance. It is clear that non-places tend to offer non-things, but increasingly the latter are not restricted to non-places—even places are now likely to offer non-things (more on this later). Thus, non-things are far more pervasive than non-places and this is even more the case because there are obviously infinitely more things than there are places. Non-things are also a much more intimate and pervasive presence in our lives than non-places. Furthermore, we may go in and out of non-places, but at least some non-things have the possibility of being with us literally all the time. Our bodies are covered by an array of non-things and even when we go to bed at night, we are likely to be surrounded by non-things (Sealy Posturepedic mattresses, Martha Stewart sheets and pillow cases, Chanel perfumes or colognes, and so on), even if we sleep in the nude and therefore without Victoria's Secret, Ralph Lauren, or even Mickey Mouse sleepwear.

There are innumerable examples of non-things in the contemporary world, such as the burritos at Taco Bell, Benetton sweaters, jeans from the Gap, even elegant and very expensive Gucci bags. Since generic products are centrally conceived and produced over and over in the same way thousands, millions, or even billions of times, any one of these products can be said to be lacking in distinctive substance. Staying with the fast-food restaurant for the time being, we can use the Big Mac as our example of a non-thing and the contrasting thing will be a Culatella ham. The latter is a distinctive product of a particular region of Italy and is produced on small farms in the area. It is cured over long periods of time hanging from the rafters of a small building (with dirt floors) devoted to that purpose. There is no large corporation conceptualizing the nature of these hams or controlling how they are produced on these farms. Not surprisingly, Culatella ham is one of those products championed by the Slow Food Movement (more on this at the close of this book) as an alternative to such fast food as the Big Mac.[43]

Analyzing Things–Non-Things

First, of course, any given Big Mac lacks anything distinctive that would serve to differentiate it from any other Big Mac; one is basically the same as any other sold anyplace in the world. All Big Macs have essentially the same ingredients and are the same size, shape, and weight. There is nothing unique about any given Big Mac; they are all more or less interchangeable. In contrast, no single Culatella ham is exactly the same as any other. Size, shape, and weight will vary depending on the pig from which it is taken, the butchering process, and the vagaries of the curing process, as well as differences between curing houses. Overall, every Big Mac will be generic, while every Culatella ham will be unique.

Second, the Big Mac is a product from nowhere. While it, and its ancestor the hamburger, may have achieved its greatest success in the United States, it has roots in Germany (Hamburg) and England (Salisbury steak). However, the Big Mac has long since lost any geographic identity as it has come to be sold, among innumerable other (non-) places, in McDonald's restaurants in approximately 130 nations throughout the world. In contrast, the Culatella ham is not only from Italy, but from a very specific region of the country. It is a product that is intimately tied to that region and its distinct culture and history. While some of it is exported, it is likely that most of it is consumed by locals in or near where it is produced.

The Culatella ham clearly comes from a place, whereas the Big Mac is part of the placeless flow of fast food from producer to consumer. The local farms that produce Culatella hams seem far from the flows of consumer products throughout the world. The hams hang in the local curing houses for long periods of time before they are deemed ready for consumption by locals or for sale outside the area. Of course, when the Culatella ham enters the world market, it becomes part of a global flow of consumer products, but it is such a minimal part of that flow that it hardly seems that way. In addition, it takes consumers much longer to work their way through a Culatella ham than a Big Mac.[44] In contrast, the Big Mac is inherently very much a part of that flow and has very little, if anything, to do with places where that flow seems to slow down or even stop for a time. The consumer does not know where, for example, the beef in the Big Mac comes from. In fact, it is part of a global flow of frozen beef patties that is hard, if not impossible, to identify with a specific locale. In fact, it is in the interest of fast-food chains to set it up in this way so that they are free to use beef from anywhere, from everywhere.

However, the third dimension of our analysis does not seem to work quite as well in terms of attempting to differentiate things from non-things. *Both* the Big Mac, at least in its most basic form—the hamburger—and the Culatella ham can be linked to a particular period of time. While the Big Mac is clearly a product of mid-20th century America, the hamburger has centuries-long ties to predecessors like its forerunners from Germany and England. Similarly, the Culatella ham has deep roots in the history of Italy and the region from which it comes. Thus, neither the hamburger nor the Culatella ham is time-less.

While both the Big Mac and the Culatella ham have long traditions, the latter has the far greater aura of permanency, whereas the Big Mac seems more ephemeral. The Culatella ham is rooted in a specific tradition, has existed in that tradition for centuries, and will likely last as long as the tradition exists. Since that tradition is so embedded in a particular local culture, it has an aura of permanency. In contrast, in spite of its roots in earlier hamburgers and Salisbury steaks, the Big Mac is clearly one of the innumerable products of 20th-century America and we have many examples of such products (e.g., McDonald's Hula Burger) that have become popular for a time only to be abandoned when they are no longer profitable. We can envision a time when McDonald's will cease selling the Big Mac because it is no longer a popular, profitable product. In contrast, even if Culatella hams were no longer profitable products, the local producers would continue to make them, at least for themselves and their neighbors.

Traditionally, it is those things with patina (a thin coating or a color change resulting from age) that are the most desirable and bring the highest prices.[45] It could be argued that because it is embedded in an ancient tradition, and is the result of a long curing process, the Culatella ham has patina and is therefore likely to bring a far higher price than a product like the Big Mac that is clearly totally lacking in patina. The latter is produced in order to be consumed almost immediately. In fact, fast-food restaurants often have rules about how long products like Big Macs can remain unsold before they must be discarded. Of course, there are better examples of things with patina, such as antiques. In fact, people are willing to pay a far higher price for certain things just because they have patina. Thus, many people are willing to pay much more for an antique than for a contemporary factory-made alternative and, similarly, some (at least those who know about the distinctiveness and quality of such ham) will pay more for a Culatella ham than for virtually any other type of ham.

Fourth, the Culatella ham is very much a human product. Individual pigs are raised on small farms, they are butchered by hand, and each ham is hand-carved from the pig. Each ham is cured on small farms by individual producers over a long period of time and when they are deemed ready, they are sold (or eaten by the producer). There is a very personal relationship between producer and Culatella ham. No such personal relationship exists between producer and the Big Mac. Furthermore, as Eric Schlosser has shown in *Fast Food Nation*,[46] the demand of the fast-food industry for massive quantities of hamburger has, among other things, led to the McDonaldization of the slaughterhouse business.[47] The latter, of course, was already a highly rationalized business a century ago with its pioneering assembly-line methods for butchering animals. However, as Schlosser shows in great detail, the pressure produced by the demands of the fast-food industry has led to an extraordinary increase in their degree of rationalization. Those who work in such slaughterhouses are poorly paid, dehumanized workers who, to say the least, have no time to develop any bonds with the steer they slaughter or the meat products they butcher. In contrast to the personal relationship between the Italian farmers and their pigs, consider the following description of the relationship of one type of worker to the steers that pass by on today's "disassembly" lines:

For eight and a half hours, a worker called a "sticker" does nothing but stand in a river of blood, being drenched in blood, slitting the neck of a steer every ten seconds or so, severing its carotid artery. He uses a long knife and must hit exactly the right spot to kill the animal humanely. He hits that spot again and again.[48]

Producers and consumers are likely to develop a stronger sense of identity with a thing like Culatella ham, than a non-thing like the Big Mac.[49] Those who produce Culatella hams certainly strongly identify with them—they may well be at the center of their lives. Those who put together and sell Big Macs (or who slaughter the steers whose meat becomes the centerpiece of the Big Mac) are unlikely to have a similar sense of identity with them. Even consumers of the Culatella ham are likely to have at least some identity with it and to strongly prefer it to the alternatives, but this is far less likely to be true of the consumer of the Big Mac who may be just as likely to eat a competing product (Burger King's Whopper, for example) as a Big Mac.[50]

Finally, there is clearly much more enchantment associated with the Culatella ham than the Big Mac. As the signature product of the paradigmatic site—McDonald's—of disenchantment (and rationalization), the Big Mac is a model for a non-thing lacking in magic. In contrast, the Culatella ham exists on the other end of the continuum and is a good example of a thing that has magical qualities, at least for those who produce and are devoted consumers of it.

Thus, the dimensions of something–nothing do a good job of distinguishing between the Culatella ham and the Big Mac and more generally between things and non-things.

In sum, just as we live in a world increasingly characterized by non-places, it is also one in which most of what we consume are non-things. But, as pointed out above (and indicating a greater proliferation of non-things than non-places), there are infinitely more things than places and much of what is sold in places as well as non-places are non-things. Thus, it could be argued that the proliferation of non-things (versus things) is an even more important development than the expansion of non-places (rather than places).

Non-People (and People)

In 1959, Erving Goffman wrote about the "non-person" (for example, the taxi driver who is treated by passengers as if he or she is not present),[51] but to most this is a counterintuitive notion. How can people be non-people? Of course, a non-person is a person, but one who does not act as if he or she is a person, does not interact with others as a person, and perhaps more importantly is not treated by others as a person. For discussion purposes, our specific example in this section of a non-person is a Disney "cast member," especially one who dons the costume of one of the Disney characters (Snow White, Mickey Mouse, etc.),[52] while our person is a bartender in a traditional tavern (clearly a classic example of a great good place and several case studies of taverns are to be found in Ray Oldenburg's *Celebrating the Third Place*[53]).

Analyzing People–Non-People

Bartenders in traditional taverns tend to be unique, one-of-a-kind characters. They have distinct personalities, are likely to be personally well known to customers (especially regulars), and they get to know their clientele quite well. Beyond perhaps the bar owner (if different from the bartender), there is no centralized organization conceiving of what bartenders should say and do and controlling their actions. This is clearly not true of the Disney cast member. The Disney Corporation is very powerful and is notorious for the control that it exercises over employees. Any number of people can and have donned the Mickey Mouse or Snow White costume and have wandered about the park greeting visitors. Those who play these parts are interchangeable. And while each might invest his or her performance with some individuality, what each does is scripted and choreographed so that it matters little which particular individual happens to be wearing the costume. There is little that is distinctive about what any cast member in such a costume does, with the result that it is easy to replace any given individual worker and, in fact, several different people might don the same costume on the same day. Any given bartender is harder to replace and when such a change occurs, the nature of the performance and of relationships to customers is likely to change a great deal. Thus, a bar might lose considerable business when a favorite bartender leaves, but business at Disney World goes on without a blip when one person replaces another in that Mickey Mouse suit.

Taverns and their bartenders tend to have deep ties to, for example, a local urban neighborhood. Bartenders are likely to come from that neighborhood or, if not, to develop ties within it over time. Ties may also be developed to particular groups within a neighborhood. Thus, an Irish pub, even when it is not in Ireland, is likely to draw much of its clientele from the residents of a local community with Irish roots. In contrast, of course, there are no local geographic ties as far as Disney World (wherever it exists—United States, France, Japan, and, soon, Hong Kong) and its employees are concerned. Employees are likely to be drawn from all over the world. Its clientele is national and international rather than local and it is far more linked to the world than to the local community. Employees are also not likely to remain on the job for very long and this inhibits their ability to develop ties to the local community. Furthermore, the area around Disney World with its many highways and modern hotels is so transient that it is unlikely to produce much in the way of a community.

Although there are types that are more long-lasting, the local bartender tends to be tied not only to a specific place, but also a particular time. Since the individual bartender is constructing his (or her) own reality during his own life course and historical time period, that reality is unique to that time and will differ from those created by bartenders with different life experiences and spans and who live in different time periods. In contrast, the Disney characters (Mickey Mouse and Snow White) inhabited by cast members are time-less. Further, even when they play more human roles, the scripts that inform their performances tend not to be time-specific.

Contrary to initial expectations, some Disney characters are, at least in some ways, surrounded by a greater sense of permanency. Characters like Mickey Mouse date back to the early 20th century, while others such as Snow White have ancient or even mythical roots and therefore have a powerful aura of permanency—we know that not only have they existed since our own childhood (if not seemingly forever), but they will be with us into the indefinite future. However, we also know that the specific individuals who wear particular costumes are highly impermanent, will be gone in short order, and will be replaced as soon as they move on. We also know that they will alternate with others who wear the same costume. We realize that the more human cast members (those without the costumes that conceal the fact that they are people) are only temporary inhabitants of those positions. While local bartenders lack the kind of permanency associated with the Mickey Mouse or Snow White characters, they appear to have more permanency that the human Disney characters. They tend to communicate a sense that as individuals they are more than temporary holders of their positions.

Because our paradigmatic bartenders work in places like the neighborhood tavern, there tends to be greater stability associated with their position. They are more a fixture in a place than part of a flow of members of the labor force freely moving into and out of transient positions. Of the regular bartender at Trena's (the African American tavern mentioned above), May says, "The bartender is an integral part of the social atmosphere in neighborhood taverns. Monique is no exception. As the regular bartender . . . she creates Trena's social atmosphere."[54] In contrast, Disney workers operate in one of the contemporary settings most defined by flows of all types with the result that there tends to be little in the way of stability associated with their work and as individuals they do little to create a sense of stability.

Such employees are part of a very mobile labor force that is steadily flowing in and out of Disney's positions and the people they deal with are part of a global flow ("touristscape"[55]) of visitors.

Clearly, the bartender is expected to develop personal relations with customers (and vice versa), especially those who are regulars, and assist them in developing relationships with one another. Said one bartender (Kenny), "I get paid to talk to people" and he concluded, "You come in here by yourself and walk out knowing 10 people." According to this bar's manager, "Kenny's a tremendous bartender. . . . No matter how busy he is, he's never too busy to be friendly."[56] In contrast, the relationship between those who don a Disney costume and visitors to the theme park approaches the highest level of dehumanization. While they may talk to and act friendly toward park visitors, Disney cast members, often occupying non-human roles and costumes, are highly unlikely to develop personal relationships with visitors and the reverse is even more the case. Similarly, even the highly scripted cast member without a costume is more likely to interact in a non-human manner than the bartender who is more likely to be on his or her own in creating "recipes"[57] for dealing with customers on a day-to-day basis, let alone in dealing with more problematic situations for which there are no recipes (in contrast, Disney employees are more likely to have scripts even to deal with such situations). Of course, the whole notion of being a "cast member" implies a scripted, dehumanized relationship with those one interacts with on the job.

Bartenders are more likely to identify with their jobs and the specific taverns in which they work. This is true, in part, because they are far more likely to be in specific jobs and settings for longer periods of time than Disney employees. Because of that fact, the latter are unlikely to identify strongly with the characters they play or with the Disney enterprise as a whole. Even if they do manage to develop such identities, they are not likely to endure because the career of the typical Disney cast member does not last very long.

Finally, genuine enchantment is far more likely to develop between bartender and customers than between Snow White and visitors to Disney World. In fact, the theme park is one of the key sites in which simulated enchantment is produced and the relationship that exists between cast members and visitors is but one example of that. However, the efforts to produce simulated enchantment are highly rationalized and are therefore better described as being disenchanted. The irony is that Disney World proclaims itself the "Magic Kingdom." There is, of course, magic there, but it is of the simulated and disenchanted variety. Nothing militates more against "genuine" magic than simulation and disenchantment.

Reflecting the latter dimension, indeed all of the dimensions employed here, bartenders are far more likely to become cultural icons than are

Disney cast members.[58] Thus, in the 1950s one of TV comedian Jackie Gleason's best-known characters was Joe the Bartender. A local barkeep, Joe always had a song and friendly word for his customers, especially the regulars. More recently, a central character in the blockbuster TV show, *Cheers,* was the bartender. First, it was Coach, but when the actor who played that role died, he was replaced by Woody. It is difficult to imagine the faceless non-person who plays a Disney character becoming a cultural icon. Indeed, if anything about them is iconic, it is the costumes they wear and this serves to reinforce the view of them as non-persons.

Non-Service (and Service)

The idea of non-service closely parallels the preceding discussion of non-people and is hard to disentangle from it. Ultimately, of course, it is non-people who are more likely to provide non-services, although it is increasingly likely that even people provide services that approach the nothing end of the continuum. And, of course, non-services are more likely to be offered in non-places and to involve non-things, but as is true in the preceding point, non-services are also increasingly likely to be found in places and to involve things.

Analyzing Service–Non-Service

In this case, we will use as our examples the services provided by waiters in gourmet restaurants and those on one of today's huge and spectacular cruise ships. Waiters in gourmet restaurants generally offer service that varies with the needs and demands of particular diners. While control is exerted by owners and headwaiters, there is generally no centralized control because gourmet restaurants tend to be one-of-a-kind operations. In contrast, since cruise ships are huge operations, usually part of increasingly enormous and centralized organizations, there is great control over waiters on those ships. What such waiters do and how they do it is likely the subject of corporate directives, guidelines, and handbooks. As a result, waiters on such ships offer service that varies little from one set of diners to another. Furthermore, while serving large numbers of people at a given meal, such waiters are unable to give customers much, if any, individual attention. Thus, each diner gets essentially the same service. In contrast, of course, the waiter in an elite restaurant is dealing with a small number of diners and is able to interact with each diner in a unique manner. To put this another way, the interactions between cruise ship waiters and diners tends to be interchangeable, while those between gourmet restaurant waiters and diners tend to be one-of-a-kind experiences. Of course, this is one of the reasons that eating in gourmet restaurants is so expensive and, conversely, why so many find a cruise an affordable vacation.

The cruise ship lacks any specific geographic ties—wandering as it does from port to port—so the services provided by waiters onboard are literally from (and in) nowhere. In contrast, those offered by the waiter in a gourmet restaurant (except those, like Wolfgang Puck's, that have grown into small chains) tend to be more embedded in local settings and linked to the expectations associated with them.

The time continuum is more problematic here. Just as there is a space-less quality to service on the cruise ship, it is also the case that there is a time-lessness to it. The diner and the waiter on the cruise ship seem to be adrift in a world without time. However, the cruise ship is a very modern creation and therefore the services provided on it do, in this sense, seem to be embedded in a particular time period. Furthermore, there is a history here of fine service on transatlantic and cruise ships and the service offered aboard today's ship is part of that sweep of history. While the service of a waiter onboard ship is diverse in terms of the time dimension, the services provided by the waiter in a gourmet restaurant seem clearly tied to a long history of service, especially to an earlier time in history when such services were more the norm, at least for society's elites. They not only appear to be little different than those offered say a century ago, but also unlikely to change very much in the future.

The services offered by the waiter in a gourmet restaurant have an aura of permanency about them. Not only do they seem unchanged and unchanging, but the settings in which they occur—gourmet restaurants—have a similar feel of permanency, even though specific gourmet restaurants (although not the broader type) come and go. On the other hand, the dining services on a cruise ship are occurring on a ship on the move and during a time period—usually a week—that is soon to end and not likely to be repeated, at least on that particular ship.[59] In the case of the gourmet restaurant, there is always the possibility that one can return for another meal, perhaps even involving the same dishes, prepared in much the same way, and served in the same manner by the same waiter.

More of a non-place, the cruise ship is a space on the move, as is everyone associated with a given cruise. As a result, the dining services offered seem to be just one more flow in a larger set of flows. Specifically, modern cruise ships are famous for the round-the-clock, non-stop availability of food, and any given meal may seem to be merely a part of a continuous flow of food. In contrast, the services offered by the waiter in a gourmet restaurant, while certainly part of a similar set of flows, occur in a place and have a strong sense of "place-ness." Maybe it is little more than a flow with a different pace, but flows associated with the gourmet restaurant seem glacial and therefore more rooted in place than those found on the cruise ship. Another big difference is traceable to the fact that while waiters in gourmet restaurants are likely to see at least some customers over and over, the cruise is a one-time experience for most people with the result that the waiter is likely to see them only during a single cruise.

Waiters in gourmet restaurants are more likely to identify strongly with what they do, the services they offer, the (often regular) customers they serve, and the settings in which they work. As a result, diners may identify a very specific kind of service with a given restaurant and even with a particular server. In contrast, waiters and diners on cruise ships, because they are part of so many different flows, are far less able to develop any of these identities, at least to any great degree.

Finally, the service at a gourmet restaurant is likely to have a magical quality about it, whereas the service provided by waiters on cruise ships, like the cruise ships themselves, is likely to be more simulated enchantment and therefore more disenchanted. In terms of the former, a good example would be one of Paris's great gourmet restaurants, especially during truffle season. Soon after diners are seated, and periodically during the evening, staff members circulate around the restaurant with a basket laden with truffles. Diners are allowed to gaze at this magical food and to inhale its aroma. The expressions on diners' faces indicate that this is clearly a magical moment. One is unlikely to experience such a moment, or such service, on a cruise ship, where the emphasis is on serving huge numbers of people lots of food quickly and efficiently.

In sum, the something–nothing continuum, and its various subcontinua, works very well, albeit in a few cases imperfectly, in distinguishing among places–non-places, things–non-things, people–non-people, and services–non-services. Not only are the various continua useful, but so are the cases in which the expected distinctions do not quite pan out as expected. This serves to give us a more nuanced picture of the nullities of concern here and their distinctions (or lack thereof) from places, things, people, and services with more substance.

The Relationship Between Forms of Nothing (and Something)

While each of the four types of nothing, as well as the broader continua of which it is part, has been discussed as if it exists in isolation from the others, the fact is that there is a powerful tendency for the types to vary together. That is, the development of nullities in one domain (say, non-places) tends to foster their development in the other domains (non-things, non-people, and non-services).

Let us start with non-places. It is largely in non-places that one finds non-things, non-people, and non-services (although increasingly not exclusively, as we have mentioned previously and will argue in more detail later). Since non-places are expanding, so, too, are the other nullities. It is true that it is in the settings that are better thought of as places that we tend to continue to find things, people, and services. However, since places are tending to give way to non-places, or at least not increasing nearly as rapidly,[60] the result is the decline of contexts supportive of things, people, and services. For example, once-unique department stores, and small chains of such stores, have been swallowed up by huge conglomerates and, as a result, have come to look increasingly alike. Federated Department Stores, Inc., now includes such formerly independent department store mini-chains as Bloomingdale's, Macy's, and The Bon Marche. In other words, and following this book's grand narrative, once something, department stores have increasingly moved in the direction of nothing. More specifically, the men's departments of such stores that once looked and operated like distinct haberdashery shops, now look increasingly alike as they are divided up into similarly looking and "logo-ed"[61] boutiques featuring much the same clothing of most of the same leading designers—Nautica, Calvin Klein, Polo, and so on. Because department stores now tend to be part of chains, they are characterized by centralized buying and by general contracts negotiated with designers and manufacturers that lead all department stores in the chain to offer many identical products and product lines. In addition, personalized service has given way to increasingly impersonal relationships between clerk and customer, and even to an ever-greater pervasiveness of a do-it-yourself system for customers. Fewer people work in these departments and those who do are likely to act more like non-people. The example of the contemporary department store makes clear the fact that the increase in nothing in one domain serves to support its increase in other domains.

The simple fact is that it is difficult for things, people, and services to survive in non-places; they do not seem to fit with non-places. First, people who consume in non-places are generally looking for non-things. They do not expect to find things (for example, a custom-made suit, a truly unique piece of handmade pottery) in non-places; they may even be jarred by the presence of things in non-places. The result is that things are likely to be met with the same reaction and experience the same fate as people. That is, they are likely to disappear from non-places. Thus, if the work of a craftsperson such as a potter from Oaxaca, Mexico, were to find its way into Target or Wal-Mart (clearly an unlikely possibility), it would not be likely to sell well and would quickly be withdrawn from the shelves. Given the low-price image of Wal-Mart, those who shop for pottery there are generally looking for low cost, mass-produced items. They are unlikely to be willing to pay the higher price for handmade Oaxacan pottery.

Second, in non-places consumers do not expect to encounter people, at least those who are full-fledged human beings, as employees. They expect either largely to serve themselves or to receive minimal assistance from non-people. Encountering an employee who is a person in such a setting would be disconcerting and might even drive the consumer away. For their part, those employees who want to act as people rather than non-people would be discouraged by management (because, for example, it is too time-consuming and labor-intensive) as well as by the negative reactions of consumers to their behavior (many do not want to deal with people in non-places). The likelihood is that those employees who want to act in this way would quickly be driven to leave such settings in search of those where their actions are more appreciated. The problem is that with the progressive disappearance of places, there are fewer and fewer settings available to them. The long-term result, at least logically, would be the complete disappearance of people (as opposed to non-people), at least in many areas of the service sector of the work world.

Third, and relatedly, customers do not expect service and the clerk who offers it is not likely to be rewarded by the consumer. That is, customers are likely to brush off, or even react negatively to, offers of assistance. More important, the personalized service that is offered is not likely to lead to higher sales and may even have an adverse effect on sales. The result is that services are likely to cease to be offered and, as pointed out above, the employees offering them are apt to leave the non-place sooner or later.

Of course, much the same arguments can be made with whatever nullity one begins. The pervasive existence of non-things leaves less and less of a role for places and makes for their progressive replacement by non-places. Non-things seem out of their element in places. The increasing tendency for people to become non-people on the job, and for consumers to prefer to deal with non-people, makes it unlikely that places will survive, because there are no people to work in such settings and, in any case, consumers prefer to deal with non-places and non-people. And the increasing preference for non-services, even do-it-yourself services, tends to drive places out of existence, leaves those who desire to be people fewer settings in which to work, and tends to drive away things that need to be sold by people in places offering full-scale services.

Thus, there is a kind of vicious, self-reinforcing process here in which non-places, non-things, non-people, and non-services tend to mutually reinforce one another, leading to their increasing pervasiveness in the social world. Of course, places, things, people, and services survive, but it is more on the margins of the social and economic world. They tend to continue to exist for the elites who can afford the high premium that has now come to be associated with that which was in the past a low-cost reality for almost everyone. However, they also continue to exist for those of more modest means in the form of rural roadside fruit and vegetable stands, craft fairs, co-ops, and the like. While those who are troubled by the increasing prevalence of nothing might be given hope by such phenomena, it is clear that these tend to be throwbacks to the past that, at best, offer highly limited and difficult-to-find alternatives to nothing.

If there is a vicious circle of the kind described above, is it possible to choose a starting point, a development that set the whole process in motion? In one sense, it is probably impossible to find such a point of origin,[62] but if one were forced to choose, it would have to be in the realm of things, specifically their mass manufacture. Thus, as good a starting point as any would be Henry Ford and the first automobile assembly line, especially perhaps the mass production of the classic non-thing, the Model-T Ford, which was available, at first, in only one style and in only one color—black! Of course, over the years Ford found a way of producing many different styles and colors of automobiles, but they were still mass-manufactured and continued to approach the non-thing end of the continuum.[63]

The problem of allowing for diversity, but still producing non-things, has long since been solved by improving technologies that allow for the mass manufacture of products that seem highly diverse. This is known as the process of *sneakerization*[64] where, for example, dozens, perhaps hundreds, of types of athletic shoes can be produced, but still be mass-manufactured and able to retain economies of scale. Indeed, even customized production that would seem to produce what are, by definition, things, is being transformed into *mass customization*[65] whereby even seemingly customized products can take on at least some of the qualities of non-things.

In any case, if we take the mass production of non-things as our starting point, it is clear that expanding production of such non-things led to an increased need for non-places in which they could be sold. True, non-things could be, and were, sold in places, but there was a clear and growing disjuncture between the two. Non-things seemed out of place, and increasingly so, in places. This disjuncture gave impetus (of course, other factors were involved) to the development of non-places—for example, supermarkets, chain stores, franchises, discounters—where the increasing number of non-things seemed to fit perfectly.

Then, of course, people began to seem odd and out of their element selling non-things in non-places. In any case their skills were no longer needed;

non-people do as good a job selling non-things, they work for less, and most generally they constitute a better fit. People were no longer needed because non-things sold themselves, or better yet were presold by massive advertising campaigns. Thus, no selling was required in a supermarket because consumers simply bought what they needed, compared prices on their own, and most important for our purposes purchased name- (or house-) brand products presold by massive advertising campaigns that sought to create invidious distinctions between the product advertised and competing products (soap is an excellent example). Furthermore, people had fewer and fewer settings to turn to for work as they were not only replaced by non-persons but also by self-service where even the non-person was no longer required.

Finally, of course, the process of non-things leading to non-places and then non-people led to non-services. Service was no longer needed to sell non-things, it was no longer needed and did not fit very well in non-places, and non-people, again by definition, did not, perhaps could not, offer anything but non-services. The supermarket and later the fast-food restaurant are, of course, classic examples of non-places where non-service is the norm.

I do not want to take this argument too far and suggest some law-like changes resulting from the mass manufacture of non-things. Furthermore, developments in the other nullities were simultaneous with the rise of large numbers of non-things and the development of all of them may have been, at least in part, the result of external changes of various sorts. For example, it is likely that the sheer increase in the population and the difficulties involved in serving ever-greater numbers of people led to the increase in non-things,[66] as well as the other nullities discussed in this chapter. Finally, there were surely changes within each domain that led to the rise of non-places, non-people, and non-services. For example, rising labor costs may have forced the substitution of non-people for people with an accompanying shift to more non-services. Furthermore, technological advances like auto-mated telephone technology led to the elimination of many phone opera-tors, with the remaining employees serving more as non-people.

It is also the case that phenomena at the something ends of the four con-tinua of concern here tend to occur together and the presence of one makes the others more likely. Without going into much detail or into all the permutations and combinations, if you start with, say, things, that is phenomena that exist at the something end of the continuum, then you are likely to need places in which to sell or offer them, people with the skills and sophistica-tion to deal with and sell them, and to offer an array of services to consumers interested in acquiring things. Following the logic used above, the mass manufacture of non-things undoubtedly was the key factor in the decline of the entire complex of somethingness.

By the way, this suggests a way of reversing the seemingly inevitable trend in the direction of nothing in all of these realms. Since it is a vicious circle, if one wants to do something about it, it can be entered at any point in the circle of non-places, non-things, non-people, and non-services. That is, either founding places, or creating things, or training people, or offering services has the potential of introducing something into the circle and, once established, it will require the creation of something in the other realms as well.

Chapter Four

Globalization

While social theorists (and other social scientists) have long been interested in globalization, in recent years there has been an explosion of work on the topic by leading contemporary thinkers.[1] The flowering of such theories (and other work) is a reflection of the fact that globalization is of great concern to, and of enormous significance for, the larger population. Virtually every nation and the lives of billions of people throughout the world are being transformed, often quite dramatically, by globalization.[2] The degree and significance of its impact is to be seen virtually everywhere one looks, most visibly in the now-commonplace protests that accompany high-level meetings of such key global organizations as the World Trade Organization (WTO), the International Monetary Fund (IMF), and the World Bank. As is made clear by the magnitude of the issues before these organizations, the level of protest against them, and the fact that these protests have taken place in widely dispersed geographic areas, people throughout the world feel very strongly that they are confronting matters of great importance.

Globalization theory also emerged as a result of a series of developments internal to social theory, notably the reaction against such earlier perspectives as modernization theory.[3] Among the defining characteristics of this theory were its orientation to issues that were of central concern in the West, the preeminence it accorded to developments there, and the idea that the rest of the world had little choice but to become increasingly like it (more democratic, more capitalistic, and so on). Other theories (for example, world system[4] and dependency theory[5]) emerged in reaction, at least in part, to such a positive view of the West (as well as the Northern versus the Southern Hemisphere) and offered global perspectives that were critical of

71

it for, among other things, its exploitation of many other parts of the world. Nevertheless, they retained a focus on the West, albeit a highly critical orientation toward it. While there are many different versions of globalization theory, there is a tendency in virtually all of them to shift away from a focus on the West and to examine transnational processes that flow in many different directions, as well as those that are independent of any single nation or area of the world.[6]

Thus, there are good reasons, both external and internal to academia, for the rise in interest in globalization in general, and globalization theory in particular, but globalization is not an idea without severe ambiguities and limitations.

We can start with a definition of *globalization* as "the worldwide diffusion of practices, expansion of relations across continents, organization of social life on a global scale, and growth of a shared global consciousness".[7] As it has come to be used, the notion of globalization encompasses a number of transnational processes which, while they can be seen as global in their reach, are separable from each other. It is beyond the scope of this book to deal with the full range of globalization processes and issues,[8] but at this point we must at least give the reader a sense of the breadth of this still-burgeoning topic and literature.

Politics[9] is a major concern of those interested in globalization with a specific focus on such issues as international governance[10] and the future of local democracy[11] and of the state (and other political entities).[12] A new type of city, the global city, is seen as emerging and it has been the subject of considerable thought and research.[13] Globalization has naturally been of great interest to those in business, especially the emergence of new global markets and the ideologies that accompany them.[14] Related to many other issues is the relationship between technology and globalization, including the role technology plays in global inequalities.[15] Of special interest and concern in this regard is the computer, the Internet,[16] and the emergence of the global digital divide.[17] Then there are such issues as the relationship between globalization and religion,[18] sport,[19] pop music,[20] and virtually every other aspect of the social world, as well as the linkage of globalization to a range of social problems such as poverty and inequality,[21] global crime,[22] global sex[23] and the international sex trade,[24] and terrorism,[25] as well as the impact of globalization on the environment.[26] All of these problems, and many others, have led to considerable interest in the morality and ethics of globalization.[27]

In his recent overview of globalization theory, Roland Robertson outlined what he considers to be *the* key issues in globalization theory.[28] While all are important, three of them lie at the center of this book and two of them are closely related to one another. The two interrelated issues are as follows: "*Does global change involve increasing homogeneity or increasing heterogeneity or a mixture of both?*" And "*What is the relationship between the local and the global?*"[29] These two issues are tightly linked since the predominance of the local would tend to be associated with heterogeneity while the dominance of the global would be associated more with homogenization. Whatever the mix (and there is always a mix) of the local and the global, heterogeneity and homogeneity, the third issue raised by Robertson remains of great importance: "*What drives the globalization process? What is its motor force?*[30] The answer to the last question(s) is highly complex since there is certainly no single driving force, nor is there a single process of globalization. However, later in this chapter, after we've specified our approach to the globalization process, we will discuss several of the motor forces—capitalism, McDonaldization, and Americanization—that will concern us here.

Whatever the answers to the above questions, to say nothing of the other central questions that he raises,[31] it is clear that to Robertson, and many other students of globalization (especially Appadurai) the central theoretical issue is the relationship between the highly interrelated topics of homogeneity–heterogeneity and the global–local. Indeed, Robertson is not only known for his interest in these issues, but for his articulation of a now-famous concept—*glocalization*—that emphasizes the integration of the global and the local.[32] While glocalization is an integrative concept, and Robertson is certainly interested in both sides of the glocal–global, homogenization–heterogenization continua, his work tends to emphasize the importance of the glocal and the existence of heterogeneity.[33] This book seeks to offer *a more balanced view* on these issues by developing a second concept—*grobalization*—to supplement the undoubtedly important idea of glocalization.

The concept of glocalization gets to the heart of not only Robertson's views, but also what many contemporary theorists interested in globalization think about the nature of transnational processes.[34] *Glocalization* can be defined as the interpenetration of the global and the local resulting in unique outcomes in different geographic areas. The concept of *grobalization,* coined here for the first time as a much-needed companion to the notion of glocalization,[35] focuses on the imperialistic ambitions of nations, corporations, organizations, and the like and their desire, indeed need, to impose themselves on various geographic areas.[36] Their main interest is in seeing their power, influence, and in some cases profits *grow* (hence the term *gro*balization) throughout the world. Grobalization involves a variety of subprocesses, three of which—capitalism, Americanization, and McDonaldization[37]—are, as pointed out above, central driving forces in grobalization, but also are of particular interest to the author and of great significance in the worldwide spread of nothingness.

It will be argued that grobalization tends to be associated with the proliferation of nothing, while glocalization tends to be tied more to something and therefore stands opposed, at least partially (and along with the local itself), to the spread of nothing. It is the fact that these two processes coexist under the broad heading of globalization, and because they are, at least to some degree, in conflict in terms of their implications for the spread of nothingness around the world, that globalization as a whole does not have a unidirectional effect on the spread of nothingness. That is, in some of its aspects (those involved in grobalization) globalization favors the spread of nothing, but in others (those related to glocalization) it tends toward the dissemination of something. This issue will be addressed in depth in this chapter and the next.

Glocalization and Grobalization

Grobalization and glocalization are rooted in competing visions of the contemporary world. Grobalization is a very modern view emphasizing the growing worldwide ability of, especially, largely capitalistic organizations and modern states[38] to increase their power and reach throughout the world. Two of the most preeminent modern theories—those of Karl Marx and Max Weber (and of their followers)—undergird this perspective. While Marx focused on the capitalistic economic system, Weber was concerned with the rationalization of not only the economy, but many other sectors of society, in the modern world.

Marxian (and neo-Marxian) theory leads to the view that one of the major driving forces behind grobalization is the corporate need to show increasing profitability through more and more far-reaching economic imperialism. Another is the need for corporations, and the states and other institutions (media, education) that buttress them, to support efforts at enhancing profitability by increasing their cultural hegemony throughout the world. Thus, from this perspective, the need for (especially) American corporations to show ever-increasing profits, and the related and supporting need of the United States and American institutions to exert ever-increasing cultural hegemony, go to the core of grobalization. American corporations aggressively export commodities for their own profit, and the nation as a whole is similarly aggressive in the exportation of its ideas in order to gain hegemony over other nations, not only for its own sake, but for the increased ability to market goods and services that such hegemony yields. Of special interest are the various consumer products and systems that the United States is exporting to the rest of the world and the ways in which they are altering what and how people consume.[39]

The second modern perspective informing our views on grobalization is the Weberian tradition that emphasizes the increasing ubiquity of rationalized structures and their growing control over people throughout the world, especially, given our interests, in the sphere of consumption. The Weberian approach attunes us to the "grobal" spread of these rationalized structures. That is, rationalized structures have a tendency to replicate themselves throughout the world and those nations that do not have them are generally eager to acquire them. While American corporations, indeed the United States as a whole, can be seen as highly rationalized, there are, as we will see, many other rationalized structures not only in the United States, but throughout the world.

While modern theories like those associated with the Marxian and Weberian traditions are closely linked to the idea of grobalization, glocalization is more in tune with postmodern social theory[40] and its emphasis on diversity, hybridity, and independence. In conjunction with local realities, the globalization of so many commodities and ideas gives communities, groups, and individuals in many parts of the world an unprecedented capacity to fashion distinctive and ever-changing realities and identities. Rather than increasing penetration by capitalist firms and the states that support them, or by rationalized structures, this perspective sees a world of increasing diversity. Although all nations are likely to be affected by the spread of capitalism and rationalization, they are likely to integrate both with local realities to produce distinctively glocal phenomena.

Thus, it should come as no surprise that grobalization and glocalization offer very different images of the impact of transnational processes. After all, they tend to stem from the antithetical bases of modern and postmodern social theory.

Globalization can be analyzed culturally, economically, politically, or institutionally. At the extremes, in the realm of *culture,* grobalization can be seen as a form of transnational expansion of common codes and practices (homogeneity) whereas glocalization involves the interaction of many global and local cultural inputs to create a kind of pastiche, or a blend, leading to a variety of cultural hybrids (heterogeneity). The trend toward homogeneity is often associated with cultural imperialism (see below), or, to put it another way, the growing international influence of a particular culture (hence, an aspect of grobalization). There are many varieties of cultural imperialism, including those that emphasize the role played by American culture,[41] the West,[42] or core countries.[43] Robertson, although he doesn't use the term cultural imperialism, tends to oppose the idea (as do others[44]) and thereby supports, as we have seen, the concept of glocalization by describing a series of cultural hybrids resulting from the interpenetration of the universal and the particular.

Theorists who focus on *economic* factors tend to emphasize their growing importance and homogenizing effect throughout the world and are therefore in tune with the idea of grobalization. They generally see globalization as the spread of the market economy throughout many different regions of the world. Recently, George Stiglitz, a Nobel Prize-winning economist and former chairman of the Council of Economic Advisors, issued a stinging attack on the World Bank, the WTO, and especially the IMF for their roles in exacerbating, rather than resolving, global economic crises. Among other things, Stiglitz criticizes the IMF for its homogenizing, "one-size-fits-all" approach that fails to take into account national differences.[45] The IMF in particular, and globalization in general, have worked to the advantage of the wealthy nations, especially the United States (which effectively has veto power over IMF decisions), and to the detriment of poor nations; the gap between rich and poor has actually *increased* as a result of globalization. While the IMF is supposed to help poor countries by providing them with economic aid, Stiglitz shows that it is often the case that the reforms that the IMF insists that poor countries undertake to fix their economic problems often end up making them worse off economically.

While those who focus on economic issues tend to emphasize homogeneity, some differentiation (heterogeneity) is acknowledged to exist at the margins of the global economy. Examples include the commodification of local cultures and the existence of flexible specialization that permits the tailoring of many products to the needs of various local specifications. More generally, those who emphasize glocalization would argue that the interaction of the global market with local markets would lead to the creation of unique glocal markets that integrate the demands of the global market with the realities of the local market.

A *political–institutional* orientation also emphasizes either homogeneity or heterogeneity. One example of a grobalization perspective in the political domain focuses on the worldwide spread of models of the nation-state and the emergence of isomorphic forms of governance throughout the globe—in other words, the growth of a more-or-less single model of governance around the world.[46] The most important example of this is the grobal spread of a democratic political system. One of the most extreme views of grobalization in the political realm is Benjamin Barber's thinking on "McWorld," or the growth of a single political[47] orientation that is increasingly pervasive throughout the world.

Interestingly, Barber also articulates, as an alternative perspective, the idea of "Jihad"—localized, ethnic, and reactionary political forces (including "rogue states") that involve a rejection of McWorld in the political realm. Jihad also tends to be associated with an intensification of nationalism and therefore is apt to lead to greater political heterogeneity throughout the world. The interaction of McWorld and Jihad at the local level may produce unique, glocal political formations that integrate elements of both the former (for example, use of the Internet to attract supporters) and the latter (for example, use of traditional ideas and rhetoric).[48]

Overall, we can, following Robertson, offer the following as the essential elements of glocalization:

1. The world is growing more pluralistic. Glocalization theory is exceptionally sensitive to differences within and between areas of the world.

2. Individuals and local groups have great power to adapt, innovate, and maneuver within a glocalized world. Glocalization theory sees individuals and groups as important and creative agents.

3. Social processes are relational and contingent. Globalization provokes a variety of reactions—ranging from nationalist entrenchment to cosmopolitan embrace—that feed back on and transform grobalization, that produce glocalization.

4. Commodities and the media, arenas and key forces in cultural change in the late 20th and early 21st centuries, are *not* seen as (totally) coercive, but rather as providing material to be used in individual and group creation throughout the glocalized areas of the world.

Naturally, *grobalization* leads to a variety of largely antithetical ideas:

1. The world is growing increasingly similar. Grobalization theory tends to minimize differences within and between areas of the world.

2. Individuals and groups have relatively little ability to adapt, innovate, and maneuver within a grobalized world. Grobalization theory sees larger structures and forces tending to overwhelm the ability of individuals and groups to create themselves and their worlds.

3. Social processes are largely one-directional and deterministic. Grobalization tends to overpower the local and limits its ability to act and react, let alone act back on the grobal.

4. Commodities and the media are the key forces and areas of cultural change and they *are* seen as largely determining the self and groups throughout the grobalized areas of the world.

Derived from this is another important difference between these two perspectives: the tendency on the part of those associated with the glocalization perspective to value it positively[49] and to be critical of grobalization as well as those who emphasize it. This is traceable, in part, to the association between glocalization and postmodernism and the latter's tendency to value positively the individual and the local over the totality—diversity over uniformity. A more specific set of examples is to be found in the essays in James Watson's *Golden Arches East: McDonald's in East Asia*.[50] The McDonald's in Beijing is described (and valued) for being more human than McDonald's in other places, especially the United States, because people can hang out there, ceremonies like children's birthday parties are more common, and there are even kindly "Aunt McDonald's" who serve as receptionists in the restaurants. In Beijing customers are allowed to linger over their meals and take about twice as long to eat as do Americans. In Taipei, like Beijing and Hong Kong, McDonald's is a hangout for teenagers, a kind of home away from home. There is something heroic about Watson's conclusion about East Asian consumers and their ability to assert themselves in the face of the grobalizing efforts of McDonald's: "East Asian consumers have *quietly*, and in some cases, *stubbornly, transformed* their neighborhood McDonald's into local institutions."[51] In these and other ways, these glocalized McDonald's are depicted positively, and they are used not only to counter the idea of grobalization, but also to be critical, explicitly and implicitly, of it.

Glocalization

A discussion of some closely related terms (and related examples) will be of considerable help in getting a better sense of glocalization. One such concept, already mentioned several times, is *heterogenization*, a term that emphasizes the diversity that is characteristic of glocalization and that stands in stark contrast to the *homogenization* that can be seen as accompanying grobalization.

Another is *hybridization*, which emphasizes the mixtures of the global and the local, as opposed to the greater *uniformity* associated with grobalization.[52] A hybrid would involve the combination of two or more elements from different cultures or parts of the world. Among the examples of hybridization (and heterogenization, glocalization) are Ugandan tourists visiting Amsterdam to watch Moroccan women engage in Thai boxing, Argentinians watching Asian rap performed by a South American band at a London club owned by a Saudi Arabian, and the more mundane experiences of Americans eating such concoctions as Irish bagels, Chinese tacos, Kosher pizza, and so on. Obviously, the list of such hybrids is long and growing rapidly with increasing glocalization. The contrast, of course, would be such uniform experiences as eating hamburgers in the United States, quiche in France, or sushi in Japan. More to the point of this book, grobalization brings with it forms and products (for example, Gap chinos,

Starbucks coffee) that tend to replace local variants and to lead to increased uniformity throughout the world.

Yet another synonym for glocalization is *creolization*.[53] The term *creole* generally refers to people of mixed race, but it has been extended to the idea of the "creolization of language", involving a combination of languages that were previously unintelligible to one another. The opposite of creolization might be conceived of as *purification*, whereby alternative languages and peoples are prevented from entering, or driven out if they succeed in gaining entree, in order to maintain the purity of a language or a race. At its extreme, grobalization involves purification as indigenous elements are driven out and replaced by purely grobal alternatives. Creolization is often used interchangeably with hybridization so that the following example could be used to illustrate both concepts (as well as glocalization): "sitting in a [Starbucks] coffee shop in London [they are now ubiquitous there] drinking Italian espresso served by an Algerian waiter to the strains of the Beach Boys singing 'I wish they all could be California girls.'"[54]

All of the above—hybridization, heterogenization, and creolization—should give the reader a good feel for what is meant here by glocalization, and, as pointed out previously, those terms will sometimes be used as synonyms for it. Similarly, although a better feel for grobalization awaits the discussion of capitalism, McDonaldization, and Americanization, the terms *homogenization, uniformity,* and *purification* are more or less synonymous with it. That is, as we will see, all three of these processes seek to replace indigenous alternatives wherever they are found in the world and in the process create increasingly pure capitalistic, McDonaldized, and Americanized forms across the globe.

Those who emphasize glocalization tend to see it as militating against the globalization of nothing and, in fact, view it as leading to the creation of a wide array of new, glocal forms of something. In contrast, those who emphasize grobalization see it as a powerful contributor to the spread of nothingness throughout the world. This being said, it must be noted that there are important similarities and differences between glocalization and grobalization and their roles in the globalization of nothing and they must be delineated as we proceed.

Grobalization

The concept of grobalization, as well as the subprocesses of capitalism, McDonaldization, and Americanization, are at odds, to some degree, with the thrust of globalization theory—especially glocalization—that have the greatest cache today. There is a gulf between those who emphasize the increasing grobal influence of capitalistic, Americanized,[55] and McDonaldized[56] interests and those who see the world growing increasingly pluralistic and indeterminate.[57] At the risk of being reductive, this divide amounts to a difference in vision between those who see a world that is becoming increasingly grobalized[58]—more capitalistic, Americanized, rationalized, codified, and restricted—and those who view it as growing increasingly glocalized—more diverse, effervescent, and free.

While there are many different subprocesses that could be discussed under the heading of grobalization,[59] we will focus on capitalism, McDonaldization, and Americanization. While it is clear that all of these processes are important, their relative significance and impact will vary (to the degree that they can be separated[60]) on a case-by-case basis (nation, export considered, and so on). Furthermore, even though each of these will be discussed separately, it is clear that while they are not reducible to one another, they are highly interrelated.

Capitalism

No force has contributed more to globalization in general, and grobalization in particular, both historically and especially today, than capitalism. As Marx fully understood over a century ago,[61] capitalist firms must continue to expand or they will die, and when possibilities for high profits within a given nation decline, capitalistic businesses are forced to seek profits in other nations.[62] Eventually, such firms are led to explore and exploit possibilities for profit in more remote and less developed regions. Thus, except perhaps for the earliest forms, capitalistic businesses have always had global ambitions; they have always been interested in grobalization and contributed to glocalization. However, their impact has greatly accelerated in the past several decades.

During the Cold War that lasted much of the 20th century there were powerful restraints on capitalism's grobal ambitions. Most important, there was a seemingly viable alternative to it—socialism/communism—and this served to temper capitalism's expansion. On one hand, the Soviet Union and China, as well as nations within their orbit, were largely closed to incursions by the capitalists. The idea, posited first by Winston Churchill in 1946, that an iron curtain had descended between Soviet-controlled Eastern Europe and Western Europe made the barrier to capitalism, and much else, perfectly clear. On the other hand, many other nations throughout the world, even if they were not behind the iron curtain, were influenced by the ideas, if not the military and political power, of the communist countries. As a result, they were at least ambivalent about participating in the capitalist system, if not overtly hostile to it. In these and other ways, capitalism's grobal ambitions were limited to some degree throughout much of the 20th century.

However, by the close of the 20th century and the beginning of the 21st century, with the death of the Soviet Union and the near-death of communism/socialism, as well as with China and Russia behaving very much like capitalistic nations, almost all limits to the grobal ambitions of capitalistic firms were eliminated. As a result, it is only now that we are beginning to see the full-flowering of grobalization in capitalism. After all, in Marx's day (the mid- to late 1800s), capitalistic businesses were comparatively small and the important technologies (computers, telecommunications, huge cargo planes and ships, and so on) that permit and encourage high levels of grobalization did not exist.[63] Today's enormous capitalistic firms, equipped with magnificent globe-straddling technologies,[64] are far better able to grobalize than their predecessors. *And,* they move into a world in which there is *no* viable alternative to capitalism. We live in an era in which, truly for the first time, capitalism is unchained and free to roam the world in search of both cheap production facilities and labor as well as new markets for its products. As two neo-Marxian thinkers, Ellen Meiksins Wood and John Bellamy Foster, put it, "humanity is more and more connected in the global dimensions of exploitation and oppression."[65] As a result, there are those who believe that the death of communism around the world will not spell the death of Marxian theory, but rather serve to resuscitate it.[66] That is, Marxian analysis will be more necessary than ever with capitalism free to exploit more and more people and geographic areas of the world. It could be argued that it is only now that capitalism exists as a truly global phenomenon and the implication of Marxian theory is that this sets the stage, for the first time, for the emergence of global opposition to it.

Capitalism is clearly related to economic grobalization, especially in the area of consumption which is of central interest here. That is, it is capitalistic firms that produce the vast majority of non-places, non-things, non-people, and non-services on offer throughout the world. However, capitalism is also related to other aspects of globalization. Without adopting a simplistic (economic) base–(political) superstructure model,[67] it is clear that much grobalization in the political realm is affected to a large degree by the capitalistic economic system. Thus, the United States' much-avowed desire to see democracy throughout the world,[68] as well as many of its military adventures, is closely related to the needs of its capitalistic system. That is, democratic societies are more likely to become capitalistic and they are more likely to be open to the incursions of capitalistic firms from other countries (especially the United States). And, in those cases where a society does not move on its own in the direction of "democracy," there is always the possibility of American military involvement in order to nudge it, not so gently, in that direction. While the state clearly has its own interests, it just as certainly shares many interests with the capitalistic economic system to which it owes much of its existence and success. Political leaders are generally safe as long as the economy is performing well; however, their situation becomes precarious when the economy falters.

Similarly, organizational–institutional grobalization is also closely related to capitalism. For example, the proliferation of the franchise system of organization (this involves a franchiser [e.g., Subway] selling others [franchisees] the right to operate an outlet, although some control remains with the franchiser, which also usually gets a share of each franchisee's profits[69]) throughout the world is driven, in significant part, by capitalist economics. That is, some franchisers have grown fabulously wealthy as a result of this system, and it is not unusual to find franchisees who have become multimillionaires from the profits from one or several franchises. However, again it is important not to reduce all of this to (capitalist) economics alone (some value the franchise system, or a specific franchise, in itself and not just for its profit potential).

We need not go into great detail here about capitalism because so much has been written about it, its operations are so well known, and it is so obviously a form of grobalization. We turn now to two somewhat less well-known forms of grobalization, although we will have occasion to return under each of them to their relationship to capitalism.

McDonaldization

This is the process by which the principles of the fast-food restaurant are coming to dominate more and more sectors of American society and an increasing number of other societies throughout the world. It fits under the heading of grobalization because it involves the *growing* power of this model and its increasing influence throughout the world. The model's principles, as we have already seen, are *efficiency, calculability, predictability,* and *control,* particularly through the *substitution of nonhuman for human technology,* as well as the seemingly inevitable *irrationalities of rationality* that accompany the process.[70] The basic concept, as well as its fundamental dimensions, is derived from Max Weber's work on formal rationality.[71] Weber demonstrated that the modern Western world was characterized by an increasing tendency toward the predominance of formally rational systems and that the rest of the world was coming under the sway of these systems. Thus, the process of McDonaldization, or at least its forerunner (increasing formal rationality and bureaucratization), obviously predates McDonald's as an institution.[72] However, that franchise is the exemplar (the bureaucracy was the model in Weber's approach) of the contemporary phase of rationalization. While the fast-food restaurant is the paradigm of this process, the process has by now affected most, if not all, social structures and institutions in the United States, as well as most nations (at least those that are reasonably developed economically) in the world. Thus, McDonaldization is restricted neither to the fast-food industry nor to the United States. Rather, it is a wide-ranging and far-reaching process of global change.

Recent work has tended to support the McDonaldization thesis. It has been applied well beyond the fast-food restaurant and even everyday consumption to such areas as higher education ("McUniversity"),[73] politics,[74] religion,[75] and criminal justice.[76] Of course, not all systems (or nations) are equally McDonaldized; McDonaldization is a matter of degree, with some settings more McDonaldized than others. However, few settings (or nations) have been able to escape its influence altogether.

In terms of globalization, the McDonaldization thesis contends that highly McDonaldized systems, and more important the principles that lie at the base of these systems, have been exported from the United States to much of the rest of the world. Many nations throughout the world, and innumerable subsystems within each, are undergoing the process of McDonaldization. While McDonaldization is traceable, most proximately, to the United States, and especially the founding of the McDonald's chain outside Chicago in the mid-1950s, the process cannot simply be subsumed under the heading of Americanization. First, it has roots outside the United States, including the German bureaucracies analyzed by Weber at the turn of the 20th century. Second, the process has taken root by now in many nations and at least some of them are in the process of exporting their own McDonaldized systems throughout the world, including back into the United States (for example, the exportation of England's Body Shops or Sweden's Ikea [it's actually owned and managed by a company based in the Netherlands] to the United States and many other nations). McDonaldization can be thought of as a transnational process that is increasingly independent of any particular nation, including even the United States, and therefore is not reducible to a specific form of Americanization. As such, it is a particularly powerful force in the globalization of nothing. In the future, paralleling the history of mass manufacturing, we can anticipate that the center of McDonaldization will shift from the United States to other parts of the world.

It is worth noting that when they have addressed the McDonaldization thesis and related ideas, some globalization theorists, especially those committed to the ideas of heterogeneity and glocalization, have tended to be critical of it for its focus on its homogenizing impact on much of the rest of the world. For example, Robertson says that "the frequent talk about the

McDonaldization of the world . . . has to be strongly tempered by what is increasingly known about the ways in which such products or services are actually *the basis for localization*."[77] Instead, those associated with this view emphasize such things as local diversity and heterogeneity, the multi-directionality of global flows, and the existence of global processes that are relatively autonomous of specific nation-states. While all of these processes exist and are significant, it is *also* the case that *some* aspects of globalization are best described as having a largely homogenizing effect on much of the rest of the world.

McDonaldization is obviously a global perspective, but it is both less and more than a theory of globalization. On the one hand, McDonaldization does not involve anything approaching the full range of global processes. For example, many economic, cultural, political, and institutional aspects of globalization are largely unrelated to McDonaldization. On the other hand, McDonaldization involves much more than an analysis of its global impact. For example, much of it involves the manifold transformations taking place *within* the United States, the main source and still the center of this process. Furthermore, one can analyze the spread of McDonaldization (once it has arrived) *within* many other nations and even subareas of those nations. In addition, one can, as we have seen, look at the McDonaldization of various aspects of the social world—religion, higher education, politics, and so on—without considering the global implications for each. Thus, McDonaldization is not coterminous with globalization, nor is it solely a global process. Nonetheless, McDonaldization has global implications and can thus be a useful lens through which to examine changes taking place around the globe.

What is clear is that McDonaldization deserves a place in any thorough-going account of globalization. There can be little doubt that the logic of McDonaldization generates a set of values and practices that has a competitive advantage over other models. It not only promises many specific advantages, but also reproduces itself more easily than other models of consumption (and in many other areas of society as well). The success of McDonaldization in the United States over the past half century, coupled with the international ambitions of McDonald's and its ilk, as well as those of indigenous clones throughout the world, strongly suggests that McDonaldization will continue to make inroads into the global market-place not only through the efforts of existing corporations but also via the diffusion of the paradigm.

It should be noted, however, that the continued advance of McDonaldization, at least in its present form, is far from ensured. In fact, there are even signs in the United States, as well as in other parts of the world, of what I have previously called *deMcDonaldization*.[78] There are, for example, the increasing problems of McDonald's: It recently lost money for the first time and, as a result, was forced to close restaurants, fire employees, scale back planned expansion, and even let its chief executive go. Internationally, McDonald's restaurants have become targets for various groups with grievances against the restaurant chain, the United States, and even globalization. In light of such international difficulties, McDonald's is rethinking its plans to expand in certain areas and is cutting back in places where it is particularly likely to be an object of protest and attack.[79] Thus, the continued growth of McDonald's is not inevitable, although the same cannot be said of the underlying process of McDonaldization (more on this later).

Nonetheless, at the moment and for the foreseeable future, McDonaldization will continue to be preeminent and it is clearly and unequivocally not only a grobal process, but also one that contributes mightily to the spread of nothingness. The whole idea behind McDonaldization is to create a formal model based on a limited number of principles that can be replicated virtually anywhere in the world.

Capitalism is clearly closely related to McDonaldization. The spread of McDonaldized systems throughout the business world is motivated largely by the high profits they tend to produce. However, McDonaldization cannot be subsumed under the heading of capitalism. For one thing, even within the economic system, there are other reasons (e.g., the cultural importance and meaning of franchises) for their spread. More important is the impact of McDonaldization on many aspects of the social world (church, education, and so on) that can be seen as largely independent of the capitalistic economic system.

Americanization

Americanization can be defined as the propagation of American ideas, customs, social patterns, industry, and capital around the world.[80] It is a powerful unidirectional process stemming from the United States that tends to overwhelm competing processes (e.g., Japanization) as well as the strength of local (and glocal) forces that might resist, modify, or transform American models into hybrid forms. Moreover, the notion of Americanization is tied to a particular nation—the United States—but it has a differential impact on many specific nations. It can be subsumed under the heading of grobalization because it envisions a *growth* in American influence in all realms throughout the world.

Americanization is inclusive of forms of American cultural, institutional, political, and economic imperialism. For example, we can include under the heading of Americanization the worldwide diffusion of the American industrial model and the later global proliferation of the American consumption model; the marketing of American media including Hollywood films and popular music; the selling of American sports such as NFL football and NBA basketball abroad; the transnational marketing of American commodities including cola, blue jeans, and computer operating systems; the extensive diplomatic and military engagement with Europe, Asia, and South America; the training of the world's military, political, and scientific elites in American universities; the expansion of the American model of democratic politics; and the development and use of the international labor market and natural resources by American corporations.

The reach of Americanization is great. A good recent example involves a traditional, century-old Scottish soft drink, Irn-Bru (containing a bit of real iron). A 2002 report indicated that for the first time in its history, Irn-Bru had been surpassed as the most popular soft drink in Scotland. The new favorite (with 41% of the Scottish soft drink market)? Coca-Cola, of course! Said an entertainer, "It really is a national icon, even the name itself conjures up something of Scotland to me. . . . I am sorry to hear it's been beaten—it was nice that Scotland was independent in a way for a time."[81]

Or, take the case of Hollywood films.[82] The American film industry has overpowered many national film industries in Europe (especially France and Great Britain) and elsewhere, to the detriment of national artistic expression. The blockbuster films of Julia Roberts and Harrison Ford not only flow through an official distribution system, but videotape and DVD versions are also pirated and sold on the streets of third world cities. While several nations, including India and China, continue to produce large numbers of commercial films, even in these countries, American films are often featured on theater marquees. Similarly, many films that are less successful in America find a global market, and this can hold true for art films as well as action movies. The result is not simply a general familiarity with American movies and many other cultural products; those products tend to have an adverse effect on local products. Indeed, in France today there is a very public debate over the so-called cultural exception, which involves, among other things, the subsidization of its flagging movie industry.

Yet this is only one part of the Americanization of contemporary cinema. Another side is that the grammars of other national cinemas are being transformed for distribution in America. The Chinese, for example, have bemoaned the fact that their leading directors (including Zhang Yimo and Chen Kaige) make films that exoticize (or "orientalize"[83]) Chinese culture and history for Western audiences. A recent example is Ang Lee's *Crouching Tiger, Hidden Dragon,* which won many international prizes, but reportedly was unsuccessful in mainland China. In short, Chinese films are being tailored to American sensibilities in order to gain prestige and sales. As a result, American film culture has, at least in some senses, become world film culture. This is not to say that American cinema is not subject to diverse interpretations depending on the cultural context in which it is viewed, but only to suggest that American cultural artifacts are an increasingly central element of global culture.

A particularly good example of Americanization, and one of particular interest to the author, is the spread of the "new means of consumption,"[84] most of which were created in the United States and are now spreading throughout the world.[85] The new means of consumption are, in the main, settings (a supermarket is one example, although one that is not very new) that allow us to consume or that serve to increase the amount that we consume. There has been an almost dizzying creation and proliferation of settings that allow, encourage, and even compel us to consume innumerable goods and services. These settings have come into existence, or taken revolutionary new forms, in the United States since the close of WWII. Building upon, but going beyond, earlier settings, they have dramatically transformed the nature of consumption.

The following are the major new means of consumption with notable examples and the year in which they began operations:

- Franchises (McDonald's, 1955)[86]
- Shopping Malls (the first indoor mall, Edina, Minnesota, 1956)
- Mega-malls (West Edmonton Mall, 1981; Mall of America, 1992)
- Superstores (Toys R Us, 1957)
- Discounters (Target, 1962)
- Home Shopping Television (Home Shopping Network, 1985)
- Cybermalls (Wal-Mart, 1996)
- Theme Parks (Disneyland, 1955)
- Cruise Ships (Sunward, 1966)
- Casino-Hotels (Flamingo, 1946)
- Eatertainment (Hard Rock Cafe, 1971)

With the exception of mega-malls and the Edmonton Mall (created in Canada, but now supplanted in importance by Minnesota's Mall of America) and eatertainment and the Hard Rock Cafe (which was created in London, albeit to bring "American" food to England), all of these are American innovations that, in recent years, have been aggressively exported to the rest of the world; that is, they have become global phenomena.

All of the new means of consumption are highly McDonaldized (and McDonald's, fast-food restaurants, and franchises are such new means), but there is much more to these settings than simply their McDonaldized characteristics. The exportation of these new means of consumption must be considered, along with McDonaldization, in the context of a discussion of grobalization.

What is it about these new means of consumption that make them distinctly American (in Germany, the new McDonaldized Starbucks have been described as "Anywhere USA"[87]), excellent examples of Americanization, when they are exported to other countries? First, and most obviously, they are about consumption and the United States has been, and is still, the world leader in consumption and in innovations in that realm by a wide margin.[88] When anyone in the world thinks of consumption, a cornucopia of goods and services, and a rate of consumption so frenetic that one can only think of "hyperconsumption," one thinks of the United States.

Second, most of the new means of consumption relate in one way or another to the high rate of mobility associated with American culture. The vast majority of them have to do with the massive addiction of Americans to their automobiles, extensive and frequent automobile travel, and the consequent development of a road and highway system unparalleled in the world. Others relate to other types of mobility by plane (Las Vegas casino hotels, Disney theme parks), boat (cruise ships), and over the Internet (cybershops, cybermalls).

Third, the sustenance of these means of consumption requires the level of affluence that is so widely available in the United States. While other nations may have higher average levels of income, no nation has nearly as many people affluent enough to afford to visit, and to consume in, these sites on such a regular basis.[89] So many Americans are so affluent that they can afford to eat more meals out in franchises, eatertainment sites, and the like than people in any other nation. Only they can afford to descend in droves on meccas of consumption such as Las Vegas, Nevada; Orlando, Florida; and Minneapolis, Minnesota.

Fourth, many of the new means of consumption reflect the American mania for that which is huge and enormous. The idea is that the United States is a huge country and that necessitates that as much as possible be done in a big way. Many of the cathedrals of consumption reflect this peculiar mania for size—the mega-malls, superstores, theme parks, cruise ships, and casino-hotels all seek to outdo each other in terms of size. Size is also reflected in the sheer quantity of products available in these settings. Malls and mega-malls are chock full of well-stocked stores (often franchises): superstores have virtually everything one could think of in a particular line of products (sporting goods, athletic shoes, linens, etc.); Disney theme parks, especially Disney World, are characterized by a number of worlds, tens of thousands of hotel rooms, many restaurants, and much kitsch for sale; and of course Las Vegas is over the top in terms of everything it has to offer and it increasingly seems to offer everything.

Then there is, of course, the tendency for fast-food restaurants of all types to be in the business of "supersizing" everything they possibly can.[90]

What of the linkage between Americanization and capitalism? Clearly, there is a strong relationship here—the American economy is the unchallenged leader of global capitalism. But, of course, the two are not coterminous. On the one hand, many other nations are also capitalistic and, furthermore, still others (most notably China) are moving strongly in that direction. On the other hand, there are forms of Americanization in, for example, the arts and basic sciences, that are, at least to some degree, separable from capitalistic interests.

The relationship between Americanization and nothing is less clear-cut than that between McDonaldization and nothing. On the surface, Americanization inherently involves something—especially the fact that fundamental American characteristics and values infuse all of its forms. The shopping mall, as we have seen, is closely linked to the importance of the automobile in the functioning of American society as well as to the value Americans place on their automobiles—the love affair Americans have with their cars.

However, many of the Americanized forms exported to the rest of the world are attractive not just because of their American character and roots, but also because they have proven to be particularly malleable and adaptable to many other cultures and nations. They often can be detached from their American roots and reconstructed in many different ways in many other places. For example, Orchard Road, the main shopping street in Singapore, is awash with huge indoor malls, but they are in a highly urbanized area and rely heavily on foot traffic and consumers who arrive by public transportation rather than by automobile.[91] Thus, many other countries have now adopted the shopping mall and still others are likely to do so in the future. While malls in other parts of the world may have some, even many, indigenous shops and products, they are still clearly malls and very much in line with their American models and predecessors.

Americanization and Nothing

Why is Americanization a greater force in the proliferation of nothing than other similar processes (say, Japanization or Brazilianization)?

First, there is simply much more Americanization than any of the competing grobal processes. As the world's greatest power, especially economically, the United States simply produces[92] more of virtually everything that is on offer around the globe than any other nation. The United States' capitalistic enterprises, as well as many other organizations, churn out

Americana of all sorts, and there are great pressures, especially the need for ever-escalating profits, to export them throughout the globe. In contrast, a nation like Brazil, for example, produces far less "Braziliana" and there is far less pressure to export it globally.

Second, American exporters are more likely to be able to afford to use the world's advertising and marketing systems to disseminate their products. Furthermore, advertising and marketing are themselves American specialties, with the result that American products are likely to be presented not only more ubiquitously, but also more expertly. Bombarded by omnipresent and clever advertisements that may well conceal the American roots of various products, natives are more likely to accept them.

Third, in order to cater to a global market, American exporters are more likely, at least at times, to conceal the roots of these exports and to transform them into ever-emptier forms that can adapt to virtually any locale.

Fourth, and perhaps most important, the United States, as Todd Gitlin has made clear, is everyone's "second culture."[93] That is, even when people are able to distinguish their own culture from American exports, they are likely to be quite comfortable with things American. Since the latter are often relatively empty forms, they are easy to accept and to infuse with whatever meaning the locals desire.

Capitalism, McDonaldization, and Americanization

The argument here is that capitalism, McDonaldization, and Americanization are all grobalization processes deeply implicated in the proliferation of nothing throughout the world. However, there are important differences among them that need to be fleshed out here.

Capitalism is certainly a powerful force in the grobalization of nothing. There are many reasons for this, but perhaps the most important is that in order to maximize profits, capitalistic firms are generally driven to reduce products to their simplest, most basic elements. To put this in terms of our definition of nothing, they seek to produce that which comes ever closer to the nothing end of the something–nothing continuum. While capitalistic businesses can and do produce that which lies toward the something end of that continuum, there is far less money to be made in the production of something than of nothing (for one thing, the demand for something is far less than that for nothing). Thus, capitalists are most likely to be drawn to that which is already nothing or to transform something progressively into nothing. This dynamic helps to explain the attraction of McDonaldized systems to other capitalistic organizations, but we must go beyond capitalism because, as we have seen, nonprofit organizations also seek to become increasingly McDonaldized.

McDonaldized systems are imperatively, and by design, minimalist; they are long on form and short on content. Thus, when McDonaldized systems are exported, especially from the United States to other parts of the world, little or nothing can or need be extracted in order to allow them to fit into the new environment. Second, in addition to the fact that there is so little substance to McDonaldized systems that there is little to remove, there is also little in the way of demand from local populations to remove offending elements because there are so few elements and those that exist are mainly generic forms that can fit almost anywhere. Third, a few local elements can be larded into the extant system, either by addition or substitution, without altering the system in any dramatic way or conflicting with the generic components. Thus, for example, McDonald's adds local items (suitably McDonaldized) to its menus in many countries, but its underlying principles remain sacrosanct and therefore almost totally unchanged. It is for these reasons, and undoubtedly others, that there is near perfect fit between grobalization, the exportation of nothing, and McDonaldization.

There is a less perfect fit between the grobalization of nothing and Americanization. The reason is that Americanized systems are, to varying degrees, laden with content, with something—fundamental American characteristics.[94] In some cases, American systems are welcomed in other nations *because* of their Americanism; it is that cultural something associated with these systems that allows them to succeed elsewhere. However, in those instances we are talking about Americanization as the grobalization of something (for much more on this see Chapter 5).

In other instances, however, Americanization brings with it, or becomes, nothing in other societies. For one thing, as everyone's second culture, the United States exports what appear to be innocuous phenomena that fit quickly and easily into other cultures. For another, that which is distinctly American about these phenomena is quickly lost sight of, or systematically extracted, rendering the American export nothing, or seemingly so. In some cases, success throughout the world depends on playing up the American roots and characteristics of these exports, while in other cases it involves playing them down or even striving to obliterate them. To the degree that things like Levi's, Coke, Mickey Mouse hats, Barbie dolls, and the like come to be disconnected from their American roots and become forms that fit anywhere and everywhere—that is, nothing—they can move effortlessly from one culture to another and be sold widely in all cultures. Thus, the success of McDonald's in Japan, and elsewhere, is aided by the fact that it is regarded by many as a local restaurant chain. This is exemplified by the case of a Japanese Boy Scout who, on a trip to the United States, was surprised to find McDonald's in Chicago—he thought McDonald's was a Japanese chain.[95]

Of Power and Purity

In the end, however, Americanization is at a disadvantage relative to both capitalism and McDonaldization in the global spread of nothing. As we have seen, the desire of capitalists to maximize profits leads them in the direction of producing nothing and aggressively exporting it to the rest of the world. For their part, McDonaldized systems are largely devoid of substance and therefore need do very little in order to fit into other cultures. In contrast, Americanized systems are defined by elements of American culture and, at least in some cases, those elements must be extracted in order for them to succeed in other cultures. Furthermore, in different countries it is not always the same elements that must be extracted and this greatly complicates matters. That is, one culture may require the removal of one set of elements, while another may demand a very different set be removed. Overall, both capitalism and McDonaldization are purer forces in the grobalization of nothing than Americanization. That is, that which emanates from capitalism and McDonaldization will generally be close to the nothing end of the continuum, while that which stems from the United States will contain at least some of the "something-ness" of American culture.[96] That is not to say that capitalism and McDonaldization are necessarily more powerful factors, but they are certainly purer factors.

In fact, overall, it is capitalism that is the most powerful force in the grobalization of nothing. To the degree that it can be separated from capitalism, Americanization is a more powerful force than McDonaldization. Furthermore, both capitalism and Americanization are more multidimensional forces than McDonaldization. That is, they are more likely to bring with them *both* something and nothing. While the impact of the United States has its ambiguities, and is not as powerful as capitalism, it is clearly an enormously powerful force throughout the world. The power of Americanization comes from its strength in all of the sectors being discussed here—cultural, economic, political, and institutional. While capitalism affects all of these realms, its greatest impact is obviously in the economic realm. McDonaldization also is found in all of these sectors, but its most profound effects are cultural and economic. Americanization is not only a potent force in these realms, but its power extends much more into the political and institutional areas, including the military. The political and military hegemony of the United States in the world today accords it enormous power. While it is possible to discuss the role of capitalism and McDonaldization in politics and the military, there is far more to those realms than simply increasing profitability and increasing rationalization.

Anti-Americanism and the
Global Attacks on McDonald's

The thrust of the argument made in this chapter is confirmed, in an odd way, by the recent acceleration of deadly attacks on American interests and on McDonald's restaurants throughout the world. In terms of the latter, the most extreme and heinous example is the destruction of the World Trade Center and part of the Pentagon on September 11, 2001 (for more on September 11th, see Chapter 7).[97] In addition, McDonald's has become a favorite target around the world, with innumerable examples of protests against (Josc Bove's efforts in France are the best-known example[98]), and even bombings of, its restaurants. As I write this, a bomb has gone off in a McDonald's in Indonesia, killing three people. In terms of the arguments being made in this book, these attacks reflect, at least in part, a growing awareness that capitalism, Americanization, and McDonaldization, and more generally the process of grobalization under which they can be subsumed, are threats to indigenous cultures. It is clear to an increasing number of people around the world that ever-increasing and accelerating expansionism lies at the heart of grobalization and that resistance is necessary if they wish their cultures to survive.

Making this argument should not be construed as a defense of the kinds of deadly actions mentioned above. Clearly, other ways need to be found to oppose these processes. Such responses are far worse than the problems they seek to deal with. Nonetheless, they do make it clear that the processes discussed here have great power and they are being met with strong, albeit sometimes misguided and even downright malevolent, responses.

The hostile reactions to capitalism, Americanization, and McDonald's (as a capitalistic organization, as American in origin, and as the paradigm of the process of McDonaldization) raises the issue, again, of whether the three sub-processes can truly be differentiated. After all, for many around the world McDonald's is both capitalistic and a key symbol of the United States and Americanization.[99] For example, on the opening of McDonald's in Moscow, one journalist called it the "ultimate icon of Americana," and on the opening of a Pizza Hut in that city, a student labeled it a "piece of America."[100] Furthermore, while many attacks on McDonald's are on the chain itself, as well as the process it represents, others, especially the most violent and deadly, are motivated by the idea that McDonald's is a worldwide surrogate for the United States and assaults on it are attacks on the United States and its interests. To those who oppose capitalism and Americanization, and want to do something about them, a McDonald's restaurant represents a far more ubiquitous and easily assailable target than, say, American embassies or General Motors factories. Thus, when Jose Bové wanted to protest increases of American tariffs on French products, he chose McDonald's as his target (there are many of them, they are easily accessible, and they do not have the guards one finds in and around American embassies and large factories throughout the world).

In addition to its association with capitalism and the United States, and its vulnerability to attack, McDonald's is an attractive target because forays against it get enormous attention throughout the world from the mass media. The reason is McDonald's enormous success and visibility world-wide, as well as the fact that it is a prime example of grobalization. It is an icon to many people around the world in both a positive and a negative sense.[101] Thus, there is great interest in news of attacks on it.

In spite of this association, we continue to hold to the view that it is important to adhere to the distinctions among capitalism, Americanization, and McDonaldization, at least for analytical purposes. While there are important overlaps among them, the fact is that there are global processes that can more easily be included under one or more of these headings than the other(s). The spread of foreign fast-food chains into the United States can be included under the heading of McDonaldization and capitalism, but not Americanization. The political and military influence of the United States throughout the world is an example of Americanization, but not of McDonaldization and only partially of capitalism. The opening of a General Motors factory in Mexico is mainly linked to the dynamics of capitalism, has less to do with Americanization, and is hard to relate to McDonaldization.

This discussion leads to another issue: Does the acceleration of attacks on capitalism, Americanization, McDonaldization, and grobalization represent the beginning of the decline of these processes? This is a complex question involving multiple, overlapping processes and predictions about the future. Let me offer four thumbnail answers to close this discussion.

First, as pointed out above, rather than slowing down, capitalism is expanding at an unprecedented level in the wake of the decline of the only global alternative to it—communism/socialism. The current wave of attacks on it is unlikely to have any impact on its continued expansion.

Second, anti-Americanism is so strong and is growing so fast in many parts of the world that it is possible to conceive of some slowdown in the incursions of Americanism throughout the world. However, there are powerful economic (capitalism!) and political forces behind Americanization, with the result that my view would be that the slowdown is likely to be mild and short-lived. Furthermore, existing side by side with anti-Americanism, is widespread and powerful pro-Americanism. Thus, a recent Pew Survey found that anti-Americanism was on the rise and that a majority of those surveyed in many countries opposed the spread of American ideas, but they also liked American culture, such as its movies, music, and television.[102]

Third, a slowdown, even reversal, of the global fortunes of McDonald's is much more likely than a similar development in the realm of

Americanization. This is clearly a corporation in trouble not only in its global operations, but it is in even more serious difficulties in the American market. However, a slowdown in the global proliferation of McDonald's, or even its disappearance, does not spell the decline or demise of McDonaldization. While the paradigm may change (Starbucks is the current star in the fast-food industry and is undergoing enormous global expansion [it is currently expanding rapidly in Europe and has just announced plans for a massive invasion of heretofore tea-drinking China]; can we think in terms of "Starbuckization"?), the underlying process of rationalization, encompassing the basic principles (efficiency, and so on) discussed above, is likely not only to continue, but to accelerate.

Finally, grobalization is the major worldwide development of the age and it is almost impossible to envision a scenario whereby it would slow down, let alone be stopped.[103] There is too much power behind the forces pushing grobalization, the forces opposing it (at least at the moment and for the foreseeable future) are far too weak, and there are far too many real and imagined gains associated with it.[104] In any case, for most nations of the world, there is little choice. Efforts to opt out, even if they were successful (and that's not likely), would push the nations that do so into the backwaters of the global system. A more likely option for most is to become active exporters in the grobal system rather than being passive recipients of that which is created and produced elsewhere, especially in the United States.[105]

Some Complexities

While this discussion has largely been set up as a confrontation between glocalization (and something) and grobalization (and nothing), the reality, even as it will be discussed in this book, is much more complex than that. As we will see in the next chapter, there is a glocalization of nothing and a grobalization of something, and their existence already adds great complexity to this discussion. However, even that only begins to scratch the surface.

As Douglas Goodman recently pointed out, there are many examples of contradiction within the social and cultural world in general and more specifically within the realm of the consumer culture that is the focus of this book.[106] Furthermore, these contradictions play themselves out at all levels from the most local to the most global and everywhere in between. It is not simply that glocalization and grobalization (and something and nothing) contradict one another, or at least seem to, but that out of their mutual interactions a wide range of other contradictions emerges. Thus, the grobalization of nothing often spawns a reaction that leads to the emergence or reemergence of a more local tradition. For example, the influx of fast food into South Korea gave impetus to the rebirth in chewing betel nuts.[107]

There is another possibility. Instead of combating the grobalization of nothing through the creation of a glocal something, it is possible that all that will be created is yet other consumer products that fit our definition of nothing—they are centrally conceived, controlled, and devoid of distinctive content. One example is an Eastern European product, Ordinary Laundry Detergent, created there as an alternative to Tide, which is advertised as "better than ordinary laundry detergent."[108] In fact, by touting the "ordinary," the Eastern European detergent could be seen as more nothing than Tide's branded version (for more on brands, see Chapter 8). Furthermore, it is not inconceivable that it, or a product like it, could become successful outside Eastern Europe as yet another example of the grobalization of nothing.

Yet another possibility is that glocal elements could respond with what Robertson calls "willful nostalgia" and purposely create products that embed themselves in the indigenous past of a particular region or nation.[109] Examples include the Shiseido cosmetics firm[110] and the makers of French chocolates,[111] both of which invoke an image of the past to sell their products in their home countries *and* internationally. Of course, these, too, become simply other centrally conceived and controlled consumer products devoid of distinctive content that are to be globalized, this time from a base in Japan or France.

Yet another layer of complexity is added when we realize that grobal firms themselves make their own use of "willful nostalgia" by creating products for a specific market that draw on the history and traditions of that market. Again, what appears to be a glocal alternative becomes simply another tool to further the grobalization of nothing. A good example is the fact that McDonald's sells *kampong* burgers in Singapore.[112] The term *kampong* refers to the local villages in which most Singaporeans lived before being resettled in the high-rise buildings that are now so common there. Thus, McDonald's is using nostalgia not to create something truly glocal, but rather to further the grobalization of nothing, this time embodied not only in itself and its usual fare, but also in the *kampong* burger, a thinly camouflaged minor variation on one of the paradigmatic examples of the grobalization of nothing—the hamburger.

The point of this is to make it clear that the use of the concepts that have been delineated theoretically in this book—in this case the grobalization of nothing and the glocalization of something—reveals interesting and important variations when we descend into the real world of grobal–glocal consumption (and much else). These ideal–typical concepts, as well as the more general theoretical perspective outlined here, are useful not only in themselves, but also for their utility in helping us analyze apparent deviations from, or variations on, them.

Chapter Five

Grobalization–Glocalization and Something–Nothing

Having now introduced the topic of globalization, at long last we get to the central issue in this book—its relationship to nothing. However, we can deal with that linkage only within the context of a more general discussion of the interrelationships among grobalization–glocalization and something–nothing. Figure 5.1 offers the four basic possibilities that emerge when we cross-cut the grobalization–glocalization and something–nothing continua (along with representative examples of places–non-places, things–non-things, people–non-people, and services–non-services for each of the four possibilities and quadrants). It should be noted that while this yields four *ideal types,* there are no hard-and-fast dividing lines between them. This is reflected in the use of both dotted lines and multidirectional arrows in Figure 5.1.

It is clear that quadrants 1 and 4 in Figure 5.1 are of greatest importance, at least for the purposes of this analysis, because their relationship to one another represents a key point of tension and conflict in the world today. Clearly, there is great pressure to grobalize nothing and often all that stands in its way in terms of achieving global hegemony is the glocalization of something. We will return to this conflict and its implications for our analysis below.

While the other two quadrants (2 and 3) are clearly residual in nature and of secondary significance, it is important to recognize that there is, at least to some degree, a glocalization of nothing (quadrant 2) and a grobalization of something (quadrant 3). Whatever tensions may exist between

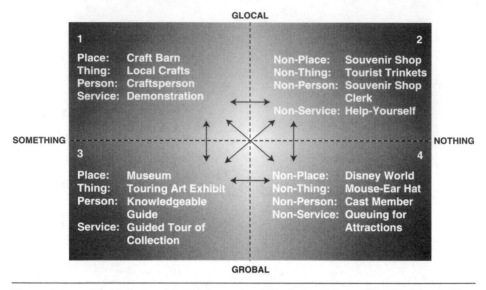

Figure 5.1   The Relationship Between Glocal-Grobal and Something-Nothing With Exemplary (Non-) Places, (Non-) Things, (Non-) Persons, and (Non-) Services.

them are of far less significance than those between the grobalization of nothing and the glocalization of something. However, a discussion of the glocalization of nothing and the grobalization of something makes it clear that grobalization is not an unmitigated source of nothing (it can involve something) and glocalization is not to be seen solely as a source of something (it can involve nothing).

Returning to the central argument, the close and centrally important relationship between (1) grobalization and nothing and (2) glocalization and something leads to the view that there is an *elective affinity* between the two elements of each of these pairs.[1] The idea of elective affinity, derived from the historical comparative sociology of Max Weber, is meant to imply that there is not a necessary, law-like causal relationship between these elements.[2] That is, in the case of neither grobalization and nothing nor glocalization and something do one of these elements "cause" the other to come into existence. Rather, the development and diffusion of one tends to go hand in hand with the other. Other ways of putting this is that grobalization–nothing and glocalization–something tend to mutually favor one another; they are inclined to combine with one another.[3] Thus, it is far easier to grobalize nothing than something; the development of grobalization creates a favorable ground for the development and spread of nothing (and nothing is easily grobalized). Similarly, it is far easier to glocalize something than nothing; the development of glocalization creates a favorable ground for the development and proliferation of something (and something is easily glocalized).

However, the situation is more complex than this since we can also see support for the argument that grobalization can, at times, involve something (for example, art exhibits that move among art galleries throughout the world, Italian exports of food like Parmiagiano Reggiano and Culatella ham, touring symphony orchestras and rock bands that perform in venues throughout the world) and that glocalization can sometimes involve nothing (for example, the production of local souvenirs and trinkets for tourists from around the world). However, we would *not* argue that there is an elective affinity between grobalization–something and glocalization–nothing. The existence of examples of the grobalization of something and the glocalization of nothing makes it clear why we need to think in terms of elective affinities and not law-like relationships.

The Grobalization of Something

While there is a clear elective affinity between grobalization and nothing, that is not to say that something is not being grobalized as well. In fact, some types of something have been grobalized to a considerable degree. This is abundantly clear throughout the world of consumption. In Figure 5.1, we have used as examples of the grobalization of something touring art exhibitions (thing) of the works of Vincent Van Gogh, the museums throughout the world in which such exhibitions occur for a time (place), the knowledgeable guides who show visitors the highlights of the exhibition (person),[4] and the detailed information and insights they are able to impart in response to questions from gallery visitors (service). To take another example, a touring series of Silk Road concerts recently brought together Persian artists and music, an American symphony orchestra, and Rimsky-Korsakov's (Russian) "Scheherezade."[5] More generally, gourmet foods, handmade crafts, and custom-made clothes are now much more available throughout the world and more likely to be traded transnationally than ever in history.

However, even with the recent increase, there is far less grobalization of something than there is grobalization of nothing and, more important, there is far less of an association between grobalization and something than there is between grobalization and nothing.

Why is there comparatively little connection between grobalization and something? First, there is simply far less demand throughout the world for most forms of something, at least in comparison to the demand for nothing. One reason for this is that the distinctiveness and complexity of something, be it gourmet foods, handmade crafts, or Silk Road concerts, require far more sophisticated tastes than nothing. Second, the complexity of something, especially the fact that it is likely to have many different elements, means that it is more likely to have at least some characteristics that will bother or even offend large numbers of people in many different cultures. For example, a Russian (or Persian) audience at a Silk Road concert might be bothered by the juxtaposition of Persian music with that of Rimsky-Korsakov. Third, the various forms of something are usually more expensive, frequently much more expensive, than competing forms of nothing (a fine, complex wine is much more costly than a jug of mass-produced wine). Higher cost means, of course, that far fewer people can afford something. As a result, the global demand for expensive forms of something is minuscule in comparison to that for the inexpensive varieties of nothing. Fourth, because the prices are high and the demand is comparatively low, far less can be spent on the advertising and marketing of something and this serves to keep demand low. Fifth, something is far more difficult to mass manufacture and, in some cases (Silk Road concerts, van Gogh exhibitions), impossible to produce in this way. The very nature of these complex phenomena serves to limit their numbers and hence their global proliferation. There are just so many world-class rock bands, gymnastic teams, and folk music troupes and the profit potential of such groups, if that is indeed the objective, is highly limited, to put it mildly. This is not the case with nothing, which, precisely because it is devoid of such characteristics, is far easier to produce in large numbers and to distribute globally. Sixth, since the demand for something is less price-sensitive than nothing (the relatively small number of people who can afford it are willing, and often able, to pay almost any price), there is less need to mass manufacture it (assuming it could be produced in this way) in order to lower prices. Seventh, the costs of shipping of something (gourmet foods, the Van Gogh paintings) are usually very high, adding to the price and thereby reducing the demand.

It could also be argued that the lesser degree of the grobalization of something (compared to nothing) helps to distinguish something from nothing. Because it is relatively scarce, something retains its status and its distinction from nothing. If something came to be mass-produced and grobalized, it is likely that it would move toward the nothing end of the continuum. This raises the intriguing question of what comes first, nothing or grobalization and the associated mass production.[6] That is, does a phenomenon start out as nothing? Or, is it transformed into nothing by mass production and grobalization? We will return to this issue at the close of this chapter.

The Grobalization of Nothing

The example of the grobalization of nothing in Figure 5.1 is a trip to one of Disney's worlds, be it in Anaheim, Orlando, Tokyo, outside Paris, or the one soon to open (2005 or 2006; groundbreaking took place in January 2003[7]) in Hong Kong, China (!). More specifically, any of Disney's worlds is a non-place and all of them are awash with a wide range of non-things (such as mouse-ear hats), staffed by non-people (the cast members, in costume or out), who offer non-services (what is offered is often dictated by rules, regulations, and the scripts followed by employees). It is the grobalization of these, and innumerable other, forms of nothing that is the central concern of this book.

The main reasons for the strong elective affinity between grobalization and nothing are basically the flip-sides of the reasons for the lesser affinity between grobalization and something. Above all, there is a far greater demand throughout the world for nothing than something. This is the case because nothing tends (although not always—see below) to be less expensive than something with the result that more people can afford the former than the latter. Large numbers of people are also far more likely to want the various forms of nothing because their comparative simplicity and lack of distinctiveness makes them relatively easy to appreciate. In addition, as pointed out earlier, that which is nothing, largely devoid of distinctive content, is far less likely to bother or offend those in other cultures. Finally, because of the far greater sales potential, much more money can be, and is, devoted to the advertising and marketing of nothing, thereby creating a still greater demand for it than for something.

Because they are so content-less, nullities are easier to extract from the given locality in which they were created and to export to other, sometimes very different, locales. As a result, it is relatively easy to grobalize that which is relatively content-less. In contrast, elaborate and distinctive phenomena may be too tied to a specific locale to be extracted from it, and their complex distinctiveness may make it difficult for them to take root in other locales. Thus, Parmigiano Reggiano is a very distinctive cheese product of a region of Italy and while it is available globally, at least on a limited scale, its market potential in locales outside of Italy dominated by other cuisines is limited. For example, it is questionable, to put it mildly, how well such a distinctive cheese would go with a Tex-Mex dish, an Indian curry, or a Chinese stir-fry.[8] In contrast, Coca-Cola, and more generally colas of any brand or even no-name versions, have proven easier to extract from their American roots, fit with virtually every cuisine (it could be, and is, consumed with Tex-Mex, curry, and stir-fry), and have, as a result, been exported successfully throughout the world; in other words, cola, especially Coca-Cola, has been grobalized.[9] In fact, a WWII soldier said he was fighting for "the right to buy Coca Cola again" and an advertising campaign in the 1990s proclaimed, "If you don't know what it [Coca-Cola] is, Welcome to Planet Earth."[10]

Beer is an interesting case in this context, especially in contrast to cola. Beer is certainly a global phenomenon, but no single brand has penetrated much of the global market for beer, at least to the extent that Coca-Cola, and to a lesser degree Pepsi-Cola, have become global soft drink brands. The beer brands that are global in reach (Beck's from Germany, Heineken from the Netherlands [described by some as the "only truly global beer brand"[11]], Foster's from Australia,[12] and Corona from Mexico, for example) tend *not* to come from the United States and to be much less important factors in the global beer business than Coke and Pepsi are in the soft-drink business. There are many reasons for this—beer does not travel as well or maintain its quality as long as soft drinks, only the soft-drink syrup, or just the formula for the syrup, needs to be exported (there is no beer syrup), and so on. However, a central factor is certainly the fact that beer is a more variable and complex drink than cola and there are important regional differences in beer tastes. In other words, beer, especially the better varieties, is more likely to be near the something end of the continuum whereas soft drinks fall nearer the nothing end of that continuum. Of course, there are such things as "gourmet" soft drinks,[13] but they tend to be glocal and to represent the glocalization of something. And, there certainly are mass-produced beers, especially dominant in the American market, but most of them are not distributed internationally to any great degree, if at all. However, such beer certainly could use inexpensive ingredients from anywhere in the world and, in this sense, be grobal.

Nullities are also easier to extract from the time period in which they were created and to be at home in other time periods. For example, stemming from an era in which there was greater tolerance, and less awareness, of drugs and the problems associated with them, Coca-Cola originally had small amounts of cocaine, but times changed and it quickly became clear that such a drug had no place in a soft drink and it was removed. Coca-Cola with cocaine would be impossible to sell today, but with the offending drug removed, it is saleable almost everywhere. More generally, there is a tendency to modify products of a given time period, to remove much of what makes them distinctive, so that they can be marketed in a different time period. The taco may have deep roots in the history of Mexican culture, but much of what was historically involved in the creation of tacos (especially the way they were made, the extremely hot chilies that gave [and continue to give] traditional tacos their spiciness) has been removed (at least outside indigenous areas where the original taco is still made and consumed) to make it the kind of time-less generic product that chains like Taco Bell can market today around the world. It is far easier to distribute such products globally—to grobalize them—than it is those that retain deep ties to a specific epoch (and local area).

Given the great demand, it is far easier to mass-produce and -distribute the empty forms of nothing than the substantively rich forms of something. Indeed, many forms of something lend themselves best to limited, if not one-of-a-kind, production. A skilled potter may produce a few dozen pieces of pottery and an artist a painting or two in, perhaps, a week, a month, or even a year (or still longer). While these craft and art works may, over time, move from owner to owner in various parts of the world, this traffic barely registers in the total of global trade and commerce. Of course, there are the rare masterpieces that may bring millions of dollars, but in the main we are talking about primarily small-ticket items. In contrast, thousands, even many millions, and sometimes billions of varieties of nothing are mass produced and sold throughout the globe. Nullities are easier to produce, and in large numbers, because they are, in the main, devoid of much distinctive and idiosyncratic content. It is far easier to centrally conceive, construct, and reproduce many times over that which is derived from a bare-bones model with minimal content (or to put it another way, a model that is far more form than content), than it is from one that is rich and elaborate in distinctive content. That is, a minimalist phenomenon, or one that comes as close as possible to it, is far easier to centrally create, reproduce, and disseminate widely than one that is rich in content. Furthermore, once one has constructed the basic model of a minimal phenomenon, then all iterations that follow from it are easy to produce since there is so little substance to the model. Also easing the way toward the proliferation of the model is the fact that only minor variations and deviations over time and across space are permitted. The proliferation of nullities obviously assumes the existence of entrepreneurs (in the broadest sense of the term) who are interested, for financial or myriad other reasons, in the expansion of their minimalist creations and their exportation to other parts of the world.

Furthermore, the economics of the marketplace demand that the massive amount of nothing that is produced be marketed and sold on a grobal basis. For example, the economies of scale mean that the more that is produced and sold, the lower the price. This means that, almost inevitably, American producers of nothing (and, as we have seen, they are by far the world leaders in this) must become dissatisfied with the American market, no matter how vast it is, and aggressively pursue a world market for their consumer products. The greater the grobal market, the lower the price that can be charged and this, in turn, means that even greater numbers of nothing can be sold and farther reaches of the globe in less-developed countries can be reached. Another economic factor stems from the stock market, which demands that corporations that produce and sell nothing (indeed all corporations) increase sales and profits from one year to the next. The stocks of those corporations that simply meet the previous year's profitability, or—God forbid—even experience a decline, are likely to be punished in the stock market and see their stock prices fall, sometimes precipitously. In order to increase profits continually, the corporation is forced, as Marx understood long ago, to continue to search out new markets, and one way of doing that is constantly to expand globally. In contrast, since something is less likely to be produced by corporations, certainly the large corporations listed in the stock market, there is far less pressure to expand the market for these things. In any case, as we saw above, given the limited number of these things that can be produced by artisans, musicians, skilled chefs, artists, and so on, there are profound limits on any type of expansion. This, in turn, brings us back to the pricing issue and relates to the price advantage that nothing ordinarily has over something. As a general rule, the various types of nothing cost far less than something. The result, obviously, is that nothing can be marketed globally far more aggressively than something.

Also, nothing has an advantage in terms of transportation around the world. These are non-things that generally can be easily and efficiently packaged and moved, often over vast areas. Lunchables, for example, are compact, prepackaged, require no refrigeration, and have a long shelf life. Furthermore, because the unit cost of such items is low, it is not of great consequence if they go awry, are lost, or are stolen. In contrast, it is more difficult and expensive to package something—say a piece of handmade pottery or an antique vase—and losing such things, having them stolen, or being broken is a disaster. As a result, it is far more expensive to insure units of something than nothing and this difference is another reason for the cost advantage that nothing has over something. It is these sorts of things that serve to limit greatly the global trade in items that can be included under the heading of something.

While the grobalization of nothing dominates in the arena of consumption as it is generally defined, we find domains—medicine, science, pharmaceuticals,[14] biotechnology,[15] education, and others—in which the grobalization of something is of far greater importance. While these areas have, as we have seen, experienced their share of the grobalization of nothing, they are also characterized by a high degree of the grobalization of something. For example, the worldwide scientific community benefits from the almost instantaneous distribution of important scientific findings, often these days via new journals on the Internet. Thus, our focus on the grobalization of nothing should not blind us to the existence and importance, especially in areas such as these, of the grobalization of something (more on this below).

The Glocalization of Nothing

One of the best examples of the glocalization of nothing is to be found in the realm of tourism,[16] especially where the grobal tourist meets the local (if they still exist) manufacturer and retailer in the production and sale of glocal goods and services (this is illustrated in quadrant 2 of Figure 5.1). There are certainly instances, perhaps even many of them, where tourism stimulates the production of something—well-made, high-quality craft products made for discerning tourists, or meals lovingly prepared by local chefs using traditional recipes and the best of local ingredients. However, far more often, and increasingly as time goes by, grobal tourism leads to the glocalization of nothing. Souvenir shops are likely to be bursting at the seams with trinkets reflecting a bit of the local culture. Such souvenirs are increasingly likely to be mass-manufactured, perhaps using components from other parts of the world, in local factories. If demand grows great enough and the possibilities of profitability high enough, low-priced souvenirs may be manufactured by the thousands or millions elsewhere in the world and then shipped back to the local area to be sold to tourists (who may not notice, or care about, the "made in China" label embossed on their souvenir replicas of the Eiffel Tower). The clerks in these souvenir shops are likely to act like non-people and tourists are highly likely to serve themselves. Similarly, large numbers of meals slapped together by semi-skilled chefs to suggest vaguely local cooking are far more likely than gourmet meals that are true to the region or that truly integrate local elements. They are likely to be offered in "touristy" restaurants that are close to the non-place end of the continuum and to be served by non-people who offer little in the way of service.

Another major example involves the production of native shows—often involving traditional costumes, dances, and music—for grobal tourists. While these could be something, there is a very strong tendency for them to be transformed into nothing to satisfy grobal tour operators and tourists. Hence these shows are examples of the glocalization of nothing because they become centrally conceived and controlled empty forms. They are often watered down, if not eviscerated, with esoteric or possibly offensive elements removed. The performances are designed to please the throngs of tourists and to put off as few of them as possible. They take place with great frequency and performers often seem as if they are going through the motions in a desultory fashion. For their part, this is about all the grobal tourists want in their rush: to see the performance, to perhaps eat an ersatz local meal, and then to move on rapidly to the next stop on the tour. Thus, in the area of tourism—in souvenirs, local performances, and local meals—we are far more likely to see the glocalization of nothing than of something.

The Glocalization of Something

This is the main interest of most of those who focus on glocalization. They tend to believe and argue that the interaction of the global and the local produces something and they tend to privilege, as we have seen, the glocal something over the grobal nothing (as well as over the glocal nothing that rarely appears in their analyses).[17] While there certainly continues to be a glocalization of something, and it represents an important counterforce to the grobalization of nothing, it is not nearly as important as glocalization theorists suggest. The example of the glocalization of something in Figure 5.1 (quadrant 1) is in the realm of local crafts like pottery or weaving. Such craft products are things and they are likely to be displayed and sold in places like craft barns. The craftsperson who makes and demonstrates his or her wares is a person, and customers are apt to be offered a great deal of service.

Such glocal products are likely to remain something, although there are certainly innumerable examples (see below for a discussion of kokopelli figures from the Southwestern United States and matryoshka dolls from Russia) of glocal forms of something that have been transformed into glocal, and in some cases grobal, forms of nothing. In fact, there is often a kind of progression here from glocal something to glocal nothing as demand grows and then to grobal nothing if some entrepreneur believes that there might be a global market for such products. However, some glocal forms of something are able to resist this process.

Glocal forms of something remain as such for various reasons. That which is derived from the glocal is, almost by definition, much more complex than that which is grobal and therefore is likely to be produced in more limited numbers. The complexity of the glocal comes from the fact that it involves an idiosyncratic mix of the global and the local and, furthermore, there may be many such combinations in many areas of the world with subtle differences in each area in the ways in which global and local elements are combined. It is difficult to produce such complex combinations in great numbers; the many different combinations speak to the likelihood of small-batch, rather than mass, production (for example, slight differences in the food served in different parts of Provence in southern France). Furthermore, there is likely to be only a minimal demand for such idiosyncratic products (for example, only relatively small numbers are likely to interested in Provencal food). Finally, that which is glocal in character is almost by definition marketed in a limited geographic area—the glocality—and this means that low levels of production might be hard-pressed to satisfy even the (g)local demand, let alone a global market. Thus, the most famous restaurants in Provence are booked long in advance and the Provencal food served in most French restaurants throughout the world has little resemblance to that served in Provence.

In addition, glocal forms of something tend to be costly, at least in comparison to mass-manufactured competitors. High price tends to keep demand down locally, let alone globally. Glocal forms of nothing are loaded with distinctive content. Among other things, this means that consumers, especially in other cultures, find them harder to understand and appreciate. Furthermore, their complex character makes it more likely that those in other cultures will find something about them they do not like or even find offensive. Those who create glocal forms of something are not, unlike larger manufacturers of nothing, pushed by market forces to expand their business and increase profits to satisfy stockholders and the stock market. While craftspeople are not immune to the desire to earn more money, the pressure to do so is more internal than external and it is not nearly as great or inexorable. In any case, the desire to earn more money is tempered by the fact that the production of each craft product is time-consuming and there are just so many of them that can be produced in a given time. Further, craft products are even less likely to lend themselves to mass-marketing and advertising than they are to mass manufacture.

Given this discussion of the four ideal types depicted in Figure 5.1, in the remainder of this chapter we turn to a variety of specific issues raised by this distinction as well as the more general ones made clear in Figure 5.1 and the analysis that ensued.

Expensive, Globally Available Types of Nothing

The thrust of this chapter might lead to the impression that it is only inexpensive goods and services that are marketed grobally, but this, it should be obvious, would be incorrect. Indeed, one of the more important recent developments in this realm is the global availability of designer products of all kinds. This, of course, is spearheaded by the dramatic expansion of such international chains as Gucci, Valentino, and Dolce and Gabbana. Chains like these are marketing expensive products throughout the world. Their success, at least from the point of view of the argument being made here, is traceable to the ways in which they have succeeded in applying the principles of nothingness to the high end of the market. The best example of this is the famous Gucci bag, which is sold in Gucci shops throughout the world. That bag was centrally conceived, its production is centrally controlled, and there is nothing to distinguish one Gucci bag of a given type from any other. More generally, there is little to distinguish the essential nature of the Gucci bag from the Benetton sweater, and even the Big Mac, other than price and, perhaps, the quality of its components. The Gucci bag is no worse and no better an example of nothing than the Big Mac, and this makes it perfectly clear that nothing can be expensive. Indeed, the wide-scale sale of knock-offs of the Gucci bag,[18] and the difficulties involved in differentiating between real and fake Gucci bags, makes the fact that it is nothing abundantly clear. Indeed, it could be argued that the high end of the market for expensive products is one of the frontiers currently being assailed and conquered by nothingness. As is clear given the problems being encountered by McDonald's, the low end of the market for nothing—in this case the fast-food market—is saturated and it is increasingly difficult to derive profits from it. However, the high end of that market, which is occupied by chains like Gucci, is still wide open with the result that many other competitors will be entering and many more high-priced products will be transformed into nothing.

Loose Cultural, Tight Structural Models

The cuisines of a number of nations throughout the world (China, Italy, Mexico, and so on) have succeeded in many other nations, and this world-wide proliferation of cuisines was occurring long before globalization became a key issue and buzzword. And, the restaurants that specialize in such cuisines have adapted to local realities (the food served in Chinese restaurants in the United States is very different from that served in such restaurants in China. It has been adapted to the American palate,[19] and adaptations, perhaps slightly different in nature, have occurred in Chinese restaurants in many other nations). However, there is a huge difference between individual entrepreneurs opening Chinese (or Italian, or any other ethnic) restaurants in many different locales and, for example, the centralized organization that owns Taco Bell (Yum! Brands) opening franchises in those same locales. It is true that both are patterned after larger models, but the former are shaped by loose cultural models that are not centrally conceived and controlled while the latter are determined by centrally conceived, highly detailed, and very tightly controlled structural models. The result is that all Taco Bell restaurants are more or less identical, while there is considerable variation from one Chinese restaurant to another.[20] Nevertheless, no matter how tight the structural model, there is always the need to make case-by-case adaptations to local realities.

The key point here is that grobalization can be impelled by loose cultural models (for example, those that lie at the base of Chinese restaurants around the world) or tight structural models (for example, those employed by Taco Bell). However, there is a huge difference between these two models. Most important, it is the tight structural models that are far more likely to produce nothing than the loose cultural models.

That there is global competition between these two models is clear in the case of Chinese restaurants. The success of the loose cultural model in producing successful, independently owned Chinese restaurants throughout the world has effectively served to block efforts to create chains of Chinese restaurants based on tight structural models. Also supporting the loose cultural model in this case is the mass migration of Chinese, creating both a pool of entrepreneurs and a ready clientele (as well as a steady supply of employees) for restaurants (and other businesses) loosely modeled on those they might have been familiar with in their homeland. However, the failure to this point to create a truly successful chain of Chinese restaurants (and there certainly have been such efforts) does not mean that such a chain will not emerge in the future.

What About the Local?

We have discussed the glocal as an alternative, and a source of resistance, to the grobal, but what about the local? Clearly, the whole idea of the glocal assumes a local that is being integrated with the grobal. However, is there a local that exists independent of the grobal? Theoretically, it is certainly possible to conceive of a local existing independent of the grobal (and glocal). Prior to the recent and dramatic expansion of the grobal, the local was empirically predominant and easy to identify. However, the fact is that it is now increasingly difficult to identify the purely local. The vast majority of that which at one time could have been thought of as local is today strongly influenced by the grobal. This means, among other things, that local products are likely now to be intertwined with imports from other parts of the world and themselves exported to other places to be integrated with that which is indigenous to them. In any case, the point is that the local, at least in the sense of anything that is *purely* local, is fast disappearing from the world scene.

This has many implications. For example, the disappearance of the truly local has dire implications for global cultural diversity. Where are the most important differences in the world to come from, if everything that we think of as local is, in fact, glocal? One answer, of course, is from distinctive glocal creations in different locales throughout the world. While this will provide some diversity, the issue is the future of cultural diversity in a world in which the local is disappearing. After all, it is the local that, at least historically, is the true source of diversity, and if it disappears, what will happen to that diversity? It seems clear that distinctive glocal mixes will continue to provide diversity, but it also seems likely that it will not approach the amount and degree of diversity that existed throughout the world when it was possible to find something approaching the genuinely local.

The point being made here is that the local is being progressively adulterated by the grobal. The glocal is, by definition, some combination of the grobal and the local. But if the local is disappearing, at least in its pure form, where is that which is truly distinctive to come from in the future? It is true that innovations will result from unique combinations of the glocal, but those innovations will be, from the outset, informed and affected by the grobal. This will inherently limit their capacity to produce true cultural innovations. More promising would be the interaction of two or more glocal phenomena producing unique entities that are not reducible to the glocalities that lie at their source. It may be that with the death of the local, the best hope for cultural innovation lies in the interaction among glocalities.

Why Now?

Why are we now witnessing this explosion in the grobalization of nothing and the extension of it to more and more areas of the world? First, there is simply an ever-increasing amount of organizational (for example, the massive expansion of the franchise system) and industrial capacity to produce and broadly disseminate nothing, and this constant increase is fueled by myriad technological and organizational advances. Further, the entities capable of producing nothing are no longer highly centralized in a few advanced industrial nations; that capacity (if not the profits from it) is now spread far more evenly around the globe (industrial production once concentrated in the United States and the West is now dispersed throughout much of the developing world) and it makes the global proliferation of nothing that much easier. Major advances in communication and transportation also make the shipping of all forms of nothing easier and less expensive.[21]

Second, the media and its influence throughout the world have grown enormously. The media are, themselves, not only purveyors of nothing (for example, the "soaps," *CNN Headline News*, sitcoms), but the major outlet throughout the world for advertisements extolling the virtues of untold varieties of nothing (including their own offerings). In fact, we are far more likely to see advertisements for nothing (for example, the wide variety of Kraft cheese products) than something (Culatella ham), and the constant barrage of advertisements for the former adds to their status as nothing. Thus, it is not only easier to produce nothing, but it is also far easier to bring it to the attention of people throughout the world, as well as to bring to their notice all sorts of reasons why they need to purchase the various forms of nothing.

Third, and more generally, several of the global flows independent of any single nation[22]—one of which is the media (*mediascapes*)—tend to operate better with nothing (for example, sitcoms) than with something (for example, cultural presentations on PBS[23]) and are excellent conduits for the global proliferation of nothing. In the world's *financescapes,* to take another example, there is a preference for currencies that are used everywhere and this gave, and continues to give, the American dollar great advantages over other currencies. Thus, the dollar (like many other things American) has tended to lose its characteristic as something—the currency specific to the United States—and has become a universal medium of exchange (the so-called "super dollar") in banking and finance throughout the world. Furthermore, in times of distress the dollar has tended to become the predominant currency de facto (Russia in the early 1990s) or de jure (Equador, as I write).

One of the best examples of the nothing associated with financescape is the euro, which in 2002 became the currency for most nations in Europe, and it is highly likely that the laggards (current exceptions are Great Britain, Denmark, and Sweden) will jump on the euro bandwagon in the not-too-distant future.[24] Relegated to the dustbin of history were currencies that really were something[25] (the franc, pound, lira, mark, and so on), at least in the sense that they had over time come to have distinctive content associated with them. These currencies were closely tied to a specific nation and had long histories and great traditions. Replacing them was the euro that had none of those things—it was largely devoid of content, but brought with it many of the usual advantages of nothing, especially increasing the efficiency with which business can be transacted and tourism undertaken.

Furthermore, gone were the familiar and unique images that adorned the face of traditional European currencies. Instead, the depictions on the euro bills[26] are of no place; they are fictional locales. Because of a fear of offending those in other nations whose locales were not depicted, a decision was made not to use any of the famous real locales in various European nations.

One would have thought there would have been great resistance to the disappearance of these fabled currencies, but the near-total absence of any reaction, let alone resistance, to it reflects the fact that we live in a world increasingly defined by nothing and any new variant of it is likely to be welcomed or at least to be accepted with little more than a shrug. Conversely, that which still smacks of something is likely to be abandoned without much ado.

Technoscape also favors nothing over something.[27] Indeed, it could be argued that technology is nothing but form; the content of any specific technology depends on the use to which it is put. An engine can be used to do innumerable things; what it actually does depends on its particular use. Much the same could be said about the media in general and television in particular. This is, of course, put a bit too strongly—technologies often do tend to favor some types of content and not others. A rifle may be put to many uses, but it does not tend to further the ends of pacifists. The media, especially those that operate in a world of profit and loss, tend to favor material that is likely to be as devoid of content as possible, or to offer the most generic of content, which therefore is apt to appeal to the largest audience or at least to alienate the smallest number of people.

However, the other "scapes," as well as the more important disjunctures among them, tend to be more ambiguous in their effects, or even to favor something over nothing. Some *ethnoscapes* do tend to foster the global proliferation of nothing. An important example, as discussed above, is the flow of tourists around the world, especially those who travel with preset tours or those who go on their own to such generic destinations as a Disney, or a Disney-like, theme park, a Las Vegas casino-hotel, or a cruise on one of the many massive cruise ships now sailing the world's waters. Then there are the tourists, discussed above, who demand that local performances and foods be watered down to suit their tastes.

Other ethnoscapes are more likely to produce something than nothing. For example, the movement of immigrants and refugees among nations and even continents, sometimes involving very large numbers of people, tends to bring with it the creation of unique enclaves rich in the style of life that they brought with them.[28] This is in line with the point made above about the difference between structural and cultural models. Immigrants are likely to operate on the basis of cultural models and therefore to be less likely to contribute to the proliferation of nothing. They are also more likely, at least initially, to participate in glocalization than grobalization.

As for *ideoscapes,* the global flow of some ideas—especially those associated with a hegemony like the United States and its efforts at obtaining and maintaining global control over ideas—tends to be associated with nothing. That is, to the degree that many nations around the world tend to buy into these ideas (for example, those associated with the market, democracy, materialism, consumerism[29]) is the degree to which there is a decline in unique idea systems that differentiate among societies and regions of the world. However, it is probably the case that, in the main, the worldwide flow of different idea systems, especially the ideologies associated with states, as well as their counterideologies, is productive of many diverse idea systems loaded with very different content.

The disjunctures that exist among all of the scapes leave room for much diversity and richness in content. In other words, disjunctures tend to limit the proliferation of nothing. Clearly, if the disjunctures did not exist, if the various scapes formed a seamless system, then there would be an even far greater possibility of the proliferation of nothing. While it is possible to imagine a scenario whereby such a seamless system would be a greater likelihood, that possibility is, at best, a long way off. At the moment, and for the foreseeable future, these disjunctures serve to limit, but certainly do not prevent, the spread of nothing.

Fourth, of course, there are great profits to be made from the creation of ever-greater markets for nothing. Thus, there are great incentives for today's entrepreneurs continually to push the global envelope on nothing in the pursuit of escalating profits. The economies of scale make it de rigeur to sell more and more nothingness anywhere it can be sold. Furthermore, the character of nothing makes each of its units highly profitable and eminently exportable; the more units exported, the higher the profits. As we know, the very nature of nothing—long on form and as devoid as possible of content—makes it comparatively inexpensive to produce and transport. Costs are low because once the form has been created, it can be repeated ad infinitum. Furthermore, content, especially when it is diverse and complex—and content (at least in comparison to form) tends to *be* diverse and complex—is far more costly both to create and to produce. As a result, because it is relatively devoid of content, nothing tends to be comparatively inexpensive and therefore profitable.

Thus, we live in an era in which a variety of its basic characteristics have led to a tremendous expansion in the grobalization of nothing. Furthermore, current trends lead to the view that the future will bring with it an even greater proliferation of nothing throughout the globe.

Which Comes First: Nothing or Its Grobalization?

Finally we need to deal with a difficult issue mentioned briefly earlier in this chapter. That is, is it possible to determine which comes first—nothing or its grobalization? The key components of the definition of nothing—central conception and control, lack of distinctive content—tend to lead us to associate nothing with the modern era of mass production. After all, it is the system of mass production that is characterized by centralized conception and control, and it is uniquely able to turn out large numbers of products lacking in distinctive content. While there undoubtedly were isolated examples of nothing prior to the Industrial Revolution, it is hard to find many that fit our basic definition of nothing.

Thus, as a general rule, nothing requires the prior existence of mass production. However, that which emanates from mass-production systems need not necessarily be distributed and sold globally. Mass-produced items may be sold initially locally and then in some cases expand to the national level. In fact, some mass-produced products (beer, for example; milk is another example) may remain restricted to a local market, although some may successfully gain a national market (Budweiser, for example). There are even a few beers (Beck, Corona, Foster's) that have come to be global, but only after they were successes within their home nation. Yet another possibility is mass-produced product that begins, and succeeds, as that which is to be sold globally.

However, as we have discussed several times in this chapter, there are great pressures on those who mass-produce nothing to market it globally. Of course, not all forms can be marketed globally, but that which has such a potentiality is likely to be pushed in that direction. Thus, there is now a very close relationship between mass production and grobalization; the view here is that *both* are crucial to the creation of nothing and are prerequisites to it.[30]

There are many different routes, and even more detours, involved in making the transition from being a local to a grobal product. Some of the most interesting examples lie in the realm of folk art that has come to be mass-produced and sold throughout the world. Take, for example, such historic examples of something as kokopellis from the Southwestern United States and matryoshka dolls from Russia. At their points of origin long ago in local cultures, these were clearly handmade products that one would have to put close to the something end of the continuum.

For example, the kokopelli, usually depicted as an arch-backed flute player, can be traced back to at least 800 A.D. and to rock art in the mountains and deserts of the Southwestern United States.[31] Such rock art is clearly something, but in recent years, kokopellis have become popular among tourists to the area and come to be produced in huge numbers in innumerable forms (figurines, lamps, key chains, light switch covers, cookies, Christmas ornaments, and so on) with increasingly less attention to the craftsmanship involved in producing them; indeed, they are increasingly likely to be mass-produced in large factories. That is, they have moved away from the something end of the continuum and toward the nothing end of that continuum. More recently, they have moved out of their points of origin in the Southwest and come to be sold globally. In order to be marketed globally at a low price,[32] much of the distinctive character and craftsmanship involved in producing the kokopelli is removed. Furthermore, offending elements are removed in order not to put off potential consumers anywhere in the world. In the case of the kokopelli, the exposed genitals that usually accompanied the arched back and the flute have been removed. The mass production and ultimately grobalization of kokopellis has moved them progressively closer to the nothing end of the continuum.

A similar scenario has occurred in the case of the matryoshka doll (from five to as many as thirty dolls of increasingly smaller size nested within one another),[33] although its roots in Russian culture are not nearly as deep (little more than a century) as that of the kokopelli in the culture of the Southwestern United States. Originally handmade and hand-painted by skilled craftspeople, and made from seasoned birch (or lime), the traditional matryoshka doll was (and is) rich in detail. With the fall of communism and the Soviet Union, Russia has grown as a tourist attraction and the matryoshka doll has become a popular souvenir. In order to supply the increasing demand of tourists, and even to distribute matryoshka dolls around the world, they are now far more likely to be machine-made; automatically painted; made of poor quality, unseasoned wood; and greatly reduced in detail. In many cases, the matryoshka doll has been reduced to the lowest level of schlock and kitsch in order to enhance sales. For example, the traditional, highly detailed designs depicting pre-communist nobles and merchants have been supplemented by caricatures of global celebrities like Bill Clinton, Mikhail Gorbachev, and even Osama bin Laden.[34] Such mass-produced and -distributed matryoshka dolls bear little resemblance to the folk art that is at their root. The mass production and grobalization of these dolls has transformed that which was something into nothing. Many other products have followed that course and still more will do so in the future.

While we have focused here on non-things (that were at one time things), much the same argument can be made about places, people, and services. That is, they too, especially in the realm of consumption, have come to be mass-produced and grobalized. This is most obvious in virtually all franchises where settings are much the same throughout the world (using many mass-manufactured components), people are trained and scripted to work in much the same way, and the same "services" are offered in much the same way. They have all been centrally conceived, are centrally controlled, and are lacking in distinctive content. They have tended to replace indigenous shops of all types that were staffed by people who tended to offer individualized services.

Chapter Six

The Ultimate Example of Nothing and Its Grobalization?

Large-Scale Consumption Sites on the Internet[1]

In the preceding five chapters a strong case has been made for the utility of the concept of nothing (and something), the increasing importance of the various types of nothing in the social world, and the elective affinity between these nullities and grobalization. However, the fact is that a discussion of what, in many ways, is the most persuasive example of nothing and its globalization—*most*[2] large-scale consumption sites on the Internet (e.g., Amazon.com, Expedia.com, Wal-Mart.com, Fidelity.com)—has been held in abeyance. If the reader is already convinced of the existence and importance of the grobalization of nothing, then this chapter will offer little more than one more set of examples of this process. However, if the reader has not been persuaded by the argument to this point, this example, and an extended discussion of it, should prove compelling. After all, most large-scale Internet consumption sites are perfect examples of nothing as empty form(s) and they are by their very nature global.[3]

It seems highly likely that those who are reading this book, and have persevered this far in it, are also likely to be avid users of, if not addicted to, the Internet and its large-scale consumption sites (as well as most of the consumer products and settings analyzed in the preceding chapters). As a result, it is likely that the Internet in general, and those consumption sites in particular, mean a great deal to most readers—that they appear to them to be quite something, the farthest thing from nothing.

Following the basic definition of nothing employed in this book, I will discuss large-scale Internet consumption sites as nothing in the sense that they are forms, in fact a potentially infinite number of forms, that are centrally conceived and controlled and largely lacking in distinctive content. This chapter will employ the various conceptual tools developed earlier to analyze these Internet consumption sites as particularly good examples of nothing.

There is a great deal about the Internet that involves consumption; indeed,x one often hears the argument that much of its potential has been undermined by the fact that so much of it has come under the sway of businesses pushing innumerable types of consumption. Nevertheless, much that characterizes the Internet is omitted because of this singular focus on consumption, although I believe that many of the points to be made below about consumption on the Internet can be extended to other things to be found on, and transpiring in, the World Wide Web.

Some Important Caveats

Yet, there are also important differences among the various domains on the Internet. For example, e-mail, chat rooms, MUDS (multiuser dimensions),[4] MMORPGS (massive mutiplayer online role playing games; "Dark Age of Camelot" and "EverQuest" are popular examples),[5] among many other things, can be seen as largely conceived and controlled by the participants,[6] (and not some central source) who endow them with much in the way of distinctive content. Much of that content comes from the establishment of distinctive human relationships. For example, of MMORPGS, it is said that, "People play online games because there are other real people in the game instead of just automatons controlled by artificial intelligence. The most successful massive multiplayer online games are designed so players can build communities inside."[7] Thus, such Internet domains do not conform to the definition of nothing employed here and this makes it clear that this concept cannot be extended in toto to the Internet. In fact, many of them are better seen as something, as that term has been defined here.

There are all sorts of complexities and difficulties involved in discussing the issue of something–nothing on the Internet. First, while things like MMORPGS mentioned above can be seen as something, they are also forms of consumption in the sense that participants must be paid subscribers. In addition, while players have considerable autonomy, there are constraints placed on them from a centralized source. Thus, while MMORPGS have elements of somethingness, they also demonstrate some fit with the nothing-ness associated with consumption in this book.

For another, e-mail has been mentioned above as an example of some-thing. We tend to think of e-mail as a realm of interpersonal communica-tion and do not associate it with consumption. In fact, while interpersonal communication by e-mail remains an important form of something, it is simultaneously increasingly moving in the direction of nothing, especially in the case of spam messages (themselves a great example of nothing) selling a wide range of products that pop up in the mail boxes of many e-mail users.[8] In fact, about 40% of e-mail in the United States is spam (it was only 8% in 2001) and it is growing at an astronomic rate.[9] This means that e-mail itself is coming increasingly under the sway of the nothingness associated with consumption.

Then there are small niche marketers (for example, NinjaTune.com) that are able to use the Internet to sell products they might not otherwise be able to sell, at least as widely. On the one hand, these sites lie more toward the something end of the continuum, at least in comparison to the behemoths (for example, Amazon.com) that dominate commerce on the Internet. On the other hand, they still fit the basic definition of nothing in the sense that they are centrally conceived, exert centralized control, and are lacking in distinctive content (as unusual as are the things they sell, those things can still can be purchased in various other immaterial and material venues).[10]

Even harder to consider as a form of nothing is the peer-to-peer file shar-ing that is an increasingly important part of the Internet.[11] The most popular of these today is Kazaa (a successor to Napster), which has been used by 160 million people; three million people are running the program at any given time.[12] Users trade media files (text, pictures, music, movies, TV shows, and so on) with one another, usually at no charge. This is illegal (shutting down Kazaa has thus far proven impossible because it is international), but the decentralized nodal structure of the Internet here permits a form of con-sumption that is closer to the something end of the continuum because it is neither centrally conceived nor controlled. Indeed, it stands in opposition to, and competes with, some of the centralized conceptions and controls of large-scale consumption sites on the Internet. Of course, what is being traded could still be the same non-things that one finds on the latter sites.

Furthermore, even if we accept the idea that large-scale consumption sites on the Internet are nothing (or approaching that end of the contin-uum), the fact remains that most people do more than just consume on the Internet. And while they may be in the realm of nothing in their dealings with Amazon.com, they are working the something end of the continuum in their personal e-mails, their participation in chat rooms, and the like, at least most of the time.

However, the most important limitation on this analysis is that there are some large-scale Internet consumption sites that cannot be seen as fitting our definition of nothing. I have in mind here auction sites like eBay.com, as well as that part of Amazon.com devoted to auctions. Such sites have few of the components of nothingness. While they are centrally conceived, control is largely[13] in the hands of those who use these sites. Because virtually everything is sold there, including such things as unique antique pieces, these sites are loaded with an ever-changing array of distinctive content. Such sites can be seen as standing more toward the something end of the continuum and contributing to the sale and distribution of the entire range of things to non-things.

Thus, for these and other reasons we must be wary of making broad generalizations about the Internet, or even about consumption on the Internet. However, our focus here is on the major Internet sites devoted to consumption (but not auctions), and in that realm it is safe to argue that we are witnessing the grobalization of nothing.

Back to the Main Argument

As already mentioned, the totality of consumption sites on the Internet (and it is a constantly growing and changing totality) can be seen as a vast field that encompasses, among many other things, an enormous number of centrally conceived and controlled forms, most of which are, in themselves, largely, if not totally, devoid of distinctive content. Previously, the argument has been made that a shopping mall, to take one example, is such a form and if that is the case, then it is even more true of Internet shopping malls. While both the brick-and-mortar and the Internet mall are centrally conceived and controlled, such conception and control are greater in the latter than the former. On-site managers (and other personnel) of brick-and-mortar malls can reconceptualize matters (at least to some degree), and should the need arise, they can alter the nature and level of control on a moment-to-moment basis. However, since no humans are present at the Internet mall, everything must be conceptualized in advance and controls cannot be altered at a moment's notice if the need arises. It is for this reason that Internet malls need to be conceptualized far more carefully and in far greater detail in advance and much more extensive controls need to be in place. It is certainly the case that, after the fact, the Internet mall can be rethought and new controls put in place, perhaps overnight (see below), but that cannot be accomplished on the fly as it might be by a brick-and-mortar mall manager.

Because it is empty, a wide range of specific content can be included in a brick-and-mortar shopping mall, but the immateriality of an equally empty

Internet mall eliminates virtually all barriers and makes an even wider range of content possible. This is true quantitatively and qualitatively. Quantitatively, the immateriality of the Internet mall makes it infinitely expandable, while the material structure of a brick-and-mortar mall, and even the totality of such malls, makes for comparatively severe restrictions on the amount and variety of content to be included.[14] Qualitatively, the Internet mall's immateriality allows for experiences that may not be possible in a "real-world" mall. For example, Amazon.com offers its users free alerts to new products and services, free e-cards, and the possibility of not only buying at its mall, but selling one's own things there, as well.

More generally, an Internet address, even one devoted to consumption, is a form that can lead one to literally virtually any type of content.[15] Furthermore, even within the context of a specific Internet address, a wide array of content can be offered. Amazon.com became known for the million-plus book titles available through its Web site, but now it offers, as we have already seen, a wide array of other types of products for sale. More generally, a portal like Yahoo.com, or one of its many alternatives, offers entry into what is literally a world of alternatives, an increasing number of which relate to consumption. Even more alternatives are to be found on Google.com, which has concentrated on continually expanding its content.[16] That content has become so extensive that it is used by Yahoo! and others. Furthermore, recently Google itself has moved more in the direction of consumption.[17]

A related point is that because they are virtual reality, Internet malls can easily, literally overnight, transform what they have to sell and how they sell it, an option not open to brick-and-mortar malls.[18] (As a result of their comparative inability to adapt, many such malls, especially the older strip malls, have become ghost towns.[19]) Again, the best example is Amazon.com, which has, in recent years, added and sometimes eliminated product lines with great rapidity. For example, at the moment, among its featured "stores" are those dedicated to health and beauty, magazine subscriptions, home and garden, kitchen and housewares, and so on. These are quite distant from the Web site's roots in the book business.

The growth and continual transformation of Internet malls lends support, of course, to this book's most general grand narrative—the dramatic proliferation of nothing—in this case in and through large-scale consumption sites on the Internet. The roots of the Internet lie in Arpanet, founded in 1969 as a conduit for messages between defense laboratories and universities. It is startling to realize that the Internet itself is, as I write this, not yet fifteen years old, having been founded in 1988 on the basis of Arpanet technology. And, of course, the Internet did not truly take off for several years, with the result that wide-scale use of it is only a decade (or less) old.

The big names in consumption on the Internet (for example, Amazon.com) did not begin operations until the mid-1990s and the entry of the brick-and-mortar firms (e.g., Wal-Mart.com) into Internet commerce came slightly later (in Wal-Mart's case, 1996). Many of the start-ups that made a big splash on the Internet in the 1990s (those that existed only online) have disappeared or been downsized substantially in the dot.com crash of the early 21st century. While some of the "irrational exuberance" (an expression made famous by Federal Reserve chairman Alan Greenspan during the height of the stock market bubble of the late 1990s) has disappeared from consumer business on the Internet, there is no question that it is not only here to stay, but likely to expand enormously in the coming years.[20]

Whatever the recent ups and downs of consumption on the Internet, the fact remains that it, and the Internet more generally, did not exist a decade or two ago, and they are now major presences in the lives of most readers of this book.

While the case for the relationship between large-scale Internet consumption sites and nothing requires considerable argumentation, no such detailed discussion is needed to make the case for the association between the Internet (and those sites) and globalization. Theoretically, anyone, anywhere in the world can log onto and consume on the Internet (assuming electricity, phone lines, credit cards, and so on). Because it is so immaterial, there are no geographic barriers to the dissemination of messages, information, and transactions across the Internet. A nation may try to block this or that (as China does on occasion), but in the main there is little that can be done about global transmissions on the Internet. Indeed, one of the hallmarks of the Internet is that it is entirely possible that one does not know, and may never know, the geographic location of a person or site with which one is dealing. The Internet is global and the size and magnitude of the globe pose few, if any, barriers to communication through, and making purchases on, it.

All of the other examples of globalization used in this book, especially as they relate to consumption, pale in comparison to the global nature of the Internet. For example, the ability to send packages quickly to virtually any place in the world via carriers like FedEx is impressive, but it is child's play in comparison to the ability to purchase and obtain stock shares (on Fidelity.com, for example) or airline tickets (on Expedia.com and other similar sites) over the Internet. The wedding of the immateriality of the World Wide Web with various immaterial goods like stock positions or airline reservations makes the Internet and consumption on it ultimate examples of globalization as it relates to consumption. After all, everyone with a computer, a modem, and a credit card anywhere in the world can engage in such transactions and almost instantaneously obtain what they are looking for.

Of course, it is true that some aspects of the Internet, and especially consumption on it, are not so immaterial, with the result that global barriers remain as impediments, at least to some degree. For example, all of the steps leading up to the purchase of, say, a book on Amazon.com are immaterial and therefore easily globalized. However, once the purchase is complete, the book (or some other product) must be sent to the purchaser (or a third party) and here the materiality of the book itself limits globalization. In effect, the more nearly limitless character of the Internet is stymied by limits associated with, for example, FedEx and its ability, no matter how great, to deliver a book that exists in a material form. While I might receive a book overnight from a nearby Amazon.com warehouse, residents in remote areas of the United States and the world may have to wait days and even weeks (and some may not be able to get the book at all). Nonetheless, Amazon.com has succeeded in making the book business (and others) a far more global business than it ever was before.

While there is a strong association between consumption on the Internet and globalization, it is also the case that the Internet is an important site and resource for both anticonsumption and antiglobalization forces. Large-scale antiglobalization demonstrations have relied, to a large degree, on the Internet to organize participants from around the world. Adbusters is an example of an anticonsumption organization that uses the Internet to great advantage for its activities, including organizing "buy nothing day."[21]

Thus, it is clear that there is an association between the Internet and globalization and we have already made the case for the elective affinity between globalization and nothing. What remains to be shown, using the tools developed earlier, is that most large-scale consumption sites on the Internet tend to be nothing or at least stand toward that end of the something–nothing continuum.

Meet the Nullities on the Internet

In Chapter 3 we described the four types of nullities of concern in this book: non-places, non-things, non-people, and non-services. What will be argued here is that not only are all four of these found on the Internet, but some of the purest examples of nothingness in each of them are to be found there.

When addressed in general terms, the large-scale consumer Web site is a near-perfect example of a non-place. That is, the Web site is almost pure form—in this case an address on the Internet—that in itself has no content, or to put it another way, can encompass any and every imaginable content. Thus, the names Yahoo.com, Google.com, Amazon.com, and so on, tell us absolutely nothing about what is on offer at those sites. However, we also deal with more specific Web sites devoted to consumption and most of those indicate and stand for at least some type of content.[22] Since just about everything is available on large-scale consumption Web sites, we find both things and non-things there. However, such sites are particularly suited to the demonstration, dissemination of information about, and sale of non-things. While one can certainly find lots of things there, it is harder to deal with them than non-things. In most cases, we do not even deal with non-people at Internet consumption sites because there are *no* people at all at the Web site. In the rare instance that we do deal with a human being, it is in the form of a phone conversation with a functionary with no name or who might as well have no name. And, as with non-people, what we get on the Web is very often non-service with the most extreme forms involving transactions like ordering books or buying airline tickets where the consumer does *all* the work and the seller provides no service at all, at least in the usual way in which we think of service. In those rare instances that we are provided with services, it is the most impersonal and anonymous of services; it is non-service.

However, we need to do more than deal with each of the types of nullities on the Internet in general terms; we also need to deal with each type in more detail. When we do, we will see that while large-scale consumption sites on the Internet are good examples of nothing, some interesting nuances arise when we analyze the non-places, non-things, non-people, and non-services found on them from the point of view of the continua outlined earlier.

Large-Scale Consumption Sites on the Internet as Non-Places

Interestingly, at first blush the major Web site, especially as it relates to consumption, poses difficulties—it seems more like something than nothing. Take our paradigmatic example, Amazon.com. It is clearly considered by most users as a *place* on the Internet. In fact, we are accustomed to thinking of specific sites as places—they even have "addresses." More generally, of course, we have taken the language of geography in the real world and transferred it to the virtual world. In fact, on the morning I sat down to begin writing this section I received the following e-mail message about my own Web site[23] with the heading "nice place": "Dear George, roaming around the Internet I landed at your virtual place. Nice to have virtually met you in person. Greetings from Amsterdam, Albert." This visitor to my Web site obviously considered it to be a place and, relating to another of our continua to be discussed later, thought of it in at least ambivalently personal terms as a place where he met me, at least virtually, "in person."

Thus, those who visit Amazon.com at least fairly regularly, probably consider it to be a place and furthermore think that this specific site, like most such sites, has lots of content—millions of books, to say nothing of toys, electronics, magazines, CDs, pet supplies, medical supplies, and even an auction site. Thus, while an Internet address may be pure form, and even Amazon.com may be a form of an address, that specific address is loaded with content. The issue of centralized conception and control is also ambiguous when one considers Internet consumption sites. On the one hand, they meet our definition of nothing since they are certainly created and controlled centrally. However, the visitor can exercise a great deal of creativity in using a site and, in some sense, can be seen as being in control of it. Nonetheless, in the end, the consumer must operate within the Web site's parameters as created and controlled by it.

The vast array of content on a Web site like Amazon.com makes it quite unique and one-of-a-kind: no other address has exactly the same content (not even direct competitors like BarnesandNoble.com). It seems to meet other criteria of something, such as the fact that it has a rich array of components, some of which (especially the auction items) may be quite distinctive, and, as discussed throughout this book, this is one of the key factors that distinguishes that which is unique from the generic. And then there is the fact that what each visitor to Amazon.com, indeed every consumer site on the Web, does there is unique and unlikely to be matched, at least exactly, by any other visitor to the site.

It would seem from this discussion of the initial aspects of nothingness that we are unable to show that a large-scale Web site devoted to consumption is nothing; indeed, it appears to be something that is unique, one-of-a-kind.[24] While other types of major Web sites devoted to consumption, say those devoted to travel (Expedia.com, Travelocity.com, and so on), may be more generic (offering much the same airfares on the same airlines), it is still hard to think of them as fitting this aspect of nothingness. If this is the only criterion on which large-scale Web sites devoted to consumption can be considered as something, or just one of a few, then we can think of this as merely adding nuance to our discussion of such Web sites. However, if, as we work our way through the other continua, it turns out that there are a number of other differences from what is to be expected of nothing, we might need to abandon our sense of large-scale Internet Web sites devoted to consumption as falling toward the nothing end of the something–nothing continuum.

Matters begin to fall more in line with our overriding perspective when we turn to the presence or absence of local geographic ties. If we considered the Internet as a geographic area (and in many ways it is quite appropriate to do so), then every address would indicate a "local" geographic area;

Amazon.com would be such a local area distinguished from other "local" areas like BarnesandNoble.com or Expedia.com. However, we are thinking in traditional geographic terms and in those terms the Internet Web site is clearly and unequivocally *not* a local geographic area. Indeed, such a Web site is perhaps the quintessential example of a non-place lacking in geographic ties. Needless to say, a defining characteristic of most Web sites is that the visitor usually has no idea from what geographic area of the world the site emanates or in which it was created. Indeed, it makes no difference because the site exists *only* in cyberspace; it has no location in the geographic world as we usually think of it, or at least its geographic location is irrelevant to the consumer. In fact, it is this near-absolute lack of any local geographic ties that is one of the defining characteristics of Web sites. The idea of the *geography of nowhere* fits the Internet to near perfection.[25]

The language used on a Web site (say Japanese) might tie it to a particular geographic area, and there are certainly many such sites on the World Wide Web. However, it is often pointed out that to succeed on the Web, especially in the realm of consumption, the text on a Web site must be in English. While there are exceptions to this rule, in the main the major consumption sites are in English. By the way, this points to the importance of Americanization in this realm. Americans have not only played a key role in creating the Web in general, and many of its key components, but many others attune their sites to the needs and demands of American users of the Internet. It is Americans who not only use the Web in great numbers, but also have the economic resources to be substantial consumers of virtually anything that is offered for sale on it (and this, of course, indicates the role played by capitalism in all of this).

A similarly good fit is found when we turn to the specific-to-the-times– time-less dimension. The large-scale consumption Web site is, of course, a product of our times and is, in that sense, specific to the times. However, great effort is made to make such Web sites time-less, that is, not easily tied to a specific time period. These Web sites have a past, but it is one that is easily forgotten as new text appears and old text disappears into the ether.

Amazon.com might feature on its booklist new offerings and current best-sellers, but what helps to define it is the fact that it offers books written decades or even hundreds of years ago. Furthermore, it is far easier to obtain most out-of-print books there than in any other way. In any case, a Web site seeks to free itself from our usual senses of time and of space. This is especially true of time during the day or night. It is clear that such Web sites are designed to operate in the same way at any time of the day or night and users may be quite oblivious to the time that they are accessing them. Indeed, one of the most important developments associated with Internet consumption sites is that they serve to "implode" most differences in time and space. As a result, all times and many more places are open to consumption. Thus, the Web site is largely time-less as well as lacking in local geographic ties—in both of these senses it clearly meets the criteria of nothingness.

Certainly, there is an absence of a sense of an aura of permanency about an Internet Web site, even the biggest and most famous of them, if for no other reason than we have seen them come and go with great rapidity. Because they are relatively recent, one does not get the feeling that they have lasted for a long time and most of them do not give the visitor the sense that they will be around well into the future (even Amazon.com was not notably successful economically). Furthermore, the many failures of Web sites of all types, especially as they relate to consumption, add to the sense of a lack of permanency. This means, of course, that there is great ephemerality surrounding Web sites and our relationship with them. Not only do many of the sites themselves have a fly-by-night quality to them, but our visits to them seem to be, and are, quite ephemeral, as we dip in and out with great rapidity, often buying nothing at all. All of this is related intimately to the immaterial quality of the Internet and of our relationship to it. By its very nature, immaterial realities seem more ephemeral as do our relationships to them; they seem to be passing us by at the very moment that we are engaged in and with them. Few things are more ephemeral than the Internet and our relationships with it in general, as well as with specific Web sites.

Relatedly, few things seem less like a locale, and more like a flow, than the Internet and its Web sites. This is the case even though, as we have seen, we tend to think of Web sites as locales (complete with addresses) and those who write their text would have us think of them in this way. (This is part of a general tendency of the Web to adopt concepts that had other meanings before the arrival of computers and the Internet. The best example, of course, is e-mail, especially AOL's ubiquitous "You've got mail" and its use of an old-fashioned mailbox as its logo.) While locales involve a sense of geographic location, the idea of flows communicates a sense of everything in flux, of constant movement rather than the apparent fixity of a locale. A Web site is, of course, a site of constant movement, although it does not necessarily appear that way to visitors who think of themselves as having arrived at some fixed point (a Web page) when they enter a Web site. What is not always so apparent to visitors is the fact that they are in movement as they arrive at a site and may almost as quickly depart for another site. At the same time, many others are either entering or leaving and this is certainly not visible to the visitor. The site itself, especially if it is a commercial site, is also undergoing constant change in order to bring new possibilities to the visitor. What visitors see may even be tailored to their own histories of interest based on their previous visits to particular sites.

While all Web sites can be seen as places of flows, this best describes large-scale sites devoted to consumption. A personal Web site may be changed (and visited) only rarely, but an important commercial Web site would employ Web masters whose job it is to see that the site is constantly revised, refreshed, and updated. Products are continually being added, emphasized, de-emphasized, re-emphasized, or even removed. And, of course, far more visitors are likely to be entering and leaving a popular commercial Web site than most other sites on the Web.

The Web sites oriented to consumption (indeed all Web sites) offer a perfect example of the dehumanization associated with nothing and the non-place end of the place–non-place continuum. This is because of the obvious fact, as mentioned previously, that *no* human beings are available on the Web site and often it is not made very clear how one can even contact a human being associated with the Web site. This is because one of the great strengths of a Web site is that once it has been created by humans, it can function on a day-to-day basis largely free of intervention by human employees. Indeed, it is likely that the only humans "on" the Web site at any given time are Web surfers who may have dipped into the site to do some quick shopping or, at least, browsing. This is the great source of economy associated with a Web site once it is up and running since, as pointed out above, the customers do all of the work associated with placing and paying for an order.[26] Think, for example, about buying an airline ticket online. Customers must find, compare, and select the appropriate flights, book them, enter various pieces of information (including credit card brand and number), and perhaps even print out their own itineraries and e-tickets on their own printers using their own paper and print cartridge. In contrast, an airline employee would need to do all of this work and more if customers ordered tickets by phone or in person at the airline's ticket office or at the airport. The cost of those activities is eliminated as the customer does all of the work of ordering tickets (and much else) online. Thus, this is a further step in the dehumanization of consumption on the commercial Web site over other consumption sites—there are *no* human beings involved online other than the customer. No human relationships are possible because there are no human employees at the other end of the Internet connection.

It is hard to imagine many, if any, consumers identifying with a large-scale Web site devoted to consumption. Can we imagine people identifying strongly with Wal-mart.com or Peapod.com? They might like and use one site more than another, but they are unlikely to identify themselves as, say, "Wal-mart.com type people." While it is not easy to imagine anyone identifying with a brick-and-mortar Wal-Mart, it is far more difficult to imagine identification with the company's Web site. Such sites lack many of the characteristics generally required to elicit a powerful sense of identity. A locale is the kind of setting that people are apt to identify with if, for no other reason than because it has the kind of stability needed for identity to develop. However, as we have seen, consumer Web sites are far better seen as flows than locales with the result that the needed stability is largely lacking. The time-lessness of Web sites poses a similar problem in terms of identity since it is far easier to identify with something linked to a specific time period than that which seems not to be embedded in any particular time. Very much related to the preceding two points is the ephemerality of Web sites and visitors' relationships with them. Ephemerality clearly militates against identity for much the same reason that it is difficult to identify with that which is not embedded in time and place. Clearly, identity would be far easier if Web sites were able to surround themselves with an aura of permanency. The presence of human beings is an important factor in the development of any significant identity and their total absence on consumer Web sites makes identity problematic, to put it mildly.

Is there any way to think of a large-scale Web site oriented to consumption as authentic? In a sense, there is. That is, they "really" are sites on the Web that perform the tasks they are designed to perform. Further, originals like Amazon.com can be seen as authentic, although they have spawned a number of (inauthentic) copies. However, they are often inauthentic in other senses. For example, they often seek to present themselves as similar in many ways to, as copies of, the brick-and-mortar stores and shops that, in many cases, they are seeking to replace. The various Web sites devoted to gambling are good examples in the sense that they emulate Las Vegas-style casinos. More important, Web sites exaggerate many of the things about themselves that are copied from the authentic; they become outrageously inauthentic.

The final continuum used here to analyze something and nothing, enchanted–disenchanted, poses some difficulties for us given the thrust of this analysis. There is no question that large-scale, consumer-oriented Web sites seem quite magical, especially to those who have not grown up with them or become intimately familiar with the way they operate. Further, great effort is made to make them seem spectacular, and the spectacle is designed, among other things, to enchant these sites, in that they follow the model pioneered by Las Vegas casino-hotels, Disney theme parks, and the like. However, the way in which these settings seek to enchant themselves is through a variety of inauthentic methods. Thus, while Disney World may have its enchanted kingdom, that enchantment is produced by its outrageous inauthenticity. Indeed, as Las Vegas has demonstrated, the more outrageous the inauthenticity, the more likely it is to seem magical.

However, this is a very different kind of enchantment than that associated with authentic settings. That enchantment comes from the essential characteristics of the settings themselves and not from inauthentic externalities superimposed on them. To the degree that consumer Web sites derive their magic from that which is superimposed on them, it is at best a second-rate form of enchantment. More important, large-scale consumer Web sites are, by their very nature, highly rationalized and rationalization is, by definition, associated with *dis*enchantment. Indeed, it could be argued, as Weber implies, that disenchantment is little more than the flip side of rationalization. Large-scale Web sites *must* be highly rationalized in order to function adequately. Among the reasons for this is the fact, discussed above, that no workers exist on the Web site; consumers must do all the work. And, in order for customers to perform the various tasks required of them, the Web site must be so highly rationalized that the customer is led through all of the steps with great precision. While traditional rationalized structures need to control the actions mainly of workers, the Web site needs to control what consumers do. Everything must be thought out, laid out, and prestructured before the customer ever enters a Web site. The end product is something approaching the highest level of rationalization imaginable with the result that, from the consumer's perspective, the Web site is highly disenchanted, even with all of its ersatz "magic."

Thus, a very strong, but not perfect, case can be made that a large-scale consumption Web site is a non-place. While there are some anomalies and exceptions (for example, auction sites), such a Web site is nonetheless an excellent example of nothingness, at least as that notion applies to (non-) places. As usual, the anomalies in this case are both interesting and instructive.

While we have dealt with non-places on the Internet in some detail, we can deal with the other nullities found there much more expeditiously, largely because many of the points made above apply as well to the other nullities on the Internet and, indeed, they have been touched on directly and indirectly in this discussion.

The Non-Things for Sale on Large-Scale Consumption Web Sites

Another of the elective affinities of interest here involves the relationship between large-scale consumption sites on the Internet and non-things. That is, the very nature of the Internet, and of large-scale consumption sites on it, makes it far easier to sell and buy non-things there than things. The main reason, once again, is the absence of human beings on the Net to sell that which is offered there. By their very nature, things have much more content and far greater complexity. As a result, they require someone like a salesperson to explain their distinguishing characteristics, what differentiates them from competing things as well as non-things, and perhaps why one should pay a premium for, or engage in the extra efforts involved in purchasing, things. Clearly, the basic information could be placed on the Web site, but obtaining it would require still more work on the part of consumers and, in any case, they might not be able to understand it as well as they might were it to be explained to them by a salesperson. In spite of this, there are things available on the Web (especially, as discussed below, on auction sites); indeed, virtually everything and anything is, or could be, for sale there.

However, it is non-things that fit best with the large-scale Web site and its fundamental characteristics and strengths. Clearly, the simpler the product—the less the distinctive substance and complexity associated with it—the easier it is to display and sell on the Web. For one thing, consumers are likely to be very familiar with many non-things and they would require little or no additional information in order to decide whether or not to purchase them. Such information that might be required could be displayed quickly and easily. Those who produce large-scale Web sites selling non-things need to do little and although whatever needs to be done is done by the consumer, it is still comparatively little in comparative terms (for example, to traveling to a brick-and-mortar mall). To put this in the terms of another of the continua employed here, it is far easier to sell generic than unique products on the large-scale sites on the Internet; it is easier to sell that which is interchangeable than the one-of-a-kind.

That being said, since virtually everything is sold on the Net, unique, one-of-a-kind products, things, are being sold there quite successfully. This is best seen on auction sites like eBay.com where all sorts of things, as well as innumerable non-things, are up for sale at any given moment. Indeed, it could be argued that while many viable alternatives exist to the Internet sale of non-things, the same is not true for things. For example, antiques could be sold in other ways—garage sales, antique dealers, antique shows—but they are poor alternatives (e.g., they are accessible to far fewer people) to the sale of such things on eBay. In contrast, there already exist many quite sophisticated places to sell non-things—malls, superstores, mail order catalogs—and the Internet and its shops and malls are simply additional ways of selling non-things. Thus, it could be argued that the Internet has meant much more to the consumption of things than non-things. That being said, it remains the case that, overall, the Internet and the large-scale consumption sites on it are best suited to the sale of non-things. Furthermore, there are infinitely more transactions, and profits, involving non-things than things.

As pointed out in Chapter 3, non-things are associated with the nothing end of all of the subcontinua while things are linked to the something end of those continua. There is no need to go into all of those linkages again at this point, but it is worth reiterating that the non-things that are best sold on the large-scale sites on the Internet tend to be generic, lack local geographic ties, and be relatively time-less, dehumanized, and disenchanted. In addition, they tend to be more ephemeral, part of a series of flows, and inauthentic. All of these characteristics are not only associated with non-things, but also make it easier for them to be consumed via large-scale Internet shops, malls, and other sites. As pointed out earlier, things, possessing, in the main, characteristics associated with the opposite (something) end of all of the continua, can be and are being consumed through the Internet. However, it is not as easy to market, sell, and buy them in that domain as it is non-things.

Non-People on Those Large-Scale, Internet Consumption Sites

As has already been mentioned, there are *no* people, there *never* are any people, on the large-scale consumption sites on the Internet. Obviously people created the Web sites and are involved in regularly monitoring and updating them. Furthermore, in some cases, it is possible to have contact with real people over the phone—although they usually act like non-people—when a consumer has a problem with a Web site or with ordering something from it.

While this is the norm, I recently had a very different experience. I purchased an airline ticket online from Southwest.com and after I ordered it, I realized I had entered the wrong month and my ticket was for July when my trip was to take place in August. I was able to find a telephone number on the Web site (that is not always so easy since the whole point is to discourage contact with people) and spoke to a Southwest representative. I expected a problem, but the agent was very pleasant and helpful and the change was made quickly and at no charge.[27] This is in stark contrast to other instances in which one tries to change airline reservations but hurdles are often imposed and penalties charged. My guess is that airlines are so eager to have customers make their reservations online—it is a great cost saving to them since, as we've seen, the customer does all of the work involved in each reservation—that they do not want to penalize those who do so for making errors. They want to do everything they can to be sure that customers continue to use the online system. When a time comes when most passengers are long-accustomed to making reservations in this way, airlines will not be so eager to make changes and will be likely to impose penalty charges for making them.

This is a point that clearly does not need to be belabored—we all recognize that consumption on the Internet has not only replaced people with non-people, but gone beyond that to eliminate people entirely. One of the things that have replaced people on Internet shopping malls and other sites are "shopbots." These are robot-like functions that are programmed to move within and between sites on the Web in search of products of interest to the consumer. For example, Google.com, not heretofore known as an arena of consumption, has recently introduced a shopbot, or what it prefers to call a *spider,* named Froogle (froogle.google.com). Here's the way it works: "Browse by category—apparel, computers, flowers, whatever—or enter a query term, and it will present a list of matching products, each with a thumbnail sketch on the left and description, price and retailer on the right."[28]

Thus, neither the human customers nor the employees are required to perform this task. While the shopbot (or spider) might be quite efficient, it is obviously an extreme case of the trend away from persons to non-persons. Indeed, it is the logical extreme where after employees have been reduced to robot-like actions it is relatively easy to replace them with mechanical, or in this case electronic, robots.

Dealing with the non-people on large-scale Internet consumption sites makes other aspects of nothingness quite clear—these non-people lack any geographic ties (except for the "geography" of the Internet), interactions with them are time-less, there are quite ephemeral relationships with them and those relationships have a flow-like quality about them, they are certainly dehumanized—even "non-humanized" (as in the case of the shopbot), it is nearly impossible to identify with something like a shopbot, the whole idea of authenticity hardly applies at all, and it is a highly rationalized and there-fore disenchanted relationship. In terms of the latter, however, it is worth remembering that all of this can seem quite magical (for example, having a shopbot fetch desired products from across a range of Internet locations) and the sites themselves seek through spectacle to enchant themselves. However, as mentioned earlier, it is a quite inauthentic form of enchant-ment with the result that the efforts are enfeebled and overwhelmed by the rationalization associated with the sites.

Non-Services on Those Large-Scale Consumption Web Sites

This nullity, too, requires little further amplification since just as the goal of a large-scale Internet consumption site is to eliminate human beings, it also and relatedly aims at reducing or eliminating service. For one thing, it is usually people who provide service and if there are no people, there is no customer service! While, as we have seen, there is a move away from providing service at brick-and-mortar consumption sites, Internet sites do not even offer the option of personalized service. Thus, Internet sites cannot do what a new department store in Buffalo did in hiring its employees. Its co-creator said, "We want positive people who are happy . . . serving the customer . . . foremost we are looking for people who embrace the concept of superior customer service."[29]

Another factor in the reduction or elimination of service on the Internet consumption site is its effort to rationalize operations by, among other things, getting the customer to do all of the work. One of the beauties of this is that customers are not paid for their work with the result that the owners of the Web site are able to achieve new heights of exploitation by getting work not just for little in the way of pay, but for *no* pay at all. With customers doing most, if not all, of the work, it is hard to think of them as receiving services—they clearly are the recipients of non-services.

Among other things, it is worth mentioning that this self-service, along with the replacement of people with non-people on the Web, represents some ultimate step in dehumanization. Customers deal with inanimate Web sites and the only human dealings, if one can call them that, are with one's self. And this is linked to the fact that the Web site achieves an unparalleled level of rationalization and this, in turn, brings with it not only dehumanization, but also disenchantment. After all, if consumers are doing all of the work, they have great understanding of what they are doing; there is little mystery about what they do.

Yet, there is a mystery, even a kind of magic associated with the way a Web site, especially a large and complex one devoted to consumption, operates. This is especially true for the vast majority of people who have no idea how computers, and what they find through them on the Internet, work. With more and more skills built into the computer, the Internet, and Web sites, users are likely to know less and less about the operation of consumption (and other) Web sites with the result that it all seems increasingly magical. This certainly brings with it a kind of enchantment, but since it occurs *because* of its high degree of rationalization, it is difficult to think of it as enchantment in the usual sense of the term—as the opposite of the disenchantment associated with rationalization. However, as I have argued elsewhere, rationalization itself can seem enchanting.[30]

Globalization

As was pointed out earlier, the Internet is by its very nature a global phenomenon and an excellent example of the process of globalization. This requires little amplification, but what of the various subtopics under the broad heading of globalization—glocalization, grobalization, capitalism, Americanization, and McDonaldization?

First, the Internet in general, and the large-scale consumption sites on it in particular, are powerfully affected by grobalization. That is, all of those entities that are interested in expanding their influence and increasing sales throughout the world have devoted considerable money and expertise in seeking to use the Internet to achieve their objectives. However, the Internet can be, and is, also used by those entities (adbusters, Slow Food, McSpotlight, and so on) opposed to the grobalization of consumption. Thus, it can cut both ways, although, as usual, the advantage lies with the forces of grobalization that have the greatest expertise and the most money to use the Internet more effectively than those opposed to them.

It is also the case that the Internet can serve as a powerful agency for glocalization. That is, it is also possible for local entities to play a central role on the Internet and, among other things, to modify grobal inputs so that they become glocal. For example, the major automobile companies are powerful forces on the Internet, but if one actually wants to buy a car through the Internet, one must deal with a local dealer. Such a dealer will combine grobal and local[31] realities in creating a distinctly glocal message and an offer that reflects the realities in a given market and the national, even international, automobile market. That is, in one market a car may be in high demand and the local dealer may not be very interested in negotiating with a customer or in discounting a car, while in another low demand may lead to aggressive negotiations and discounting.

Under the heading of grobalization, capitalism is obviously increasingly implicated in the Internet, especially the large-scale consumption sites of interest in this chapter. However, there is clearly much else on the Internet (chat rooms, e-mail) that is independent, at least to some degree, of capitalism. Furthermore, there is even a significant amount of anticapitalistic activity on the Internet. However, many observers worry that the potential of the Internet has been subverted, and will be subverted further, by the incursions of capitalism.

Americanization is a major force and factor on the Internet. After all, the Internet is an American creation and it is dominated by American (capitalistic) companies and organizations (Microsoft, Yahoo!, Google, Amazon, and so on). The Internet, or at least that portion of it devoted to consumption, is a major conduit for the sale of American goods and services throughout the world. However, it is obvious that the businesses of every other country can and do sell themselves and their wares via the Internet and especially into the lucrative American market. While American businesses and other entities have the advantage on the Internet, and for the usual reasons, it is clear that while it is far from a level playing field, innumerable counterforces, or at least alternative forces, play a role on the Internet, especially in the area of consumption. Furthermore, it is likely that in the future organizations associated with other parts of the world will close the gap that exists between them and their American competitors in terms of their ability to use and to exploit the Internet. Thus, we can anticipate a decline in the Americanization of the Internet, although it is difficult to envision a time when anyone will threaten America's position as the single most important player on it.

Turning to the issue of McDonaldization, the argument is unequivocal—we will see a continuation of the McDonaldization of the Internet in general and of large-scale consumption sites on it in particular. That is, to operate successfully on the Internet, operations *must* be efficient, predictable, and calculable, and are, by definition, dominated by non-human technologies. Any Web site oriented to consumption must be organized on the basis of these principles. To put it in negative terms, any Web site that a visitor cannot navigate and utilize efficiently, that operates unpredictably from one time to the next, that does not rely on a high degree of calculability, and that does not offer hospitable and effective non-human technologies will rapidly fall into disuse and disappear. Those sites, wherever in the world they are created and from whatever area they emanate, must learn from the most successful Web sites because if they do not, they are likely to fail.

The unequivocal trend in the direction of McDonaldization stems from the basic character of the Internet in general and specifically large-scale consumption sites. When operating on a Web site the consumer must do all of the work (as we saw earlier, one of the basic facts of life in McDonaldized systems). As a result, great care must be taken in building a Web site (really a non-human technology that controls the consumer), so that the site operates efficiently, predictably, and calculably from the perspective of the consumer (and the seller). The major alternative would be a human being—a salesperson—who would guide the consumer through the various steps involved in consuming on an Internet site. But since, as has been often repeated, one of the keys to the success of an Internet site is the elimination of the human salesperson, all of the rationality must be built into the site.

Of course, this great pressure to maximize the McDonaldization of Web sites and the Internet brings with it various manifestations of the irrationality of rationality. The above makes it clear that the most obvious of these irrationalities—dehumanization—is an inherent part of successful large-scale Web sites and Internet operations. Thus, it seems inevitable that we will see more McDonaldization on the Internet and accompanying it will be a steady increase in dehumanization and other irrationalities of rationality. While the latter may be worrisome to some, to most they seem like a small price to pay for the advantages of McDonaldizing the Internet and its consumption sites, especially the largest of them.

However, the central point about McDonaldization, at least from the perspective of this section of the chapter, is that Web sites, especially large ones, throughout the world will be forced to McDonaldize if they hope to survive. Furthermore, Web sites will compete on the basis of which one can offer the most McDonaldized sites and services. The most McDonaldized sites, wherever in the world they exist, are likely to be the ones that survive and succeed. And, of course, they are the ones that are most likely to offer nothing and to offer it globally.

Chapter Seven

A Few (by Necessity) Concluding Thoughts on Nothing (and Its Globalization)

The preceding chapters have raised or suggested a wide range of issues that relate to the main concern in this book: the globalization of nothing. The final two chapters deal with many of these topics. In this chapter the main focus is on various concerns relating to the issue of nothing, although it is inevitable the topic of globalization will arise here and there. In Chapter 8 the focus will be on issues relating to globalization, although we will certainly not be able to avoid (nor would we want to) the topic of nothing. While the emphasis is different in the two concluding chapters of this book, taken together they deal with a wide range of issues that has arisen throughout this analysis.

The Increase in Nothing! The Decline in Something?

We begin this penultimate chapter by returning to the key argument made in Chapter 1, and pervading everything to this point in the analysis, that there is a long-term trend in the social world in general, and in the realm of consumption in particular, in the direction of nothing. More specifically, there is a historic movement from something to nothing. Recall that this is simply an argument about the increase in forms that are centrally conceived and controlled and are largely devoid of distinctive content. In other words, we have witnessed a long-term trend *from* a world in which indigenously conceived and controlled forms laden with distinctive content predominated *to* one where centrally conceived and controlled forms that are largely lacking in distinctive content are increasingly predominant.

There is no question that there has been an increase in nothing and a relative decline in something, but many forms of something have not experienced a decline in any absolute sense.[1] In fact, in many cases forms of something have increased, but they have simply not increased at anything like the pace of the increase in nothing. For example while the number of fast-food restaurants has increased astronomically since the founding of the McDonald's chain in 1955,[2] the number of independent gourmet and ethnic restaurants has also increased, although not nearly at the pace of fast-food restaurants. This helps to account for the fact that a city like, to take an example I know well, Washington, D.C. has, over the past half century, witnessed a massive increase in fast-food restaurants *at the same time* that there has been a substantial expansion of gourmet and ethnic restaurants.[3] In fact, it could be argued that there is a dialectic here and the absolute increase in nothing sometimes serves to spur at least some increase in something. That is, as people are increasingly surrounded by nothing, they are driven to search out, or create, something. However, the key point is that the grand narrative presented here is more about the relative ascendancy of nothing and the relative decline in something, and not about absolute change, especially as it relates to the decline of something.

Nonetheless, at least some forms of something have suffered absolute declines and may have disappeared or be on the verge of disappearance. One example is the "greasy spoon,"[4] the small café likely staffed by a short-order cook and perhaps a cashier and/or waitress. These were not noted for the quality of the food (the name is derived from the fact that the food was often greasy), but it was cooked to order and over time the cooks came to know regular customers and their preferences. Friendly, if not intimate, relationships were likely to develop between customers and cooks, waitresses, and perhaps other regular customers. Greasy spoons continue to exist here and there, but in the main they have been supplanted by fast-food restaurants. They are most likely to continue to be found in areas—small towns and rural areas—where the population base is not large enough to sustain many, if any, fast-food restaurants.

A similar fate has befallen the small, local grocery store which has been driven to the wall, and often out of business, by the supermarket (clearly lying toward the nothing end of the continuum). Likely a "mom and pop" operation, local grocers were apt to know many of their customers quite well. As a result, they were likely to do such things as put together and deliver regular orders and allow customers to run up tabs that were to be settled up on payday. If times were tough, the tab might have been extended for weeks, even months.

Yet another example is the cafeteria, with perhaps the best-known example being the New York and Philadelphia chain known as the Automat.[5] Unlike the previous examples, the Automat falls more toward the middle of the something–nothing continuum. For one thing, it was a (small) chain and for another, as its name suggests, some of its operations involved automatic technologies. There was a fair degree of rationalization in the Automat, with the best example being the windowed slots along one wall of the restaurant that held various food items. A customer inserted a few coins, originally nickels, into a slot next to the desired food and was then able to open the door and remove the food. Eliminated was "non-rational" interaction between employee and customer. However, the Automat was far from being totally dehumanized. It also had what defined most cafeterias—a food line (along another wall) with a variety of stations (vegetables, meats, desserts, and so on). A customer moved down the line selecting various items (which were doled out by employees behind the counter) and then moving on to the cashier to pay for the food. Furthermore, customers often became regulars and many looked forward to regular interaction with people behind the counter, cashiers, and other customers. Like the greasy spoon, and in spite of its rationalized elements, the Automat gave way to the fast-food restaurant, as well as to other chain restaurants.

It could be argued that all of these are examples of what Joseph Schumpeter called "creative destruction."[6] That is, the greasy spoon, the neighborhood grocer, and the cafeteria, among many others, have largely disappeared, but in their place has arisen successors like the fast-food restaurant, the supermarket, and the "dinnerhouse" (for example, Cheesecake Factory).[7] While there is no question that extensive destruction of older forms has occurred, and that considerable creativity has gone into the new forms, one must question Schumpeter's one-sidedly positive view of this process. Perhaps some things have been lost, even some measure of creativity, with the passing of these older forms. It may be that the destruction has not been so creative.

However, no overall value judgment needs to be made here—forms laden with content (something) are not inherently better than those devoid of content (nothing), or vice versa. In fact, there were and are many forms rich in content that are among the most heinous of the world's creations. We could think, for example, of the pogroms that were so common in Russia,[8] Poland, and elsewhere. These were largely locally conceived and controlled and were awash in distinctive content (anti-Semitism, nationalism, and so on). Conversely, forms largely devoid of content are not necessarily bad. For example, the bureaucracy, as Max Weber pointed out, is a form (and ideal type) that is largely lacking in content. As such, it is able to operate in a way that other, more content-laden, forms of organization—those associated with traditional and charismatic forms of organization—could not. That is, it was set up to be impartial, to *not*, at least theoretically, discriminate against anyone.

There is very strong support for the argument, especially in the realm of consumption, that we are in the midst of a long-term trend away from something and in the direction of nothing. By the way, this implies a forecast for the future—we will see further increases in nothingness, further erosions of somethingness, in the years to come. There seems to be no scenario short of a global nuclear conflagration (obviously much too high a price to pay) that would serve to return us in the direction of something. In terms of the kinds of examples discussed throughout the book, we are increasingly leaving behind a world dominated by local diners, Parmigiano Reggiano, gourmet chefs, home-cooked meals, and haberdashery services and moving in the direction of one increasingly populated by fast-food restaurants, Gap wear for children, telemarketers, Lunchables, and self-service clothing sections of department stores.

This brings us to two issues of concern here that were anticipated in Chapter 1—the pros and cons of this historical development. If one endeavors to look at the spread of empty forms as objectively as possible, it is clear that one can enumerate a variety of *both* positive and negative effects. The proliferation of these forms, as well as the relative decline of forms loaded with substance, is neither an unmitigated good nor entirely problematic.

The Positive Side of Nothing and Its Spread

There is no question that global proliferation of nothing has brought with it a number of benefits. To argue otherwise would be to believe that people are demanding, purchasing, and flocking to that which is without merit (we will discuss the issue of rational choice later in this book and in the Appendix). However, there are, as we have seen throughout this book, many different forms of nothing and each of them has its own set of benefits. Let us see what might be some of the positive characteristics that most, or all, of these forms have in common.

We would need to start with the perception, and in at least some cases the reality, that nothing is *comparatively inexpensive*.[9] A credit card costs little to acquire and may even be "free." Furthermore, if one pays one's bill in full each month, free credit is also obtainable.[10] Fast-food restaurants these days offer a number of menu items for a dollar and there are the "value meals" for those who want more than just, say, a sandwich. Those tract houses in suburban developments offer a lot of rooms, square feet, and amenities for what appears to be a comparatively low price. A week on a cruise ship for one low price—including all the food you can eat—seems like a steal. The list could be extended indefinitely, but the key point is that the various types of nothing seem inexpensive, at least in comparison to the possible alternatives.

A second advantage of nothing is *convenience,* which can take many different forms.[11] A Lunchable is an entire lunch neatly prepackaged in its own tray that can be stored in the closet and will not spoil or deteriorate while waiting to be eaten. Disney World offers everything one could want on a vacation—attractions, entertainment, shopping, hotels, and so on—at one self-contained location. Much the same could be said of cruise ships and Las Vegas casino-hotels. The credit card is undoubtedly far more convenient than carrying large amounts of cash, especially when one is traveling between countries with different currencies. A similar point can be made about the euro, which makes it far more convenient not only to travel in the nations that use it, but also for those nations to do business with one another.

All of the examples of nothingness discussed in this book are character-ized by the *efficiency* with which they can be produced and consumed. Mass manufacture and batch processing are intimately associated with all forms of nothingness. That is, the efficient production of products (non-things) and the efficient handling of consumers (in non-places, by non-people, and with non-services) are characteristic of nothingness. This efficiency is a lure to producers and managers because it promises not only great profits, but systems that make for easy handling of products, sites, and people. Efficiency makes it easy for consumers to obtain and use the various forms of nothing.

Perhaps most important, nothingness has made a veritable cornucopia of virtually anything one can imagine available to more people throughout the world than ever before. It could be argued that nothingness has contributed significantly to the *monumental abundance* that is characteristic of the developed world, especially the United States, today. Furthermore, the promise is that this is just the beginning and the range of that which is available, and the ease with which everything it encompasses can be obtained, will increase exponentially in the coming years.

We could undoubtedly enumerate many more advantages of nothing, and in the process extend this list enormously, but this is enough to illus-trate the point that there are certainly good reasons for the proliferation of nothing.[12] However, with most consumers and many scholars extolling the virtues of the many forms of nothing, it is important that we turn to a discussion of the downside of its spread.

The Negative Side of the Spread of Nothingness

The most important criticism of the spread of nothing throughout the globe is that because it tends to expand inexorably into the nooks and crannies occupied by something, in most cases[13] there is less and less room for the latter. With the explosion of non-places, non-things, non-people, and non-services, there is progressively less room for places, things, people, and services. We live in a world increasingly denuded of something in its many forms. Take, for example, the case of Ikea. "The low prices draw people away from small neighborhood shops, the nodes of community exchange; the volume of business attracts other mass retailers, creating big-box strip malls."[14] More generally, *The Harvard Design School Guide to Shopping* describes the implosion of shopping into museums, churches, schools, libraries, and hospitals and it concludes: "In the end, there will be little else for us to do but shop."[15] We end up with a world in which that which has, from time immemorial, been of great importance and meaning to people is either disappearing or turned over, in whole or in part, to nothing. This impoverishment of the world is, paradoxically, coming at the same time that the (developed) world is awash in an unprecedented number and variety of (non) -places, -things, -people, and -services. It is an odd kind of privation, *loss in the midst of monumental abundance,* but it is an apt description of a major problem of the age in the developed world, at least from the point of view of this analysis. This diagnosis of a central problem of the contemporary world—loss amid unprecedented affluence—means that even though we find ourselves surrounded by a plethora of (non) -places, -things, -people, and -services, we nevertheless are deprived of the distinctive content that has always characterized places, things, people, and services.[16] We could be said to be dying of thirst even though we are surrounded by water.

This rather unique diagnosis of societal ills reflects the fact that we are living in an extraordinary era. Thus, the judgments of the classic social theorists either no longer sound accurate or, at least, do not get to the heart of contemporary realities. For example, while, as we saw in Chapter 4, Karl Marx's ideas on capitalism are perhaps more relevant than ever, his notions of alienation and exploitation are too work-related to have much relevance to the contemporary developed world where consumption is increasingly central (although it is probably more relevant than ever to the less-developed world where much of the kind of production-oriented work analyzed by Marx is increasingly done). Emile Durkheim's ideas on anomie (a sense of normlessness, of not knowing what we are expected to do) seem quaint in a world in which it is not only quite obvious that we are expected to consume, but also crystal clear how, and how much, we are supposed to consume. There is certainly a "tragedy of culture" in this deprivation amid unprecedented affluence, but it is not one that has anything to with, as Georg Simmel argued, a growing gap between objective (cultural products) and subjective (the ability to create those products) culture. Finally, Max Weber may have been closer to the mark with his ideas on the "iron cage of rationalization," that we are increasingly surrounded and constrained by rational structures (like bureaucracies). However, Weber's theories had little direct relevance to consumption, and even when they are extended in that direction, they do little to help us understand loss amid unprecedented affluence.

The critique of nothing being offered here is beautifully illustrated in the movie, *One Hour Photo,* discussed in Chapter 1. First, the superstore depicted in the movie, Sav-Mart, is absolutely crammed full of stuff; it is a metaphor for the unprecedented affluence of the United States (and much of the developed world) today. Second, Si, the photo lab employee, and several of his customers seem to be deprived even as they find themselves enmeshed in this affluence. Third, in spite of its stocked shelves, Sav-Mart seems barren and this is made abundantly clear in the dream sequence where Si finds himself surrounded by shelves that have been emptied of all their stuff (non-things). A sense of loss pervades the store, and the movie, but it is not made clear exactly what has been lost. From the point of view of this discussion, what has been lost there, and in the developed world more generally, is the locally conceived and controlled forms with distinctive substance associated with places, things, people, and services.

Turning to the examples of nothing used throughout this book, it is clear that it is possible to associate many, if not all of them, with the idea of loss. Let us begin with the example with which we began the book—the credit card. Many problems have been associated with easy access to credit cards. For some users, credit cards open up a magical world of a cornucopia full of life's delights, but for others it becomes a nightmarish void where it is impossible to extricate themselves from debt in a world characterized by a continuous round of often empty and unfulfilling consumption of unneeded and unnecessary goods and services. Many who are deeply enmeshed in the credit card world complain about its emptiness and their inability to find meaning in it (of course, many others revel in it). Clearly, it is hard to find much in the way of substance in an unsolicited letter (or phone call) making a largely impersonal offer of a credit card and loan associated with it. Recently, a journalist pointed out the emptiness of the credit card world in general, in part through the metaphor of a description of the barrenness of the center of the credit card business in the United States (and therefore the world)—Wilmington, Delaware ("Plastic City"):

> I walked all the way around MBNA's four, beigey-blah, interconnected green-awninged buildings, where I saw *nothing,* and nobody: I looped around the Chase building, too, and then walked seven blocks down toward the Christina River, to ponder First USA's buildings. This is a lot of concrete and *empty* plazas and walkways. . . . The *emptiness* here left me wishing I could write a song about credit card problems. . . . [17]

There is some indication that the story told in the movie, *Fight Club,* is set in Wilmington. That movie's protagonist is not only employed by a financial corporation like one of those mentioned above, but he is deep into a consumerism heavily financed by credit card use. Among other things, he is shown on the telephone ordering inexpensive, mass-produced furniture from the global chain, Ikea. Both that firm's stores (examples of a non-place) and its products (non-things) are, has been mentioned several times before, prime examples of what is considered in these pages to be nothing. Purchase of these non-things in that non-place is made possible in the movie, and for most people on a regular basis, by the credit card. Living a boring and meaningless existence dominated by non-places and non-things, dramatic changes take place when the movie's "hero" is introduced to the Fight Club, a place where he is able to find at least part of what has been lost in a modern, consumerist society. This is

> where men beat each other senseless as a response to the *numbness* they feel living in an *empty,* consumeristic culture.
>
> By the movie's end, the narrator learns that his Fight Club is an hallucination; and as a metaphor and tragic finale, he blows the skyscrapers of this pseudo-Wilmington to smithereens. It's not a bad movie for anyone who ever had credit card debt and entertained notions of an Armageddon that would set people free.[18]

The club devoted to fighting and depicted in this movie may be many things, but it is *not* empty! What transpires in the Fight Club is something—it is conceived and controlled by the fighters themselves and each of the fights is quite distinctive in its content.

This article is not only a critique of the credit card (and its associated culture and home base), but also the emptiness and loss associated with the consumer goods that its author (like the hero in *Fight Club*) acquired with it over the years:

> I would like to be able to tell you that in all those thousands of dollars there was a three-week trip to Italy when I was 24, during which I fell madly in love.
>
> Unfortunately, I have to be honest: There was never an Italy.

There was Banana Republic, there was Barnes and Noble, there were new Midas brakes for the car. There was the removal of my wisdom teeth at 24, paid for in part on my Citibank MasterCard, because insurance only covered half. There were motel rooms, and even a few hotel rooms, but they tended to be in places like Yuma, Az., and Lexington, Ky., and Shreveport, La., because I have always seemed to be just driving through.

. . . There was something Gucci, but there was so much more Gap. . . . For every nice meal charged to my plastic, there are, I am sad to report, many more charges to what appear to be Chinese takeout joints.

There were glasses of wine that I bought in hotel lobby bars while I waited.

Sometimes I was waiting for someone in particular, and sometimes I was waiting for *nothing* at all.[19]

This critique of the emptiness associated with the credit card, as well as the credit card culture and the hyperconsumption it plays such a great role in supporting, can be extended to all of the forms of nothingness associated with contemporary consumption and discussed in this book. Indeed, a number of specific examples of them—Banana Republic, Barnes and Noble, Midas, (all) motel and (most) hotel rooms, Gucci,[20] Gap, Chinese takeout joints, (most) hotel lobby bars—are enumerated in the previous quotation. Implied is the absence of a variety of things that would be considered something in terms of this analysis—trips to Italy, love, nice meals, and so on.

The fast-food restaurant lends itself easily to being considered in terms of emptiness and loss. It is hard, to put it mildly, for most customers to find meaning in these empty structures, much less the drive-through lanes through which the fast-food restaurant prefers to shunt as many customers as possible. In a sense, the drive-through lane implies not only that no meaning is going to be derived from the restaurant experience, but it is preferred that the customer not even dare enter the restaurant itself in the (nearly hopeless) pursuit of meaning. The consumption of the same food over and over, produced in a kind of assembly-line process, is hardly likely to give the food itself much in the way of distinctive substance. Because they are so impersonal, routine, and even scripted, relations with the counter people or those who staff the drive-through window are unlikely to have much in the way of substance. Finally, it is virtually impossible to find meaning in the service, which is all but nonexistent. Implied in all of this is a loss, especially of all that is associated with great good places where things are offered by people who also provide service.

Then there is the TVGnetwork.com (as well as online casinos and many other large-scale consumption sites). This is an interactive Web site that allows bettors to wager on horse races without going to the racetrack (it is possible to watch the races online or over a cable television network run by the same company). This clearly has many advantages as far as horse players are concerned—convenience, efficiency, the ability to bet on many different races at a number of racetracks, and so on. But just as clearly, it involves a loss associated with no longer actually being at the racetrack. While we must be wary of romanticizing race tracks, they do have many characteristics of a great good place. Racetracks usually have a number of regulars who form a community and look forward to interacting with one another, renewing old acquaintances, telling stories associated with the track and its lore, sharing tips on horses, and so on. Furthermore, there is the experience of actually being at the track, watching the horses run, and rooting for one's favorite. On the relatively rare occasions that one actually wins, there is not only the joy of collecting the winnings in cash but bragging about it immediately after with friends at the track. All of this, and more, is lost when bettors stay at home, bet on TVGnetwork.com, and watch the races on television. Of course, in spite of the loss, many opt to do this (racetrack attendance is way down) because of its many advantages.

There is another very real kind of loss associated with the TVGnetwork. Betting on horse racing is made so efficient and so easy that horse players can descend into an endless round of wagering and losing (since, because of the way odds are set, everyone in the long run must lose). To put it another way, it is far easier for people to get lost in an endless round of consumption (betting is a form of consumption) on the Internet. Furthermore, while betting at a racetrack might be possible for say five hours a day, races on the Net and the related TV channels are available for twice that amount of time. In the future, we are likely to see the availability of races from other parts of the world making betting on, and watching, races possible around the clock. This greatly expands the void of betting (and losing) into which people can descend. Overall, it is far easier now to bet than it was in the not-too-distant past when people actually had to trek to the racetrack[21] to wager and see the races on which they bet. The immateriality of online wagering makes it more likely to be, and seem like, a void, and that void is increased in the likely event that people lose large sums of money, perhaps larger than they can afford, thereby plunging into an abyss of indebtedness. For example, all-star professional hockey player Jaromir Jagr accrued $500,000 in losses betting on sports events on Caribsports.com.[22] After all, if, as has been shown, it is generally far easier to spend electronic money that it is cold, hard cash,[23] then it is easier to charge bets on the Internet than it is to wager cash at the track.

This applies to all consumption on the Internet. That is, basically the only way to pay for things purchased on the Internet is by credit card (including bets on the TVGnetwork). It is not only easier to spend money when it is an abstract number that will show up at some later date on one's credit card bill than cash, but it is so easy and seemingly distant that the numbers add up quickly and the amounts owed can quickly get out of hand. The marriage of the credit card and consumption on the Internet makes it easy for an economic void to develop that large numbers of people have tumbled into and from which many have had great difficulty extricating themselves.

Then there is an even broader and deeper void associated with the Internet, only a portion of which is associated with consumption sites. While we can easily imagine people totally losing themselves in eBay or the TVGnetwork.com, the much greater likelihood is that people will get lost in a far wider range of Internet activities that might include keeping up with one's e-mail, playing an MMORPG, reading a newspaper online, spending time in a chat room, and, of course, making purchases at Amazon.com. While the idea of a void leads to a fear of losing one's self in the abyss of the Internet, another fear is of the rending of the self[24] into many different and perhaps conflicting parts as one jumps around among the different selves expressed in chat rooms, MMORPGs, MUDs, and in e-mail relationships with many different people. This serves to make it clear that consumption may be only a part of a broader set of problems involving the Internet, consumption,[25] and the void.

While some people do experience a sense of loss in the worlds of fast-food restaurants, credit cards, the TVGnetwork, or more generally hyper-consumption, the evidence is that many, probably the vast majority of, people not only have no such sense of loss, but seem to experience these phenomena as quite substantial and to endow them with a great deal of meaning. This, of course, brings us to the important issue of subjectivity, a topic that we will deal with much more extensively in the Appendix. People can and do experience nothing quite differently from the way it is portrayed here. That is, they can view the various forms and types of nothing as being full of distinctive content; as being extraordinarily meaningful, full, and involving anything but loss; and as that which they can exert control over and even reconceptualize. As W.I. and Dorothy S. Thomas taught us long ago, if people define situations as real, they are real in their consequences.[26]

However, we can distinguish between the objective loss (there are gains, as well) being discussed here and people's feelings about those phenomena that involve such a loss. The point here is that something is lost when we go from personal loans to credit card loans, from great good places to fast-food restaurants, from races tracks to the TVGnetwork, and so on. Most generally, in the historic movement toward that which is centrally conceived and controlled and lacking in distinctive content, there is a tendency to lose that which is locally conceived and controlled and is brimming with distinctive content. Thus, this is an objective, material loss that can be defined subjectively in many different ways. That is, the subjective definition need not be, indeed often is not, in accord with the objective circumstances.

Grobalization and Loss

The argument made in Chapter 5 about the grobalization of nothing fits perfectly with this argument about loss. That is, grobalization has brought with it a proliferation of nothing around the world and while it carries with it many advantages (to say nothing of those associated with the grobalization of something), it has also led to a loss as local (and glocal) forms of something are progressively threatened and replaced by grobalized (and glocalized) forms of nothing.[27]

Indeed, the reality and the sense of loss are far greater in much of the rest of the world than they are in the United States. As the center and source of much nothingness, the United States has also progressed farthest in the direction of nothingness and away from somethingness. Thus, Americans are long accustomed to nothingness and have fewer and fewer forms of somethingness with which to compare and evaluate it. Each new form of, or advance in, nothingness creates barely a ripple in American society.

However, the situation is different in much of the rest of the world. Myriad forms of something remain well entrenched and actively supported. The various forms of nothing, often at least initially imports from the United States, are quickly and easily perceived as nothing since alternative forms of something, and the standards they provide, are alive and well. Certainly large numbers of people in these countries flock to nothing in its various forms, but many others are critical of, and on guard against, it. The various forms of something thriving in these countries give supporters places, things, people, and services to rally around in the face of the onslaught of nothing. Thus, it is not surprising that the Slow Food Movement (see below and the next chapter), oriented to the defense of "slow food" against the incursion of fast food, began in Italy (in fact, the origin of this movement was a battle to prevent McDonald's from opening a restaurant at the foot of the Spanish Steps in Rome) and has its greatest support throughout Europe.

Explaining the Gap

How do we explain the disparity between the above argument about loss and the fact that most people, especially in America, fail to perceive a loss and, in fact, are quite happy with all of the forms of nothing described above and involving such a loss? One possibility is that many, and that number is increasing, have no experience with that which is being described here as something. Without such experience, without such a comparison base, it is very difficult, if not impossible, to see the loss involved in many contemporary forms of nothing. Thus, those who rarely if ever have personally negotiated a loan, eaten in a great good place, or gone to the race track will find it difficult, if not impossible, to see the loss associated with credit card loans, fast-food restaurants, and the TVGnetwork.

This problem is exacerbated by the fact that many forms of something are rapidly declining in number or are fast disappearing. It is hard to use something as a comparison base if it is hard to find or has disappeared completely. Furthermore, those born in recent years may know only the various forms of nothing and would have little reason to know about these forms of something, let alone to take the time and energy to try to root them out.

Another possibility is that people are well aware of these forms of something and the fact that there is loss in the various forms of nothing, but the disadvantages of the former (for example, seedy racetracks) and the advantages of the latter (for example, lower cost) are so great that the losses seem bearable, if not insignificant. Thus, the ability of a horse player to stay at home and bet on innumerable races may far outweigh the losses associated with no longer going to the racetrack and experiencing that which it can uniquely provide.

Thus, for these and other reasons, most people are either largely unaware of the loss being discussed here or, if they are cognizant of it, see it as a small price to pay, or perhaps even a gain. Of course, there are also many people who are aware of this loss, but feel that they are unable to afford the remaining forms of something. While this is sometimes true, it should be remembered that nothing is often more expensive than it appears and may actually be more expensive than something. Cooking a hamburger meal at home is less expensive than one purchased at Burger King. Given the number of races offered on the TVGnetwork, the fact that they go on for many hours more each day than the races at any single track, and that they take place seven days a week (few bettors can get to a race track that often), bettors are likely to lose far less at the track than online.

Nostalgia?

This discussion of loss, indeed the very term, seems to be rooted deeply in a nostalgia for that which has existed in the past. Loss implies that we had something in the past, but we no longer have it. I think there is much truth in the idea that those entities that are associated with something in this book—personal loans, great good places, race tracks, and so on—tend to be associated with the past. Indeed, this is closely tied to this book's grand narrative of a historical transition from something to nothing.

However, all of these forms of something and many others (for example, home cooking, authentic ethnic restaurants, and so on) continue to exist in the United States and to a far greater extent in most other parts of the world. More important, there are many ongoing and very active efforts to sustain if not resuscitate places, things, people, and services. A good example is the Slow Food Movement that we will discuss in more detail at the close of this book. This is a lively and growing movement that is devoted to protecting endangered foods and to sustaining and reviving traditional small farms and their farming techniques, small and excellent facilities for food production, high-quality restaurants, traditional and high-quality foods, and those who know how to prepare and serve such foods.[28] While there is a strong element of maintaining the past in the Slow Food Movement, it is very much oriented to the present (it explicitly does *not* want to become a museum for dead or dying foods) and the future.

A critique of the loss associated with the growth of nothing and the decline of something must not remain rooted in the past, but must be oriented to the present and especially the future. That is, it is not just a matter of reviving past, or sustaining extant, forms of something, but also, and perhaps more important, building on them as well as creating entirely new forms of something. Surely all of the magnificent advances of recent decades need not be restricted to aiding the increasing predominance of nothing. For example, advances in science and technology can be used to create new types of gourmet foods and meals, new great good places, and people with skills that extend far beyond those of their predecessors and that enable them to offer undreamed-of services. It could be argued that the golden age of something is not to be found in the past, but awaits us in the not-too-distant future.

Changes Over Time

One of the tendencies in this discussion has been to categorize phenomena as either something or nothing. However, it is clear that such categorizations can and do change over time. For one thing, at their creation, various forms are likely to be local, decentralized, and heavily laden with content—to be something (e.g., the original McDonald's restaurant created by the McDonald brothers in California). However, over time, especially if the objective is to have the forms grow dramatically, there is a tendency to centralize conceptualization and control further and to denude them of as much of their content as possible so that they can proliferate more rapidly and extensively. For example, the founder of Kentucky Fried Chicken, the "real" Colonel (Harlan) Sanders, was very proud of his chicken, especially the gravy and secret seasonings originally made at home by his wife. In fact, his goal was to create such delicious gravy that people would have little interest in the chicken. However, when Sanders sold his business in 1964, the new owners dramatically altered the gravy in order to cut costs, simplify the product, and speed up the time it took to prepare. Sanders expressed his outrage to his friend Ray Kroc (founder of the McDonald's chain): "That friggin' . . . outfit . . . they prostituted every goddamn thing I had. I had the greatest gravy in the world and those sons of bitches they dragged it out and extended it and watered it down that I'm so goddamn mad."[29]

At the same time, as content is reduced or eliminated, the form is elaborated in ever-greater detail so that it can be recreated and used easily in diverse settings by many different people. Thus, for example, the company manual, frequently many volumes in length, grows to explain more and to take more contingencies into account. An organization develops more and more subgroups, departments, and divisions to handle various matters. Specialized personnel are hired and trained to handle increasingly detailed issues and transactions.

For another, that which was once considered involving a loss can come to be seen as full of meaning and, in contrast, that which once had meaning can come to be viewed as involving a loss. In terms of the former, an example might be a cafeteria like the Automat that, in its day, might have been seen by many as involving a loss, at least in comparison to small restaurants that it tended to supplant. After all, it represented, to at least some degree, a step in the direction of McDonaldization and therefore was likely to be found wanting by some who regretted the growth of such cafeterias at the expense of full-service restaurants. Specifically, some were likely to have complained about obtaining their food from compartments rather than directly from a cook or human server. Now, however, perhaps because it has passed into history (there is a display in the Smithsonian dealing with it) and been romanticized, the Automat, at least retrospectively and in comparison to the fast-food restaurant, seems to be anything but a loss and is now described as a "masterpiece."[30]

On the other side, an example of a phenomenon that once was full and is now seen, at least by some, as empty is the strip mall. When such malls first opened (beginning in 1939), they must have appeared to many to be full of content; to involve anything but a loss. Now, however, that they have become numerous, routine, and routinized, such malls are more likely to be seen by at least some people as empty. In fact, while shopping malls, especially those that are fully enclosed, continue to increase in importance, older malls, especially uncovered strip malls, are being abandoned in large numbers.[31] Their content (their shops) has literally been lost (they've gone out of business); they have become "derelict landscapes"[32] slowly disintegrating by the side of the road.

Judgments about loss (and emptiness) are certainly affected by temporal changes. Standards change, as do the systems being judged, and this affects such judgments. The most important change affecting these systems is that they become routine, subject to the same basic blueprints. Thus, while they may have been full of content when they were newly minted innovations, they come to lose that meaning as they are recreated endlessly and come to resemble one another to a great degree. At the same time, that which one may not have thought of as loaded with content (for example, the greasy spoon) comes to be redefined over time as a function of its decline as well as the rise of alternatives that seem comparatively devoid of content. As older systems decline, or even disappear, nostalgia sets in and that which in its day may have seemed devoid of content comes to be seen in a completely different light.

This makes another point very clear—judgments about fullness and loss depend upon one's comparison base. Initial visitors to the first supermarkets may have seen them as great wonders and full of content because of all that was combined under one roof, of the cornucopia of goods available in one place. Others may have seen them as involving a loss in comparison to the content-rich (especially in terms of interpersonal relations) grocery stores, fruit and vegetable stands, butcher shops, and bakeries that they were replacing. Today, the prevalence of fast-food restaurants may make the greasy spoon seem like something to at least some diners, but in their heyday many may have seen greasy spoons as largely empty.

However, the proliferation of nothing, including its global spread, raises an important issue about one's comparison base. If nothing becomes so predominant that it drives out, or relegates to the margins, places, things, people, and services, then many people lose a base from which to compare nullities. If virtually all one knows, if all that is available, is shopping malls, Gap clothes, telemarketers, the TVGnetwork, and the "services" of ATMs, then how is one to conclude that these involve a loss? The coming crisis implied here is that people will increasingly come to live their lives surrounded by centrally conceived and controlled settings devoid of distinctive content, consuming things that lack distinctiveness, having interactions with people that are largely indistinguishable from all other such interactions, and receiving similarly indistinguishable services. And, it is entirely possible since more and more of us will be living our lives increasingly immersed in nothingness, that we won't even be aware of this trend and how it is affecting our lives. It could be argued that since loss is, at least in part, in the minds of consumers, they are not aware that a loss has occurred (at least in comparison to more content-laden alternatives that no longer exist or have been relegated to the margins of society). It may well be that nothingness will cease being seen as involving a loss and come to be seen as full.

How Can We Make So Much Out of So Little?

Among all of the paradoxes inherent in this analysis (the globalization of nothing, nothing is nothing, and so on), none is more perplexing than the fact that so many of us are so capable of making so much out of the various forms of nothingness discussed here. How can this be explained?

First we need to differentiate between peoples' thoughts and actions. Starting with latter, the point is that there are many things that people *do* to modify the largely empty phenomena of concern here so that they are closer to being something, to being fuller of distinctive content and being able to provide people with meaning. Oddly, because they are so empty, the various forms of nothing make it much easier to take various actions to change them so that they can be more laden with content and, therefore, meaningful.[33] Take jeans, for example. Here is a form of apparel that is very simple in conception and contains very few design elements. Although there are exceptions (very expensive designer jeans), and even design changes in jeans (for example, the current craze for jeans that look as if they have whitened with age), in the main jeans are of a uniform design, are made of denim, and are the familiar blue in color. The standard pair of jeans is a pretty empty form; one pair is much like all the others. Because jeans are so empty people can do all sorts of things to them in order to give them content; accord them more meaning. In fact, their emptiness invites such modification. Examples include cutting them off in mid-leg, allowing them to fray at the bottom, creating holes in all sorts of places (some quite revealing), plastering them with all sorts of appliqués, washing them in a wide range of ways to give them certain characteristics, and so on. Of course, even the most unadorned and unadulterated pair of jeans can become meaningful to its owner over time as it grows more comfortable, frays on the edges, and is marked by stains that bring back fond memories. Most important, simply wearing a pair of jeans over a long period of time can give it meaning as it comes to be associated with past events and activities.[34] In these and many other ways, that largely empty pair of jeans purchased in the store is transformed into apparel that can be extraordinarily meaningful to those who own and wear them.

While jeans as a form of nothing can be easily modified in these and other ways, this is less true of clothing that is rich in content; that is something. For example, custom-made slacks, or those made by a fashion designer, out of expensive cloth and with elaborate design elements, are more likely to be something (rich in distinctive content) with the result that there is little need to do anything to them. In any case, there is already much content in such slacks. Adding design elements (for example, appliqués) becomes more difficult because, among other things, they might conflict with those that are already part of the slacks. In contrast, because they are so empty of content, jeans seem capable of absorbing virtually any alterations. Removing some elements from designer slacks might be a form of action that gives them more meaning (although this is highly unlikely, as well), but adding things to something already rich in content is simply more difficult than if it was lacking in content.

The case of jeans is interesting from the point of view of this book because of their popularity around the world. It may be that one reason for that popularity is the emptiness of the form. However, we know that jeans have had great meaning in the world, especially in the old Soviet-bloc countries. To them, it was a prime example of the United States and much of the content, and there was a lot of it in their eyes, was traceable to its roots in American society, especially the old West.[35] In the main, this represents the other meaning of Americanization employed in this book. Rather than succeeding because they are empty products, some American exports succeed because they are infused with key elements of American culture or because those elements can be attributed to them by those who consume them. In fact, in the case of jeans, their enormous success globally is traceable to the fact that many buy them because they see them as symbols of the United States, many others because they are empty forms, and still others for many other reasons (cost, durability, flexibility, and so on). We will return to this issue of the subjective meaning associated with nothing–something, but before we do let's return to the issue of the actions taken by people.

Turning from a pair of jeans (a non-thing) to the fast-food restaurant (a non-place), the basic argument is, of course, that one of the sources of its national and international success is its relative emptiness as far as distinctive substance is concerned—simple structures, utilitarian tables and chairs, limited menus, few options for those menu items that do exist, and so on. In fact, as was pointed out earlier, the increasing popularity of the drive-through window means that virtually all substance associated with the structure of the restaurant has been removed, at least as far as those customers who use those windows are concerned since they never enter the structure at all.

However, in spite of the emptiness, and even the negativity, diners throughout the world continue to come to fast-food restaurants in droves. One reason they do so is that the settings are so empty that they can make of them what they want (even if that is opposed to what the owners and managers want). Thus, pensioners are known to use the fast-food restaurant as meeting places for coffee in the morning and some restaurants have allowed their restaurants to be used for bingo games during nonpeak hours. In spite of the best efforts of management, teenagers, among others, do use the fast-food restaurant as a hangout. Internationally, fast-food restaurants have come to be used in all sorts of unexpected ways. Thus, as mentioned before, in Japan teenagers with only small apartments in which to do their homework stop off at a fast-food restaurant after school and use it as a place to meet friends and do their homework. They spend hours there, a nightmare from the perspective of an American fast-food restaurant manager since they are likely to occupy space for long periods of time and spend comparatively little money.

Of course taking actions to alter the nature of nothingness usually depends on developing an alternative construction of the reality of nothingness. Again, the point is that since so little of substance is associated with nothing (at least in comparison to something), creating alternative constructions of reality is relatively easy. Furthermore, since those who are behind the various forms of nothing are obsessed with expansion nationally and internationally (grobalization), they often care little what sort of reconstructions (especially mental and even in some case physical) people undertake as long as they buy the product or service. Thus, the manufacturer of jeans doesn't care how customers reconstruct them, or what they do with them, after they have been purchased. If the buyer wants to define jeans as a source of cut-offs or a blank slate for a wide range of artwork of various kinds, that is just fine with the manufacturer. This is less true of the owner of a fast-food restaurant because certain definitions, and more importantly actions, might serve to reduce business (rowdy teenagers defining the restaurant as a place in which to monopolize tables for long periods of time and then acting on that new definition), but even there, if an unanticipated redefinition leads to increased business, it may well be welcomed.

The reverse is true in the case of something. For example, a gourmet restaurant is what it is because of its extraordinarily rich content. It is unthinkable that diners would seek to redefine and reconstruct it so that it was something other than what it was. Thus, one would not demand a quick hamburger and fries (perhaps to go) at one of Provence's renowned French restaurants, or request plastic utensils with which to eat one's meal.

Thus, one of the reasons for the global success of nothing is that its emptiness makes it particularly easy to define and use in many different ways, many of which are totally unanticipated by the owners, manufacturers, and disbursers of nothing.[36]

Of course, this is only part of the story, maybe even only a small part of the story, since it is also the case that whatever their substantive character-istics (or lack thereof), various forms of nothingness (including blue jeans and fast-food restaurants) have come to be defined by large numbers of people around the world as something. For example, Coca-Cola is little more than sugar, some flavoring, and lots of (carbonated) water. It is largely indistinguishable from innumerable other brands of cola, yet people around the world seem to think that Coca-Cola is something and they are eager to ask for it by name and even to pay a premium for it.

Part of the reason for this, of course, is the power of advertising. Coca-Cola, for example, spends billions of dollars on advertising around the world to convince people that it is Coca-Cola, and only Coca-Cola, that they want and need to drink. (Of course, one of the reasons Coca-Cola can spend so much on advertising is that the product itself—largely devoid of distinctive substance—costs so little to make. It is another one of many products where the container or the packaging may cost more than what's inside.) As a result, many people have come to define Coca-Cola as some-thing. Of course, it is also possible for nothing to come to be defined as something informally, by word-of-mouth and not as a result of advertising campaigns. The enormous popularity of jeans in the old Soviet bloc is a case in point. Even high-end products like the Gucci bag can achieve popularity more by word-of-mouth than as a result of advertisements and marketing campaigns.

As a general rule, the emptier the product, the less money spent on sub-stance, the more that is available to be spent on promotion. Furthermore, the greater the degree of nothingness, the greater the need to advertise. After all, it is more likely to be true that distinctive substance sells itself (at least to those who are interested in, open to, and can afford it), but nothing needs to be sold, and very aggressively (there are exceptions such as the word-of-mouth successes like jeans). The result is the expensive, elaborate, and often brilliant advertising campaigns that lead people to endow nothing with a great deal of meaning. In effect, it is the substance of the ads and the images created, and not the substance of the product, that leads consumers to think of certain products as having great meaning. There is something approaching a general rule here: The less the substance in a product, the more it is nothing, the greater the need to use marketing to endow it with meaning (for more on this see the discussion of brands in Chapter 8).

Breakfast cereals offer another example of a product that is nothing, costs pennies to produce, yet huge advertising budgets have successfully endowed at least some of them (for example, Rice Krispies, Frosted Flakes) with great meaning. One brand of rice puffs or corn flakes is pretty indistinguishable from any other brand, or even the "no-name" brands that may be secretly manufactured by the same company that makes the name brand. Yet, some consumers define Kellogg's Corn Flakes as something and will have no other brand (or non-brand) for breakfast. Of course, this is the essence of advertising—manufacturing substance (and difference) where there is little or no substance (and difference). That which is truly substantially different, and in important ways, has less need to advertise and, in any case, has fewer resources to devote to advertising because more is invested in the substance of the product.

A third reason that nothing has great meaning is that even though various forms of nothingness are largely devoid of distinctive content, people develop a personal history with them. It is that personal history, rather than the content (or lack thereof), that accords nothingness meaning.

There is a fourth reason: In a world increasingly defined by emptiness, people prefer to surround themselves with nothingness which, in a perverse way, comes to be defined as something. It often takes hard work (and money—more on the economics of something–nothing below) to engage with and appreciate something (a fine wine, a gourmet French meal). In contrast, nothing is usually easily appreciated largely because of its relative emptiness, including the simplicity of its components and characteristics. Thus, while a fine wine (and a good beer) may be quite complex and require some skill to discern its diversity and quality, a glass of cola has a few, very obvious characteristics that are easily discerned (for example, the sweetness, the familiar cola taste). It is that simplicity and the familiarity that come to be defined as something. The same can be said of McDonald's French fries, where the overriding taste is saltiness; it is almost impossible given the amount of salt and the thinness of the fry, to say nothing of the fact that it was frozen, to taste the potato that is the base of those French fries. In contrast, homemade French fries are more likely to taste like potatoes, although people increasingly familiar with and who prefer McDonald's fries may salt their homemade fries to death so that all they taste is the salt and not the potato (an increasingly unfamiliar flavor). Not only is there a preference for nothing, it becomes the standard against which all else is judged. Another irony: Judged against the standard of nothing, something fails precisely because it is something, because it is rich in the kind of content absent in nothing!

The preference for salty French fries and sweet colas is part of the general trend toward a world largely composed of near-emptiness. Given that trend, people come to prefer the empty to the full: They define the empty as the full and the full as the empty. Of course, as we have seen above, that which is empty can more easily be redefined and acted upon to be made full. While this is true, it does not negate the fact, indeed it reinforces it, that we increasingly live in a world in which people prefer nothing to something.

Making Something Out of Nothing on the Internet

Since we devoted a whole chapter to it, let us take a look at the issue of making something out of nothing as it applies to large-scale consumption sites on the Internet. It is certainly the case that on Internet Web sites, especially those that permit interaction between and among people on the Web, the emptiness of forms does not prevent people from making something out of them, perhaps something quite important to them and others. Thus, a chat room would be a good example of a Web site that, while it is formally empty, can be made into something quite important by those who happen to be participating at any given time. However, large-scale consumption sites tend to offer little or nothing in the way of interaction with the result that the ability to transform them into something is much more limited. Furthermore, such consumption Web sites are centrally created and controlled. As a result, they are crammed full of preprogrammed mechanisms that involve set responses to actions taken by consumers on the Web site. This often seems like interaction, but it is one-sided and there is little possibility of a meaningful relationship developing between consumers and a "dumb" Web site.

Of course, those who are deeply enmeshed in the computer, and the life possible on and through it, will find large-scale consumer Web sites as one more component of what is to them a quite meaningful way of life. While some might question how meaningful such an isolated life can be, the fact remains that many do find meaning there. There is no question that it is possible to turn the Internet into quite something, and large-scale consumer Web sites can be part of that meaningful life.

Certainly, those who find meaning in consumption, and who are deeply enmeshed in such a life, will find the huge variety of Web sites available to them quite meaningful and an important addition to the many other ways of consuming. For those who simply find that they must purchase something—a new car, a new house, insurance, and so on—the Internet can be something in the sense that it puts an unprecedented amount of information and power in the hands of the consumer. For example, for someone in the market for a new car, the Internet provides a near limitless amount of information that can be of great help to the consumer—list price, invoice price, stock on hand in a particular dealership, automobile specifications, expert reviews as well as the views of owners of the car in question. More generally, comparison-shopping services like DealTime, BizRate, and My Simon allow people to be knowledgeable consumers of a wide range of things by providing them with prices (ranked by lowest price), as well as taxes and shipping costs. The Internet makes it possible for people to be far more knowledgeable consumers. Furthermore, it gives them much more power in the negotiating process. Prices can be solicited over the Internet from a number of dealers and the consumer can pit one dealer against the others. Negotiations can be conducted over the Internet with the result that the consumer is less likely to fall victim to the various interpersonal sales devices at the disposal of a salesperson.[37] Successfully completing a purchase through the Internet at the best possible price can certainly mean something to the consumer. Indeed, it can free people from what many consider the most odious aspects of consumption such as negotiating in person with automobile salespeople.

However, while the Internet can be used to the advantage of the consumer, it can, as pointed out before, also make it easy for the consumer to plunge into the depths of the void associated with the nothingness of consumption. That is, it is all too easy to consume over the Internet at all times of the day and night and on every day of the year. One who is already involved in hyper-consumption can easily find Internet consumption irresistible . . . and it is all likely to be made easier, and for some insidious, because the preferred mode of payment on the Internet is the credit card.

The Economics of Nothingness

We have mentioned the economics of nothing (and something) at several points in this book, especially earlier in this chapter where we discussed low cost, or at least the perception of it, as one of the advantages of nothing. Let us try to clarify our general position on the economics of nothing.

First, it is clear that, in general, there is an inverse relationship between income and nothing. That is, those with money can still afford to acquire various forms of something, whereas those with little money are largely restricted to nothing.[38] Thus, only the affluent can afford expensive bottles of complex wine or gourmet French meals with truffles. Those with little means are largely restricted to Coca-Cola, Lunchables, microwave meals, and McDonald's fries.

Second, there is an economic floor to this, and those below a certain income level cannot even afford that which is categorized here as nothing. Thus, there are those near or below the poverty line in the United States who often cannot afford a meal at McDonald's or a six-pack of Coca-Cola.

More important, there are many more people in the less developed parts of the world who do not have access to, and cannot afford, such forms of nothing. Interestingly, extreme poverty relegates people to something—homemade meals and brews made from whatever is available. However, in this case it is hard to make the argument for something. These forms of something are often meager and those who are restricted to them would love to have access to that which has been defined as nothing throughout this book and by many people throughout the world.

Third, looking at the society as a whole, some minimum level of affluence and prosperity must be reached before it can afford nothing. That is, in the truly impoverished nations of the world there are few ATMs, fast-food restaurants, and Victoria's Secrets. There simply is not enough income and wealth for people to be able to afford nothing; people in these societies are, ironically, doomed—at least for the time being—to something. Thus, they are more oriented to bartering, preparing food at home from scratch, and making their own nightgowns. It is not that they would not eagerly trade their something for the forms of nothing described above and throughout this book, but they are unable to do so. It seems clear that as soon as the level of wealth in such a country reaches some minimal level, the various forms of nothing will be welcomed and, for their part, they will enter eagerly.

Fourth, even the wealthiest of people often consume nothing.[39] For one thing, as has been pointed out previously, nothing is not restricted to inexpensive (non-)places, (non-)things, (non-) people, and (non-services). Some forms of nothing—a Four Seasons hotel room, a Dolce and Gabbana frock, the salesperson at Gucci, and the service of a waiter at a Morton's steak-house—are very costly, but they still qualify as nothing—relatively empty forms—as that term is used here. The consumption of these very expensive forms of nothing is obviously restricted to the uppermost reaches of the economic ladder.

For example, I recently visited a very exclusive resort in Sardinia, Porto Cervo on the Costa Smeralda. The potential for this area, marked by a beautiful harbor, surrounding hills, and a fine Mediterranean climate, was discovered several decades ago and it was developed as a resort for the very wealthy. Since many residents arrive by yacht, huge concrete piers were built in the bay. While it may be a beautiful site when the piers are lined on both sides by magnificent yachts—mainly in August—the rest of the year the view is badly marred by these concrete abutments. Thus, most of the time, it looks much more like a harbor for commercial shipping than a charming Mediterranean inlet. In other words, an inherently beautiful harbor (something) has been transformed into nothing (yet another harbor for ships) in order to accommodate wealthy tourists and summer residents.

The developer placed tight restrictions on the nature of the housing that could be built in Porto Cervo. The result is that there is great uniformity in the housing and the town has the feeling of a sort of very expensive Levittown, albeit one that is built in a beautiful location with magnificent weather: There is little individuality associated with the architecture of the houses in the town and that dominate the hills surrounding the harbor. Thus, the nothingness of the houses looks down upon the nothingness in the harbor.

The town center turns out to be an outdoor shopping mall. However, since it is catering to the well-to-do, it is not characterized by low-end chains—no McDonald's or Wal-Mart is to be found. However, virtually all of the shops are outlets of the high-end chains of Italy (Valentino) and the world (Cartier). There are few local shops (places) and there are no small bakeries, grocers, butchers, and greengrocers. There was a supermarket, but even that is better thought of as a non-place than a place.

Adding to the sense of nothingness, at least in the off-season—and most of the year is off-season for the wealthy visitors and (part-time) residents of Porto Cervo—is the fact that virtually no one lives in the town most of the time. The wealthy are likely to be there in August and perhaps on one or a few other occasions during the year. Interestingly, virtually no Sardinians live in Porto Cervo—it is simply too expensive for the vast majority of them. Those who work there travel in from the surrounding mountains and villages where the cost of living is a fraction of what it is in Porto Cervo. Thus, most of the year Porto Cervo is a sort of ultimate form of nothingness—a virtual ghost town with similar looking houses and chain outlets that are both literally and figuratively empty. At those times, Porto Cervo almost seems like an exclusive Potemkin Village.[40]

Ironically, local Sardinians are "doomed" to live in small villages (places), to eat local fare (things), to be served by people they know very well, and to receive personalized service. Nonetheless, and this, once again, is the perversity of nothing, most local Sardinians would sacrifice something in an eye-blink if they had a chance to obtain the various forms of nothing, including the ability to live in Porto Cervo.

Fifth, the wealthy are drawn to many of the same low-priced forms of nothing that cater to the mass of the population, even those who would be considered poor or very close to it. Thus, a credit card knows no income barriers, at least at the high end of the spectrum, and the same is true of ATMs. The wealthy, especially wealthy teenagers, are just as likely to be attracted to fast-food restaurants as those from virtually every other income group.

What all of this adds up to, then, is that there is no simple relationship between wealth and nothingness.

A Lot of Nothing Is Still Nothing

Another of the paradoxes pointed to by this analysis relates to the fallacy that quantity, especially large quantities, is related to quality. At the individual, collective, and societal levels there seems to have emerged a widespread belief that more is better (supersizing everything is one contemporary example[41]). However, if much of what is being produced and distributed in the world is at the nothing end of the continuum, then more of nothing, even a lot of nothing, does not necessarily translate into something. Indeed, it could be argued, paralleling Gresham's law as it relates to money,[42] that increases in nothing tend to leave less and less room for something. Thus, not only does a lot of nothing not add up to something, but the increasing quantity of nothing leaves less space for something.

At the individual level, we see increasing numbers of people eating more meals at fast-food restaurants, wearing Gap clothes, staying at Holiday Inns, and so on. Earlier in this chapter we quoted a journalist who, when he reviewed his credit card bills, found that he had lots of charges for various types of nothing, but regretted that there were woefully few charges for something—a three-week trip to Italy, a nice meal in a gourmet restaurant, and so on. We may now be able to do and acquire lots of nothing, but that tends to leave little time, money, and desire for something.

One of the striking new developments in the realm of nothing—the cell phone and the innumerable phone calls (from anywhere and everywhere, any time and every time) that they make possible—is a good example of this. Certainly the cell phone is a welcome addition to our technological arsenal and it has many important uses. However, just as certainly, it, and many of the innumerable phone calls it has made possible, would fall under the heading of nothing. That is, most of these calls are by any standard empty and unnecessary calls that add little to peoples' lives, except for the fact that they are able to have much more interpersonal contact than ever before. Lots of time and money (cell phones, call plans, and especially those expensive calls above the contracted limits, are certainly forms of consumption) are being spent on these conversations. Furthermore, things that not long ago were accomplished with minimal prior communication—arranging a meeting or a date—now seem to require numerous contacts, often by cell phone. Again, the point is that time and money spent in this way may allow for less of both to be invested in activities that lie more toward the something end of the continuum.

To be fair, the other interpretation of this is that the cell phone permits more of a very important type of something—interpersonal contact—and given the thesis of this book (especially its emphasis on human relations), it should be something to be welcomed. There is much merit in this position and time will tell whether the cell phone is a technology that increases activities at the something end of the continuum or has the opposite effect.

At a more collective level, we can look at towns or even large cities. It is abundantly clear that the arrival and spread of nothing tends to sound the death knell for many forms of something. Perhaps the best example is the arrival of a Wal-Mart in a small town, often on its outskirts, and the resulting decline and even demise of downtown small businesses. Not only do these small businesses tend to disappear, but so does the downtown business district and the community it supported. Instead of congregating there, people drive to the Wal-Mart. Of course, the Wal-Mart tends to lead to the development of a whole series of satellite business, many of which are likely to be chains of one kind or another. The nothingness of this environment replaces the somethingness, or at least the possibility of it, in the life of the center of the small town.

The impact in the large city is not nearly as profound. A city like New York or London was, and is, the site of virtually every form of something one can think of. Of course, such cities have not been immune to the spread of nothing, but they are so large and diverse that the impact of the spread of nothing is diffused and may itself give birth to new forms of something. One can rue the passing of various forms of something in, say, New York—the aforementioned cafeteria, especially the Automat, the Jewish delicatessen, the Italian grocery, the Irish pub, and so on—but there are also many new bodegas and small restaurants serving things like jerk chicken that have tended to replace them. True, there are now also many fast-food restaurants, superstores, and the like in New York, but they seem to coexist with many forms of somethingness. Furthermore, it is there that one sees the simultaneous expansion of new forms of somethingness—for example, the rise of an enormous variety of ethnic restaurants from all over the world.

Nevertheless, it is hard to escape the view that the world's great cities all have witnessed the explosive growth of nothing with the result that there is much more in each of these cities that closely resembles what is to be found in the others.[43] This tends to leave at least some visitors with a sense that some of the forms that made a given city distinctive (something) have been supplanted by various forms of nothing. Thus, the cities themselves seem to have moved in the direction of nothingness even though in a broader sense they may be more diverse than ever before; offer a greater a variety of somethingness.

For example, in the last few years London has witnessed the opening of numerous Starbucks coffee houses, especially in the downtown areas most likely to be seen and visited by tourists. Thus, the areas around Piccadilly Circus and the West End (the theater district) are awash with Starbucks coffee houses. Such a uniform chain is one of the prime examples of nothing and its proliferation in the most visited areas of that city tends to give it the feeling of nothingness.

However, the proliferation of Starbucks is not restricted to the tourist areas. The Fleet Street area, populated by business people, lawyers, and the like, seems to have at least as great a concentration of Starbucks as London's tourist areas.

A more mid-size city, say in the Midwestern United States, is another story. Those cities are more likely to resemble the small town described above than they do New York or London. It is in those cities that nothing is more likely to replace something. Furthermore, in comparatively new cities of this ilk, or ones that have experienced their growth relatively recently, there were likely to be few forms of something in existence prior to the explosion of nothingness. Thus, it was not a matter of nothing replacing something; nothing had the field virtually all to itself. The forms of nothingness did not need to compete with, or overcome, parallel forms of something and that made their spread throughout mid-size American cities that much easier.[44]

A similar point applies at the societal level. That is, as societies grow more affluent, they have increasing interest in acquiring what the wealthiest countries have, and much of that can be included under the heading of nothing. The wealthier such societies grow, the greater their interest in acquiring nothing. For their part, the affluent nations (the centers of nothingness), especially the states that represent them and their most powerful companies, are deeply interested in exporting the goods, services, ideas, and so on that reflect and manifest nothing to whatever country will accept and pay for them (and often even those that are not eager to accept them). There are countries that are largely, perhaps even totally, ignored, perhaps because of the hostility or lack of openness to these things, but in the main every nation is at least a potential market for nothing. As nations that once fell below some economic (and perhaps political) threshold achieve a minimal level of economic success, they are likely to be bombarded with many things, including large amounts, and an incredible variety, of nothing. Of course, this is not one-sided. The people of such nations have seen these things in the media and they generally crave what is swamping the more developed world. Furthermore, there are indigenous entrepreneurs eager to meet this demand, and to stoke it further, because of the great profits that are likely to await them.

The result is that an ever-increasing number of nations and areas of the world are coming to be penetrated by nothing and the more affluent they become, the greater the nothingness.

Chapter Eight

Concluding Thoughts on Globalization (and Nothing)

Contrary to appearances, and in spite of the great amount of attention devoted to it throughout this book (and especially in the last chapter), the central issue here is *not* nothing per se, but rather its globalization. The complexities involved in the concept of nothing have required that we devote much space to it. While the concept of globalization has its own ambiguities and difficulties, there is far more work on it in the social sciences than on nothing, we know far more about it, and it is far easier to deal with than nothing.

In order to analyze the globalization of nothing we introduced the concept of grobalization as a complement to the idea of glocalization; the two together are seen as the central processes under the broader heading of globalization. Grobalization, in turn, was dealt with in terms of three of its key subprocesses—capitalism, McDonaldization, and Americanization. While there are many other grobalization processes, these are seen as not only the most important in the world today, but also the ones of greatest interest to the author.

It is grobalization in general and capitalism, McDonaldization, and Americanization in particular that are the key forces in the global spread of nothing. While there is not a law-like relationship between grobalization and nothing, there is an elective affinity between them; one tends to call into existence the other. On the one hand, an increasingly global market insists on large numbers and great varieties of nothing to satisfy the increasing demand for it, at least part of it fabricated (through advertising and marketing) by the forces (corporations, states) that profit from the widespread distribution and sale of nothing. On the other hand, production of so much nothing, and the requirement that it be profitable or successful, leads to increasing pressure to find ever-more remote global markets for nothing. It is far easier to grobalize nothing than something; the production of nothing, especially in large numbers, is amenable to grobal proliferation. Grobalization is inherently expansionistic—it is by definition oriented to growth—and a global market offers the largest possible venue for expansionism. And, it is far easier to sell (relatively) empty forms—nothing—in diverse settings around the globe than it is to sell phenomena laden with content—something.

Capitalism spreads throughout the globe because of the incursions of capitalistic firms and the desire of those in other areas to emulate them. Because empty forms are easier to create, produce, and sell throughout the world, capitalist firms tend to largely prefer them. As another variant of grobalization, McDonaldization expands globally because of a belief in both the host nation and the receiving nations in the basic model and the fact that such a model has demonstrated that it can work everywhere with few, if any, modifications. Behind Americanization and its spread throughout the world is the belief, again in both host (the United States) and receiving nations, in the American way of doing things—a view that Americanization has a kind of manifest destiny. While those phenomena that emanate from America are inherently something because they are touched, if not infused with, that which defines America, many of them have shown a peculiar capacity to shuck their American characteristics and become many different things to many different cultures and to melt seamlessly into other cultures (Coca-Cola and Levi's in many nations around the world are excellent examples). The capacity for that which is American to lose its cultural characteristics, to become nothing (or nearly so), is linked to the view that the United States is everyone's second culture and therefore its exports are easily modified, denuded, and integrated into local culture.

While capitalism, McDonaldization, and Americanization can be seen as key forces in the grobalization of nothing, McDonaldization is the purest force because it is by its very nature oriented to the creation of phenomena that are as long on form and as short on content as possible. Capitalism (as a general rule it will produce anything that is profitable, including something) and Americanization (its products reflect American culture) are not nearly as pure forces, but they are both probably more powerful than McDonaldization. In any case, in reality it is difficult, and in some cases impossible, to distinguish among these three processes with the result that in the real world they are mutually reinforcing. For example, McDonald's, as the paradigm of the process of McDonaldization, is (or was, until recently) a highly successful capitalistic firm and it is also intimately associated with Americanization.

The above seems to imply that supporters of a particular organizational form and of American culture are key forces behind grobalization and while there is some truth to that view, the fact is that the overriding factor (at least in the economy) is undoubtedly the need on the part of capitalist enterprises not only to show a profit, but an increasing profit from one year to the next. The stock market is a cruel master, and any corporation that fails to show increasing profitability is likely to be hurt badly by it. This imperative is in perfect accord with the notion of grobalization since it is the need for profits to grow that is a major factor fueling the exportation of all sorts of goods and services. Most McDonaldized entities, or at least those active in the global arena of consumption, are profit-making organizations and it is the need to show increasing profits that is a major explanation for their global proliferation. Similarly, a large portion (although not as large as McDonaldization) of Americanization involves American firms seeking to increase profits through increased penetration of the global marketplace. Thus, much of grobalization is traceable to the demands of a modern capitalist economy.

However, it would be wrong to think that all of grobalization is the result of capitalist dynamics. For one thing, there are believers in grobalization in general, and McDonaldization and Americanization in particular, who push them as articles of faith and not necessarily, or focally, for their profit potential. For another, grobalization extends beyond the realm of profit-making enterprises and into such domains as religion, penology, and education. It is not profits that fuel grobalization in these domains, but rather belief in the advantages of McDonaldized or Americanized systems. It may be that these systems bring with them various economic advantages (such as lower costs) than extant systems, but that is not the most important factor behind grobalization in these domains.

Grobalization Versus Glocalization

As pointed out earlier, one of the key contributions of this work is the argument that the key dynamic under the broad heading of globalization is the conflict between grobalization and glocalization. This is a very different view from *any* of the conventional perspectives on global conflict. For example, I think a large number of observers have tended to see the defining conflict, where one is seen to exist, as that between globalization and the local. However, the perspective offered here differs from that perspective on several crucial points.

First, globalization does not represent one side in the central conflict. It is far too broad a concept, encompassing, as it does, all transnational processes. It needs further refinement to be useful in this context such as the distinction between grobalization and glocalization. When that differentiation is made, it is clear that the broad process of globalization already encompasses important conflicting processes. Since globalization contains the key poles in the conflict, it therefore is not, and cannot be, one position in that conflict.

Second, the other side of the traditional view of that conflict—the local—is relegated to secondary importance in this conceptualization. That is, the local, to the degree that it continues to exist, is seen as increasingly insignificant and not a key player in the dynamics of globalization. Little of the local remains that has been untouched by the global. Thus, much of what we often think of as the local is, in reality, the glocal. As the grobal increasingly penetrates the local, less and less of the latter will remain free of grobal influences. That which does will be relegated to the peripheries and interstices of the local community. The bulk of that which remains is much better described as glocal than local.

In community after community, the real struggle is between the more purely grobal versus the glocal. One absolutely crucial implication of this is that *it is increasingly difficult to find anything in the world untouched by globalization.* The major alternative in an increasing portion of the world seems to be the choice between that which is inherently and deeply globalized—grobalization—and that in which global and vestiges of local elements intermingle—glocalization. This clearly implies the near-total triumph of the global throughout the world.

Ironically, then, the hope for those opposed to the excesses of globalization, that is grobalization, seems to lie in an alternative form of globalization—glocalization. This is hardly a stirring hope as far as most opponents of grobalization are concerned, but it is the most realistic and viable one available. The implication is that those who wish to oppose globalization, specifically grobalization, must support and align themselves with the other major form of globalization—glocalization.

Yet, glocalization does represent some measure of hope. For one thing, it is the last outpost of most lingering, if already adulterated (by grobalization), forms of the local. That is, important vestiges of the local remain in the glocal. For another, the interaction of the grobal and the local produces unique phenomena that are not reducible to either the grobal or the local. If the local alone is no longer the source that it once was for uniqueness, at least some of the slack has been picked up by the glocal. It is even conceivable that the glocal is, or at least can be, a more significant source of uniqueness and innovation than the local. Another source of hope lies in two or more glocal forms interacting to produce that which is distinctive in content.

Can the Local Be Resuscitated?

Is it possible that globalization in both of its major guises—glocalization and grobalization—can give new life to the local? After all, if one of the reasons for development of glocalization is that it was a counterreaction to grobalization, then the combination of the two forms of globalization can, at least theoretically, have the effect of alienating locals and forcing them to turn inward (assuming it is not too late) in search of alternatives to *both* forms of globalization. While grobalization can certainly offend locals (Victoria's Secret in nations dominated by religious fundamentalism), the bastardizations produced by glocalization can have much the same effect. Some locals will look at glocal forms arising around them—for example, in the case of McDonald's, McSpaghetti in the Philippines, McHuevo in Uruguay, McFalafel in Egypt, and Teriyaki Burger in Japan—and yearn for a return to the original local forms. It is unlikely, to put it mildly, that, for example, McDonald's falafel or teriyaki is going to measure up to indigenous versions. Thus, one local's reaction to the new McArabia sandwich (chicken patties on flatbread) in Kuwait was, "It's not real Arabic taste."[1] Some may even be driven to ransack their past in search of traditional local practices that could be resuscitated in an effort to provide alternatives, and counters, to both the grobal and the glocal.

While such scenarios are possible, and even likely, it is difficult to be hopeful about the revival of the local and its prospects for countering globalization (although we will close this chapter on a hopeful note). This pessimism is based on several factors. First, any local revival is, from the outset, implicated in globalization since it is a reaction against it. Second, if it succeeds in attracting enough interest, firms, eventually those with global interests, will move in and seek to gain control over it. Finally, even greater success will bring it to the attention of entrepreneurial exporters who will aggressively seek to export it—to grobalize it (can we, for example, anticipate a global trade in betel nuts if the chewing of them is revived in Korea?). Thus, revivals of anything local, especially those that are successful, are likely to be grobalized and thereby lose their local character.

While it may be doomed eventually to be co-opted completely by the forces of grobalization and glocalization, what remains of the local continues, at least at present, to play a key role in the world as a source of both diversity and innovation. While one can envision a scenario in which diversity and innovation increasingly come from the glocal, it can never be quite as good a source of innovation as the local. After all, by definition, the glocal is modified from the very beginning by a variety of forces that seeks to make it acceptable to a wide range of consumers, perhaps in many different locales throughout the world. In this way, linkages to the original place and thing are progressively lost as they are increasingly watered down to suit diverse tastes and interests. In contrast, the local, again by definition, has not been so modified, with the result that it is generally more unique and a source of greater diversity.

Because of this, it is possible to argue that the world grows increasingly impoverished as the local declines in importance and perhaps disappears. The paradox is that grobalization brings with it unparalleled development in some parts of the world at the same time that it impoverishes others culturally (and, according to Joseph Stiglitz, economically) by reducing or eliminating the role of the local.[2] This point leads nicely into an aside on the 2001 terrorist attacks on the United States and their relationship to the impoverishment of the local and more generally the globalization of nothing.

The Globalization of Nothing and September 11, 2001

On the surface, it seems difficult to argue that the spread of nothing had any relationship to the events of September 11th. How can nothing have anything to do with events that have clearly meant something of such monumental importance to perpetrators and victims alike? Part of the answer, of course, is that nothing means a great deal to many people, as does the grobalization—including capitalism, McDonaldization, and Americanization—of nothing. I am not arguing that there is some sort of direct link between September 11th and the grobalization of nothing. However, it is my view that the latter provided at least some of the fuel, if not for that attack, then at least for the kind of atmosphere that exists in many parts of the world that is conducive to the development of the kinds of feelings behind assaults on American interests including embassies, military installations, and that most favorite of all targets—McDonald's!

In saying this, I am not excusing the attacks, dignifying them, or according them any sort of rational basis. I am simply saying that we need to understand the contexts in which September 11th occurred and one of those contexts is the grobalization of nothing.

The attacks of September 11th were aimed at key American symbols—the World Trade Center, the Pentagon, and perhaps the White House. Among other things, these structures symbolized America's grobal reach economically (including in the realm of consumption), militarily, and politically. In attacking such cultural icons, the attackers were clearly trying to make a statement, in fact many statements—that the United States was vulnerable, that such attacks could have long-term disastrous consequences for a complex society, *and* that there is bitterness in the world about the United States' grobal ambitions and what they are doing to local institutions that remain dear to at least some people in almost every culture.

While our focus here is on consumption, and therefore the economy, as well as culture, it is important to underscore the point that the concept of grobalization is robust enough to encompass both politics and the military. With the demise of the Soviet Union, the United States reigns supreme in the world and it is difficult to think of any serious competitors in these realms.[3] The fact is that grobalization is a good term to describe the United States' efforts to exert its power both politically and militarily throughout the world. Recent examples include the 1991 war with Iraq, the ousting of the Taliban in Afghanistan in 2001–2002, the successful late 2002 effort to get the United Nations to support a tough resolution on weapons inspection in Iraq, and the 2003 war that led to the ouster of Saddam Hussein and his regime.

In these cases, it is clear that Americanization is part of grobalization since such a high proportion of political and military grobalization stems from the United States. And it is clear that capitalistic interests are involved in, for example, the large quantity of oil that exists in Iraq (and elsewhere in the Middle East), as well as the military hardware that was used, and needs to be replaced, because of the war. McDonaldization can also be associated with these processes and, at least to some degree, be distinguished from capitalism and Americanization. For example, much of the advanced, highly rationalized weaponry that was developed in the United States is being used to support military and political grobalization. Examples that come to mind are drone aircraft, cruise missiles, smart bombs, and the like. These are certainly not only non-human technologies, but in many cases are designed to all but completely eliminate the human combatant. They are also clearly efficient. Because of the heightened accuracy, fewer of them need to be employed than more conventional alternatives. They are highly predictable since their advanced technology means that they are highly likely to end up almost exactly where they are sent. They are precisely calibrated, and elaborate and detailed calculations are involved in giving them such precision.[4] Of course, like all other manifestations of McDonaldization, they are subject to the irrationality of rationality. For example, wars are more likely to be undertaken, and these weapons deployed, because there is a far smaller risk of human casualties, at least on the American side.

Returning to our focal concern with consumption, the exportation of largely empty forms to other nations is likely to be deeply offensive to some, especially when they serve to threaten, reduce the importance of, or replace local forms rich in substance. To many, the threat to, and the replacement of, local phenomena rich in substance by those that are largely devoid of substance is likely to represent a great loss and a great insult—after all, nothing has usurped a position formerly held by something. Thus, grobalization is likely to lead to great resentment among some (and it is likely to be openly embraced by others), especially the empty forms associated with capitalism and McDonaldization as well as the easily emptied forms linked to Americanization.

As discussed previously, Americanization (and those forms of capitalism and McDonaldization hard to distinguish from it) is likely to be resented for exactly the opposite reason, as well. That is, some are likely to react negatively to the growth of forms heavily saturated with Americanism within the context of their own cultures and societies. Of course, there is a large element of subjectivity in these judgments and some in other countries may see a form as empty while others may see it as the epitome of American cultural imperialism, and still others may see it as both. There is also another possibility here—empty forms can come to be seen as the product of the United States, an inherent characteristic of American culture that is being aggressively exported throughout the world. Thus, empty forms—nothing—may be resented not only in themselves (for their emptiness), but also because they seem so American.

Whatever the form, and however it is perceived, nothing is likely to take on enormous symbolic importance when it is exported to other cultures. Another paradoxical aspect of this line of analysis is the argument that nothing is often of enormous symbolic importance, especially in nations and cultures to which it is exported. Whether the Visa credit card is seen as nothing, a manifestation of capitalism, a form of McDonaldization, a form of Americanization, or some combination of all of them, it is an important symbol in many nations around the world. While many welcome, use, and accept the card, many others are likely to be offended by it, especially when it is taken together with the many similar forms that are likely to accompany it. How do those who are offended respond? There are many ways—refusing to use or accept the card, for example—but more symbolic responses are possible, especially when the threat is viewed in symbolic terms. Thus, cutting up a Visa card, perhaps in public, might be one such symbolic response. Smashing the window of a locally owned shop that displays the Visa logo would be another, more dramatic, response. However, such responses are unlikely to have much impact on the banks that support Visa (although assaults on those banks would) or on one's own society, let alone the society—the United States—that is the creator and main exporter of these cards and all that they mean and symbolize.

Thus, those who want to have a greater impact are likely to strike at more visible and important symbols and they are likely to choose targets to which damage is likely to attract great public attention. It is in this context that we can think about such things as the looting, bombing, and destruction of McDonald's restaurants, attacks on American embassies, assaults on American ships, and, of course, the crimes committed on September 11th. The World Trade Center was a powerful symbol of grobalization, and its collapse seemed to its perpetrators and supporters as a dramatic symbolic blow against grobalization. If the World Trade Center symbolized grobalization in the economic realm, then the Pentagon is a powerful symbol of military grobalization. The collapse of one of its walls had an impact in the military realm similar to that of the collapse of the twin towers on the economic sector. And just think of the impact that a direct hit on the White House might have had on the political system and America's propensity toward political grobalization.

Just as the impact of grobalization is far more than symbolic—peoples' lives are altered in innumerable ways—much the same thing can be said about the assaults against the symbols of grobalization on September 11th. Grobalization is viewed by many as having a deleterious effect on the economies of many nations.[5] For example, at the moment, the Argentinian economy has collapsed and many in that country blame the collapse on what is here being called grobalization[6]. Similarly, the attacks of September 11th, especially the implosion of the World Trade Center towers, had stunningly negative consequences on the American economy in general (and especially that of New York City) and more specifically on American industries like the airlines and tourism. As I write this, well over a year after the event, the American economy is still a long way from recovering from the shock of that day and its myriad reverberations. For example, major American airlines continue to be in deep economic trouble and the second largest of them, United Airlines, recently declared bankruptcy.

Back to the paradoxes involved in this analysis, the argument being made here is that the grobal spread of nothing provides at least a context for gaining a better understanding of one of the most meaningful (and heinous) events of our time.

Consumption and Beyond

The substantive arguments made in this book, and most of its examples, are derived from the realm of consumption. However, as has been made clear at several points in this analysis, consumption is a rather elastic concept that can be applied to domains that one does not usually think of in these terms. The two examples discussed earlier, at least briefly, are education and medicine. That is, it is easy to think of these in terms of consumption with, for example, students and patients being consumers, schools and hospitals seen as consumption settings, and education and medical help being that which is consumed.

This being said, we can then go on to argue that these are domains that have also been affected by the grobalization of nothing. For example, one could argue that in the realm of higher education the textbook falls toward the non-thing end of the thing–non-thing continuum.[7] The textbook is largely an American invention, produced by profit-making corporations, *and* it can be seen as a book oriented to rationalizing, McDonaldizing, the communication of information. That is, instead of having to read many books, or excerpts from them, the student is given a textbook that offers the authors' summaries of those works. It further McDonaldizes reading by eliminating overly complex texts and ideas, and it offers a single accessible voice rather than that of diverse authors, many of whose voices may not be easily comprehended by students. After all, the authors originally wrote for an audience of peers, not students, and frequently the works were written quite some time ago when the norms that applied to writing were very different.

In any case, the textbook has come to be grobalized. In many nations where the American use of the textbook was ridiculed or frowned upon not too long ago, one now finds American textbooks in use and indigenous textbooks that are growing in popularity. In some cases, successful American texts are revised by local academics to reflect better the nature of a field in a given country. Especially important is the replacement of examples from the American social world by local examples. There are even "grobal" textbooks—books that have been written in such a way that they can be used in many different nations.[8]

Turning to health care, it could be argued that the global market for drugs or for routine medical procedures (even for such extreme problems as heart transplants) are examples of the grobalization of nothing. These examples also make it clear, once again, that the grobalization of nothing is often a welcome and positive development (even in the realm of consumption that we have criticized heavily for it). While the global proliferation of, for example, textbooks can be looked at in a negative light (the fact that students are reading non-books rather than the original books on which the texts are based and that are rich in substance), that is not the case with the global spread of drugs and standard medical procedures. The latter are nothing in the sense that they are centrally conceived and controlled forms largely devoid of distinctive content (for example, there is now a standard procedure for performing something as complex as a heart transplant), but in most cases they are to be welcomed.

In contrast, a textbook can be looked at as *both* an empty form and as a non-thing that is not to be welcomed because it plunges students into the void of an educational system dominated by textbooks. The focus on texts means that fewer original works, with their unique and distinctive content, are required (another loss!). In fact, it is because of this content that they are dealt with in textbooks. But instead of reading these originals, students read greatly simplified summaries of them in textbooks.

In an earlier work, I criticized textbooks for the cookie-cutter format imposed on textbook writers by publishers. That is, to be published, textbooks, especially those for the large introductory courses, must follow the general pattern laid down by the successful texts in the field. It is centralized conception and control exercised by publishers that are major factors in making textbooks nothing. In the end, they lead to texts in which there is little to distinguish one from another. In contrast, of course, the original books, the ones on which texts are built, are loaded with distinctive content—there is no cookie cutter for truly original scholarly works. In addition, such scholarly books are much more the product of individual authors, in stark contrast to the textbooks that, as we have seen, are likely to be conceived and controlled by publishers. Of course, there is great variation in the degree and extent to which this cookie-cutter approach can be applied, both in and out of the educational system. For example, introductory textbooks and Big Macs lend themselves very well to it, while in open-heart surgery, there is a standard approach, but because of the complexities and contingencies involved, there is great variation from one operation to the next.

However, we need not stop with education and health care—many other domains can be seen as involving consumption and therefore subject to the grobalization of nothing.

• For example, the public, especially criminals, can be viewed as consumers of police services. The grobalization of nothing here would involve, among many other things, the development of standard police practices that are disseminated throughout the world.[9]

• In the same domain, convicted criminals can be seen as the consumers of prison services. The development of standard structures within the penal system (for example, panopticon-like structures that permit total visibility of inmate behavior, the rise of "supermax" prisons) create the likelihood that such structures, if they are deemed successful, will be picked up by prison systems in many geographic locales throughout the world.[10]

• The church certainly has its "customers" (those who attend, or whom the church would like to see attend), and churches develop techniques for attracting and keeping a flock that, if successful, are copied by churches around the world.[11]

- Even in politics it is possible to view the public as consumers of the political system. It is clear that democratic principles have proven to be the most stable and reliable way of dealing with the public with the result that those principles have proliferated throughout the world.[12]

These examples make it clear that the basic theses of this book are not as delimited as it first appears. If so many domains can be seen as falling under the heading of consumption, then clearly the grobalization of nothing is affecting not only many countries, but a wide range of structures and institutions in those societies, as well. However, the grobalization of nothing applies beyond the realm of consumption in general, as well as consumption within each of these domains. For example, it certainly applies as well to consumption's other face—production. We literally could not have the grobalization of, for example, non-things without the existence of systems that produce massive numbers of the non-things that are to be sold and distributed worldwide. But even production, or the production–consumption nexus, is too narrow a domain for examining the grobalization of nothing. Nothing spreads globally within politics, or the church, or the criminal justice system, for myriad reasons, many of them specific to each of those domains, that have nothing to do with production or consumption.

For example, a set of common problems has led entities around the world to search for models that have proven successful in handling them. Thus, police departments throughout the world are often confronted by unruly mobs, demonstrations, and protests—for example, the now frequent anti-grobalization (to use the term developed here) demonstrations—and they often rely on, or turn to, examples of procedures where such crowds have been contained without too much disruption, destruction, and injury or death to demonstrators, police, and bystanders. To the degree that the latter objectives are achieved, those who oppose such demonstrations would see it as an example of the grobalization of nothing where the disadvantages outweigh the benefits, although this view is not shared by the demonstrators whose objectives might be better served by less pre- and well-planned crowd control.

There is no better indicator of the rampant spread of nothingness than the fact that *both* pro- *and* anti-grobalization forces have been affected by it. This entire book has been devoted to the ways in which the former have been affected, but what of the latter, the forces that oppose grobalization, especially of nothing? The fact is that in order for such a mass movement to succeed, it must rely on methods that would fall, according to the criteria developed and employed in this book, at the nothing end of the continuum. The best example would be the development, routinization, and wide-scale dissemination (especially over the Internet) of tried-and-true techniques for gaining attention for the anti-grobalization movement. Rather than developing their own techniques (something), these groups tend to rely on methods that have worked in other times and places. Of course, there is much that is spontaneous about the actions of these groups, but they also fall prey to the lure of nothingness.

This point has been made in a slightly different way by Benjamin Barber in *Jihad vs. McWorld*.[13] As we saw earlier, Barber describes the global spread of McWorld, an argument that has close similarities to the one being made here about nothingness, especially the role played by McDonaldization in its grobalization. McWorld, were it to come into existence fully, would be a world replete with nothingness. Jihad is Barber's term for a wide range of forces opposed to the spread of nothingness. They would clearly fall toward the something end of the continuum employed here. Interestingly, this makes it perfectly clear, yet again, that something is *not* necessarily to be preferred to nothing. In this case, while they have many meritorious issues and goals, and are something in the sense of being rich in distinctive content, the forces of Jihad have also committed many heinous acts (as we saw in the previous discussion of September 11, 2001). In any case, the central point to be made here is that those who support Jihad must use the techniques of McWorld (for example, television, the Internet) in order to succeed. In other words, like much else in the world, Jihad is drifting, if not racing headlong, in the direction of nothingness.

The Role of Brands

Many brand names have been touched on throughout the course of this book. Up to this point, however, our concern has been with the phenomena being branded—things, places, people, and services—rather than with the brands themselves, or the branding process. In this section we turn to brands and branding and a discussion of how they relate to globalization in general and the grobalization of nothing in particular. A brand may be defined "as a name, logo, or symbol intended to distinguish a particular seller's offerings from those of competitors."[14]

We can begin with the point that brands, especially the most successful of them, are global. To achieve this transnational notoriety, powerful grobalizing forces lie behind the most notable and successful brands. While efforts might be made to glocalize brands, what defines the success of the best-known and most successful brands is grobalization.

If the most successful brands are defined by grobalization, are we describing the grobalization of nothing or the grobalization of something? Given the definitions of something and nothing, it is not easy to think of brands as something (even though they mean a great deal to many people) in that they are *not* locally conceived and controlled. However, brands are forms with distinctive content; the (ideational, emotional[15]) content associated with one brand is different from that associated with other, especially competing, brands. Thus, brands are centrally conceived and controlled, but they are also endowed with distinctive content. As a result, they *cannot* be thought of as nothing, or something for that matter, at least from the perspective of the definitions employed here. Thus, thinking of brands as either something or nothing is a difficult matter and it would require considerable time and effort to try to unravel the complexities involved in this issue. I will leave such analysis for another occasion, but I do want to deal with another aspect of the relationship between brands and something-nothing in this section. That is, I want to argue that it is the increasing proliferation of nothing, nationally and internationally, that makes branding increasingly important.

The mass production of nothing is closely related to branding. This is clearest in the case of non-things (for example, Nike shoes), but it also applies to non-places (for example, Niketown), non-people (Niketown's salespeople), and non-services (self-service at Niketown). While we are accustomed to thinking of brands as applying to things (and especially non-things), there has been a dramatic trend toward trying to brand not only things but also places (for example, Niketown), people (the characters, played by cast members, that populate Disney World—Mickey Mouse, Snow White, and so on), and services (AOL's "You've got mail").

In the likelihood that there are several competing iterations of nothing in each of these realms, a strong need exists to create and aggressively market a brand in order to distinguish one variety of nothing from all the others. For example, there is little to distinguish Nike's running shoes from many other brand-name or even no-name shoes. Thus, great amounts of money and attention are devoted to promoting the brand and the icon—the Swoosh—that has become inextricable from it. Indeed, Nike is almost a pure example of this because the corporation itself produces little other than the brand and the infrastructure to support and perpetuate it (see below).

The importance of brands and branding is especially clear in the case of the mass-produced non-things. If one manufacturer's mass production creates non-things, and the mass-production processes of other manufacturers fabricate almost identical non-things, then producers are faced with the task of seeking to differentiate their non-things from those of their competitors; to create difference where little or none exists. A brand, especially one that is successfully marketed and imprinted in the minds of consumers, often serves to differentiate that which has little or no difference from its competitors.

Of course, *the* best example of the branding of nothing is bottled water.[16] Bottled water is centrally conceived and controlled and it's perhaps the ultimate in a non-thing lacking in distinctive content. There is little, if anything, to distinguish one brand of bottled water (Perrier) from another (Evian), to say nothing of that available from our faucets. As a result, there is a very aggressive effort by these brands to create difference where absolutely no difference exists.

While all of this might not be so clear to consumers, indeed there are active efforts to conceal it from them, it is clear to experts in the field. One such expert argues, "Marketing is a battle of perceptions, *not products. . . . There is no objective reality.* There are no facts. There are no best products. All that exists in the world of marketing are perceptions in the minds of customers or prospects. The perception is the reality. Everything else is an illusion."[17] In fact, in this world of illusion, that which is nothing has a great advantage over something. That is, since there is no distinctive substance to constrain it, the perceptions surrounding a given brand are free to be led, and to roam, anywhere and everywhere. In contrast, a brand that represents something is much more constrained by the distinctive content it represents.

Furthermore, there is relatively little need for branding when we are considering *things* (as well as *places, people,* and *services*). Not only is the mass production of things generally a contradiction in terms,[18] but a thing is usually defined by the fact that it is locally conceived, controlled, and produced, and little mass production takes place in and for local areas. A thing is further defined by its possession of truly distinctive content and therefore there is little or no need for branding to differentiate that which is already well differentiated. That is, the more there is something on offer, the less the need for a brand. To a large degree, something sells itself. In one sense, there is little or no need to brand something. In another sense, something more or less automatically brands itself (a Picasso, or a Michael Jordan[19] dunk, for example). This is not to say that there are not active efforts at times to brand something. The examples that come to mind are tourism and the cases where great efforts are made to "brand" a locale (for example, Acapulco, Jamaica).

Thus, the central points to be made here are that a major reason for the existence of brands is to deal with the problem of nothingness in the world of consumption and that branding has grown exponentially because of the tremendous expansion of such nothingness. This is not only the case in the obvious growth of non-things, but in non-places, -people, and -services. Great expenditures and efforts are made to make that which brands represent seem like something. This need is inversely proportional to the degree of nothingness of that which the brand represents. In addition to the obvious example of bottled water, what could be more prosaic, more lacking in distinctive content, than a cola; innumerable companies can and do make colas and there is little to differentiate one from another. Similarly, Nike's shoes are famously manufactured by independent contractors in Southeast Asia (and other places) that, on the same assembly lines and perhaps on the same day, may produce very similar running shoes under other brand, and no-brand, names. With little to distinguish the product, there is little choice (other than the price competition that most companies despise because it cuts into profits[20]) for the aspiring manufacturer than to create the illusion or image of difference through the creation and active promotion of a brand. Thus, Coca-Cola (and Pepsi-Cola), as well as Nike, are among the companies that spend the largest amounts on the "care and feeding" (to say nothing of the advertising) of their brands.

A very interesting example of this is the arrival in late 2002 of Mecca Cola in France and its spread to England (and elsewhere) in 2003. The content of the product is not the issue since Mecca Cola "is aimed at Muslims who like the taste of the classic American drink but do not want to contribute to American economic success."[21] The motivation of the founder of Mecca Cola is both economic (to make money) and political. In terms of the latter, 10 percent of the profits go to Palestinian causes (and another 10 percent to other charities) and the soft drink's Web site offers pictures of Palestinians battling Israeli soldiers on the West Bank. More important, for the purposes of this discussion, this involves the creation of a brand that not only seeks to distinguish itself from Coca-Cola, but also to make it clear that it is of the same genre. Thus, the packaging, including white lettering on a red background, is very similar to that of Coca-Cola. However, of greatest importance is the fact that ultimately the content—cola—is indistinguishable from that of Coca-Cola or many other brand and non-brand colas. It is the brand, and its politicized call to Muslims to support one another and not the United States, that is being sold in this case.

The commonness of branding, and its proliferation, is not only related to the proliferation of (non-) things, but also of the other nullities. That is, those who offer non-places, non-people, or non-services, either on their own or in conjunction with non-things, are confronted with the problem of creating brands that distinguish that which is not distinctive. Thus, for example, H&R Block (and other chains offering income tax services) offers uniform services to taxpayers; indeed, most of those services are derived from computerized computations and decisions that taxpayers themselves could do and make if they had access to those programs. Indeed, computerized programs are available to taxpayers that do much the same thing as those employed by companies like H&R Block. Furthermore, H&R Block offers services that are indistinguishable from those offered by many other companies and independent tax consultants. Indeed, if there is anything distinctive about what that company has to offer, it is that its services are apt to be offered by less skilled personnel who are less likely to give great personal attention to each client. Given all that, H&R Block clearly has a great need to promote its brand of service aggressively in order to compensate for the nothingness that is the essence of the tax services it has to offer.

Thus, another old-fashioned grand narrative is being offered here. The tremendous expansion of non-things, -places, -people, and -services has led to an ever-expanding need to distinguish among competitors within each of them. Since they are all nullities, there is by definition little or nothing distinctive about any of them. Thus, it is not their inherent qualities that serve to distinguish among them. There is, therefore, a need to create the illusion of distinction and one of the most important ways that is accomplished is through branding. As a result, the proliferation of nullities of all types has led to a tremendous expansion in the number, types, and importance of brands.

Responding to the Grobalization of Nothing

The most obvious response to grobalization is that no response is necessary. For one thing, this is a global trend that is clearly going to continue and there is little that any nation (even the United States), let alone any individual (or small group), can do. It is difficult to conceive of a circumstance (except, perhaps, for a global disaster) that would lead to a slowing down, stopping, or reversing of the grobalization of nothing. For another, this is a trend with many positive benefits. In the world of consumption, more things are available to more people at lower prices and often in magnificent "cathedrals of consumption" *because* of the grobalization of nothing. The vast majority of people around the world like the proliferation of nothing and those who have yet to experience it would be delighted to have that experience. There are certainly many who benefit little from globalization and are even victimized by it. However, they seem to lack the power to deal with the process in their own nation, let alone on a global basis.

Yet, as we have pointed out, there are problems beyond being relative or absolute losers in the grobalization of nothing and there are those who are acutely sensitive to them. For those people, the answers to the problem of nothingness lies in somethingness, in the grobalization or glocalization of something. While there is, as we've seen, a powerful elective affinity between grobalization and nothing, there is some tendency, although not nearly as strong, for grobalization and something to coexist. Glocalization is more likely to lead to something (although, as we've made clear, there is also a glocalization of nothing). Thus, those unhappy with the grobalization of nothing should support the grobalization, and more importantly the glocalization, of something.

In either case, what is needed is the creation, use, support, and so on of those phenomena that fall near the something end of the continuum, that is, places, things, people, and services. While it is certainly the case that entre-preneurs are crucial, all non-places, non-things, non-people, and non-services continue to exist because consumers use them and, in fact, seem increasingly to prefer them. In a world increasingly characterized by nothing, consumers prefer to shop in non-places (for example, malls), buy non-things (for exam-ple, Dockers khakis), and deal with non-people (counter people at a fast-food restaurant) and non-services (ordering books from Amazon.com). There are clearly many good reasons for such preferences, not the least of which is the *perception* of lower cost. In some cases, of course, the costs *are* lower, but in others the savings are largely illusory. In other cases, much is invested in giving nothing the feeling of magical enchantment so that consumers feel they must visit, buy, or use a given form of nothing.

For those concerned about these trends, the first thing that is needed is a *defense* of the ever-shrinking remnants of something at the local level. This is based on the conviction that much of what is something has, at least historically, flowed from the local. It is also based on the view that the local is under assault by the grobal and in the fact that it is likely to be either destroyed, minimized, or glocalized. In any case, the local, in anything approaching its pure sense, is rapidly disappearing. The defense of the local is premised on the idea that it is far easier to protect that which is already in existence or in process, than it is to recreate phenomena that have dis-appeared. When phenomena have disappeared, interest will wane or disap-pear, among other things, and the artisans, or even artists, who created local phenomena may well pass from the scene or move on to some other undertaking. Consumers' memories of these phenomena will fade and begin to disappear. Whole generations will be born with no direct knowledge of local phenomena once considered something.

Building on that which is being protected and defended, it becomes possible to expand production of forms of something already in existence and to produce new forms of something. What is needed is the defense *and* further creation of places, things, people, and services. That is, we want to prevent a further erosion *and* encourage the creation of new places, things, people, and services that are unique and one of a kind; have local geographic ties; are specific to the times; involve human relations; and are enchanted.

Secondarily, this means support for those places, things, people, and services that have an aura of permanency, are locales, offer people a source of identity, and are authentic.

It is certainly not being argued that the flood of nothing emanating from grobalization ought to be reduced or eliminated. Clearly, there is great demand for nothing in its multitudinous guises and there are many advantages associated with them. However, if current trends continue, something will be increasingly reduced and pushed into more remote and narrower corners of the world. Grobalization will threaten something more and more, and that which is something will be increasingly glocalized and thereby moved toward the nothing end of the continuum (at least in comparison to the truly local). Capitalism and McDonaldization are particularly powerful forces here both because of their grobal aspirations and because of their involvement in the production of nothing. The impact of Americanization, as always to the degree that it can be separated from capitalism and McDonaldization, is less clear-cut. It is clearly extraordinarily powerful, and while it is often involved in the worldwide dissemination of nothing, or that which becomes nothing, it is also involved in the export of that which is something, at least to the degree that it is imbued with American characteristics.

While grobalization and glocalization are to be supported for various reasons, there also must be a coordinated and sustained effort to support that which is left of the local, especially those aspects of it involved in the creation of something. It is important not to over-romanticize the local—it is the source of much that is not so desirable and perhaps even destructive and reprehensible. It is not that one would want to return to a world dominated by the local; grobalization and glocalization have given people throughout the world much that has advanced their lives and that seems to have made many of them happier. What is needed is a world in which people continue to have the *option* of choosing the local—a world in which the local has not been destroyed as a viable alternative by grobalization and glocalization.

What of the argument of economists and others in the social sciences who adopt a rational choice[22] perspective? That is, what of the argument that people the world over are freely choosing nothing—non-places, non-things, non-people, and non-services—and therefore there is no need to defend the local—the natural home of places, things, people, and services—because it is clear that increasingly few want that which is local? However, the view here is that the struggle between the local on one side and the grobal and glocal on the other is a highly uneven one—one that is being won by the twin forces of globalization. Virtually all of the power—economic, marketing, advertising, and so on—lies with the forces that support globalization. In the so-called free market, the grobal and the glocal are rapidly destroying the local. The result is that there must be active efforts to support and sustain the local. The goal is not to push the world back centuries to an epoch in which the local was virtually all there was for the vast majority of people on the planet. Rather, the goal is the retention of at least some aspects of the local so that people can make a truly rational choice between it, the grobal, and the glocal. But this is not merely a matter of permitting greater choice; it is also a matter of sustaining a crucial source of innovation in the world. Without ideas and innovations bubbling up from below, from the local, the world will be much more stagnant and greatly impoverished. This is certainly not true of innovations in areas like medicine and science that are highly dependent on grobalization (although there are problems here, as well, such as the stifling of new and alternative medicines from many local areas around the globe), but it is true in the domain of culture conceived in its broadest terms. We need grobal innovations in medicine, science, and the like in order to survive (although many of them—in military technology, for example—threaten us as well) and to live the kinds of lives we wish to live, but we also need culture and cultural innovations in order to be truly human beings. Continued cultural innovation depends, at least in part, on the sustenance of the local in the face of grobal processes that are, at this moment, well on their way to overwhelming it.

However, we can go beyond generalizations to discuss, at least in brief, a tangible example of an organization—Slow Food—that is actively engaged in keeping the local alive.

Slow Food can be seen as a grobal organization. It has sought, quite successfully, to become a force throughout the world and now has about 70,000 members in over forty-five countries.[23] However, unlike virtually all others of its ilk, it is a grobal organization interested in sustaining that which is locally conceived and controlled and is rich in distinctive content (in other words, it is interested in both the maintenance of the local and the grobalization of something). The Slow Food Movement

- supports traditional ways of growing and raising food that is exceptional in quality and taste.
- favors the eating of such food as opposed to the alternatives produced by grobal corporations.
- seeks to continue local traditions not only in how food is produced, but in what is eaten and how it is prepared.
- favors food preparation that is traditional and as close to handmade as possible.
- favors raw ingredients that are as specific to the place in which the food is made as possible.

- fights against environmental degradations that threaten local methods of producing food.
- supports the local shopkeeper and restauranteur (it favors "local inns and cafes"[24]) in their efforts to survive in the face of the onslaught of powerful grobal competitors.
- creates local "convivia" that meet and engage in actions to further the above causes.
- has created an "Ark of Taste" which lists hundreds of foods that are endangered and in need of protection. "Ark foods must live in the modern world—must withstand the threats posed by bland, synthetic, mass-produced and menacingly cheap food."[25]
- seeks to involve restaurants, communities, cities, national governments, and intergovernmental agencies in the support of slow food.
- offers annual Slow Food awards, especially to those "who preserve biodiversity as it relates to food—people who may in the process save whole villages and ecosystems."[26]
- offers special prizes and support to third world efforts and it seeks to help organize local efforts there to help conserve "prizewinners' plants, animals, and foods."[27]

In these and many other ways, Slow Food is fighting to sustain the continued existence of something within the realm of food. Something-ness in all realms and of all types needs organizations like Slow Food, and efforts such as these, if it and we are not to be inundated by a sea of nothingness. There is no reason why similar global organizations cannot be formed with the objective of sustaining something, and warding off the onslaught of nothing, in various realms.

In addition to more general organizations like Slow Food, we can conceive of four specific types of global organizations oriented to sustaining and defending places, things, people, and services. Of course, innumerable, much more specific organizations would need to be created to sustain and defend specific places, things, people, and services. Following the basic dimensions laid down in Chapter 2, all of these organizations would be devoted to the maintenance and defense of that which is unique, has local geographic ties, is specific to the times, involves human relations, and is enchanted. Indeed, the Slow Food Movement is devoted to just such things and therefore stands as a successful grobal model for those interested in protecting and furthering something in a world increasingly characterized by the grobal spread of nothing.

While the maintenance and defense of something are both important, it must be remembered that the Slow Food Movement does not want to be seen as creating a museum. That is, it is not interested in simply maintaining the past and present, but it is also concerned with creating the future.

This means that it is important for it, and all organizations like it, to be actively involved in encouraging the creation of *new* forms of something. This may involve new combinations of that which already exists, or the creation of entirely new places, things, people, and services. The latter is no easy task, but it must not be lost sight of in the maintenance of extant forms of something.

Appendix

Nothing

Theoretical and Methodological Issues

In order to keep the main body of this book focused on substantive matters relating to nothing and its grobalization, a range of theoretical and methodological issues have been relegated to this Appendix. While the book can be read without knowledge of the issues covered in this Appendix, one's understanding of the issues raised and the arguments made will be enhanced by it. Let us look, at least briefly, at what previous thinkers have to say about nothing (and related issues) and to what degree they inform our understanding of nothing.

Nothing: Previous Work

Nothing is an awe-inspiring yet essentially undigested concept, highly esteemed by writers of a mystical or existentialist tendency, but by most others regarded with anxiety, nausea, or panic.[1]

This is obviously not the first effort to deal with nothing. The ancients were clearly concerned with nothing, particularly as it relates to the number zero. Early Greek philosophers such as Parmenides and Zeno grappled with nothing and their ideas remain influential. Medieval thinkers such as St. Augustine struggled with the meaning of nothing (equated with the Devil) in the context of religion and God. In literature, it is notable how many times Shakespeare dealt with the issue of nothing, most famously in

Much Ado About Nothing. Barrow offers a good summary of the various ways in which Shakespeare addressed nothing and in the process gives us at least some sense of the range of meanings associated with this concept:

> Shakespeare explored all the meanings of Nothing from the simplicity of zero, the nonentity of the cipher, the emptiness of the void, and the absence of everything it witnessed to the contrast between the whole and the hole that was zero, the circle and the egg, hell, oblivion and the necromancer's circle.[2]

Furthermore, Shakespeare dealt with both the positive ("the power of nothing to generate something") and the negative ("the absence of things, on denial, apathy and silence").[3] While Shakespeare and others "were plumbing the depths of the moral vacuum, others [like Galileo and Pascal] were seeking to create nothing less than a real physical vacuum."[4] The problem of nothing has concerned physicists from Newton to Einstein to today's physicists (and mathematicians).

The most eminent philosophers and social thinkers, including Immanuel Kant, Georg G. W. Hegel, Martin Heidegger, Jean-Paul Sartre, and Jerry Seinfeld (yes, *that* Jerry Seinfeld), have dealt with the issue of nothing. This is not a work in philosophy, and this is not the place to go into a detailed exposition of the recondite thoughts of these worthies. However, a brief overview will prove useful if for no other reason than to show that while the way nothing is used in this volume is not unrelated to these efforts, it is completely different from their senses of nothing.

In fact, the thinking of arguably the greatest philosopher of them all, Immanuel Kant (1724–1804), lies at the heart of this work, especially the distinction—form versus content—that is central to his thinking. As we have seen, nothing is defined here as a particular social *form*—one that is comparatively devoid of distinctive *content*. The use of the terms form and content seems to imply that this analysis is based on Kantian philosophy. Kant defines form as "that which causes the manifold matter of the phenomenon to be perceived as arranged in a certain order."[5] Content, then, is the matter that form arranges. The forms with which Kant is concerned exist in the mind and both precede and organize content: "The matter only of all phenomena is given us *a posteriori;* but their form must be ready for them in the mind . . . *a priori;* and must therefore be capable of being considered as separate from all sensations."[6] While the concepts of form and content inform this work, they are clearly *not* the same as those of Kantian philosophy. This is especially true in the case of forms, since to Kant forms exist in the mind while the forms of concern in this work exist in the social world. Furthermore, within the context of form and content, Kant would reject the idea of nothingness since he dismisses the ideas of pure form, of empty form, of empty space. From Kant's point of view, it would be inaccurate to say that a form (or its content) is empty, that it is nothing. Rather, to Kant, such a statement would be a reflection of the poverty of our conceptual resources. However, this is all of little relevance to the argument being made here since Kant's forms exist in the mind while those discussed here exist in the social world. While it may be that Kant's forms logically cannot be empty of content (they cannot be nothing), that has little or nothing to do with the argument that centrally conceived and controlled *social* forms can be, and increasingly are, (largely) lacking in (distinctive) content.

Georg W. F. Hegel (1770–1831), quite typically, takes a dialectical approach to nothing, examining the dialectical relationship between nothing and being. He argues that they cannot be disentangled because neither exists outside of the relationship of *becoming*. That is, being becomes nothing and nothing becomes being; they disappear, pass over, into one another. They are inseparable, but at the same time they are distinct. The following gives the reader the flavor of this in Hegel's own words:

> *Pure being* and *pure nothing* are, therefore, the same. What is the truth is neither being nor nothing, but that being does not pass over but has passed over—into nothing, and nothing into being. But it is equally true that they are not undistinguished from each other, that, on the contrary, they are not the same, that they are absolutely distinct, and yet that they are unseparated and inseparable and that each immediately *vanishes in its opposite*. The truth is, therefore, this movement of the immediate vanishing of the one in the other: *becoming*, a movement in which both are distinguished, but by a difference which has equally immediately resolved itself.[7]

Such a dialectical approach is, of course, picked up by Marx who analyzes the nature of capitalism in this way. Yet, while Marx sees any number of dialectical relationships in capitalism—forces and relations of production, capitalist and proletariat—he is nonetheless able to separate them out for analytical purposes. Similarly, while we accept the view that there is a dialectical relationship between form and content and, more important, between something and nothing—that each is continually becoming the other—we, too, have in fact had to separate them out for analytical purposes.

Of course, a concept like nothing is anathema to Marx. It is too abstract, too philosophical for his tastes and interests. After all, Marx has a materialistic interest in a concrete analysis of a specific economic form—capitalism. He is interested not only in understanding it, but in helping to hasten its demise. Given such an orientation, ruminating on form and content, their dialectical relationship, and whether form can be devoid of content, would not only not be issues of interest to Marx, but they would be abhorrent to him.

If Kant, Hegel, and Marx are of little direct relevance to this analysis, what of one of their most important successors in sociology—Georg Simmel? After all, the problem may lie in their philosophizing about the concepts and not in the concepts themselves. However, Simmel's conceptualization and utilization of the form–content distinction is too close to that of Kant to be of much use to us.[8] Here is the way Levine expresses the relationship between form and content in Simmel's thinking: *"The world consists of innumerable contents which are given determinate identity, structure, and meaning through the imposition of forms which man has created in the course of his experience."*[9] This is very similar to Kantian thinking except for the fact that rather than being built into consciousness, forms, while they are mental constructs, are human creations and change over time. This gives Simmel's conceptualization of form a more dynamic and more social dimension than that of Kant, but still restricts it to the mental realm.

Of more direct relevance to this work is Simmel's argument that just as people impose forms on the contents of the social world, it is the task of the social theorist to do much the same thing in an analysis of social reality. Thus, Simmel develops such forms as exchange, conflict, and superordination–subordination to analyze the social world. These forms are similar in function to nothing and its major forms—non-places, non-things, non-people, and non-services—used in this volume. That is, these forms have been created by the author to permit a better understanding of the diverse social phenomena that are brought together under each of them and, more generally, the nature of contemporary society.

While this is all within the realm of epistemology, there is also an important ontology that is central to both Simmel's work and this one. Most generally, Simmel is concerned with the "tragedy of culture," which for him involves the growing gap between subjective (the ability to create cultural products) and objective (those cultural products) culture. Because of the division of labor and the specialization of individuals, objective culture proliferates at an exponential rate while subjective culture grows little, if at all. The result (and the tragedy) is that people increasingly lose the ability even to understand, let alone control, the objective culture proliferating around them. Thus, Simmel depicts a world in which people are increasingly alienated from, and oppressed by, their objective culture.

In terms of Simmel's thinking, the concern here is with one aspect of contemporary objective culture: the proliferation of nothing in the form of non-places, non-things, non-people, and non-services. The tragedy today is that those who continue to search for something are likely to be increasingly frustrated by, alienated from, and oppressed by the nothingness that increasingly characterizes today's world. Even more tragic is the fact that more people will be born into, and know little other than, nothing. The result is that we may well be witnessing the birth of a generation for which not only is nothing all they know, but what they value is nothing in its various guises—non-places, non-things, non-people, and non-services. In other words, that which is rich in distinctive substance (something)—places, things, people, and services—may increasingly come to be seen as lacking in comparison to the ubiquitous examples of nothing. The vision of the future, and the tragedy of culture, is one in which virtually all of what most people know and desire exists in the realm of nothing.

Martin Heidegger (1889–1976) and Jean-Paul Sartre (1905–1980) are undoubtedly the two most important philosophers to deal directly with the issue of nothing. Indeed, Sartre's (1943/1958) famous *Being and Nothingness* involves, in part, an effort to critique, and develop an alternative to, Heidegger's sense of nothing. While there are overwhelming differences between them on this issue, and many others, it is important to remember that they are *both* not only philosophers, but also existentialists. This limits the utility of their ideas from the point of view of this work for two basic reasons. First, and most obviously, they operate with a philosophical perspective on nothing rather than the sociological orientation of this work.[10] While the work of both has influenced social theory, the abstractness of their philosophy is difficult to connect with the more mundane concerns (diners, Tommy Hilfiger jackets) of this book. Second, the fact that they are both existentialists means, most fundamentally, that they are led away from a focal concern with the mind[11] and in the direction of individual action in the social world, especially the either/or choices inevitably encountered in that world. Existentialism has a complex relationship to what is undertaken in these pages. On the one hand, existentialism tends to point in a more microscopic direction—actors and the choices they must make—than the generally more macroscopic direction taken here (for example, the grand narrative of increasing forms of nothingness). On the other hand, there is a concern in existentialism for the weakness, the feebleness of people in the face of the large-scale developments taking place around them in the social world. This book does depict a large-scale development in the direction of nothingness and a loss that people seem to have little ability to affect, let alone stop. Thus, the existential perspective is of at least some utility from the perspective of this work.

Heidegger is a famously impenetrable thinker and to try to present even a few of his ideas briefly and clearly is a daunting, if not impossible, task.[12] Perhaps the heart of Heidegger's thinking, and his best-known concept, is *Dasein,* or the field of being. *Dasein* is "solidly in that banal, public, everyday world of our experience."[13] One of the beauties of focusing on *Dasein* is that it dissolves various dichotomies—subject–object, micro–macro— that have dogged both philosophy and social theory. As a result, people exist not in the mind or mental processes, but rather they exist totally in the world. To Heidegger, being "is held out into the nothing,"[14] and at the same time nothingness penetrates *Dasein* and comes to open up within our being. Nothing has both positive and negative implications. On the negative side, it is associated with anxiety, radical insecurity, death and the finitude of life, and a world from which God has withdrawn. Furthermore, nothing is "the *non-sense* that constantly threatens the *sense* of the world . . . everything threatens to lose its significance."[15] However, "Our finitude is such that positive and negative interpenetrate our whole existence."[16] Thus, there is also a positive side to nothingness in Heidegger's philosophy. Most generally, nothing plays an absolutely central role in being. To Heidegger, being is finite and would not develop and expand were it not for nothing. *Dasein* is led into nothing and it is there that being is able to reveal itself. In other words, being must be able to transcend itself in order to be fully human. It is expansion into nothingness that also makes possible the development of selfhood, freedom, fresh illumination, and openness, among other things.[17] For example, if anxiety over our own death is allowed to remain separated from *Dasein,* within nothingness, we are likely to be crippled in various ways and apt to take on only limited projects. However, if *Dasein* embraces death (as part of nothingness), if we accept death and take it into ourselves, then we are liberated to take on essential projects that can enrich our lives and that otherwise might not have been undertaken because of the fear and anxiety over death.

Sartre criticizes Heidegger on various grounds in *Being and Nothingness.* Fundamentally, Sartre is critical of Heidegger's separation and privileging of nothingness. On the latter issue, Sartre emphasizes that Heidegger sees "man a lieutenant of the nothing"; nothing as "belonging to the Being of beings."[18] In contrast, as implied by the title of his book, Sartre privileges being and sees nothingness as integral to it: "Nothingness if it is to be supported by being, vanishes *qua nothingness,* and we fall back upon being. . . . if nothing can be given, it is neither before nor after being, nor in a general way outside of being. Nothingness lies coiled in the heart of being—like a worm."[19] While to Heidegger it is in nothingness that humans express themselves, to Sartre nothing is derived from humanness (being), "from an act, an expectation, or a project of the human being."[20] Similarly, Sartre criticizes the active role accorded nothing by Heidegger. As pointed out above, Heidegger sees nothing penetrating being. Furthermore, in a famous phrase, Heidegger argues, that "nothing nihilates" (or, "nothing nothings").[21] This phrase is subject to multiple interpretations, but however it is interpreted it clearly accords an active role to nothingness. That is, anxiety brings us face to face with nothing, and it is in the confrontation with nothing that the source of the openness of our being is revealed;

nothing sheds light on the nature of being itself.[22] Sartre disagrees with the idea of granting priority to nothing. It is only being that can be active. Nothing cannot nihilate itself; only being can nihilate itself. Nothing is given existence by being, not the reverse. As a result, to Sartre, being is haunted by nothingness (or the void associated with loss). Thus, Sartre sees nothing as derived from being and argues against Heidegger's view that nothing (and being) stems from nothing.

More positively, Sartre has a sense of nothingness that is part of a broad existential perspective. From that point of view, it is generally associated with notions like the "void," "emptiness," and the "meaninglessness of our daily lives."[23] In an essential existentialist text, Samuel Beckett's famous play, *Waiting for Godot,* "Nothingness [in these senses of the term] circulates through every line from beginning to end."[24] It is Beckett who said, "Nothing is more real than nothing."[25] Sartre's own novel, *Nausea* (1938), deals in part with peoples' disgust with the decay and dreadfulness of the nothingness of life.

Thus, Sartre associates nothingness with the world in which we live. Although there are overpowering forces associated with this world, it is important that people resist, say no to, these forces. Thus, the solution to the problem of nothingness lies in the freedom to say no. Freedom, saying no, is by its very nature negative, but it is a creative form of nothingness.

Implicated with the nothingness of the existentialist's world is the absence of God, or of a widely shared set of values. Thus people are on their own; all they have is their own *existence.* Man "exists, and out of the free project which his existence can be he makes himself what he is. When God dies, man takes the place of God."[26] On their own, it is incumbent on people to go beyond themselves, to transcend themselves. This is closely linked to the need for revolutionary activity on the part of individuals. Thus, what people do matters, matters a great deal, and surrendering one's ability to act in this way constitutes "bad faith" as far as Sartre is concerned.

Given this brief overview of the work of Heidegger and Sartre, how do their ideas relate to the way nothing is employed in this work? It is difficult to see much relationship between Heidegger's sense of nothing and the way that concept is used here. Interestingly, however, much more relevance can be found in some of his ideas on technology[27] leading to a world much like the one portrayed by Aldous Huxley in *Brave New World,*

> where everyone is satisfied and pleased ... But what has been lost is depth, awareness and freedom. .... Heidegger's fear is that once we have gained complete control over ourselves and our natural environment, we will have lost our openness to Being ... we will be so entrapped in technology that we will have no suspicion that there are other, richer ways in which beings can show themselves.[28]

In their analysis of my work on McDonaldization from the point of view of Heidegger's thinking on technology, Deena and Michael Weinstein argue that we are enframed by technology, and instead of collaborating with the world, we believe that we are in a position to command it.[29] This line of thinking is clearly related to our discussion of loss in Chapter 7. In this case what is lost is depth, awareness, freedom, openness to being, and the ability to collaborate with the world.

In the case of Sartre, his thinking also has little relevance to our sense of nothing—centrally conceived and controlled forms that are largely devoid of distinctive content—but it too is of great relevance to the idea of loss. Sartre sees nothingness as loss in the sense that God has deserted people and, as a result, they have been left without anything to believe in. Thus, "When God dies, man takes the place of God."[30] However, people must confront the world not only without God, but also without fundamental essences and a basic value system. As a result, people are doomed to both radical insecurity and contingency. All people have is their existence and it is there that they can freely create who they are. Thus, people are left to their own devices in the void. And the void is, among other things, full of that which is morally reprehensible. And Sartre, unlike Heidegger with his more positive view of nothingness, is involved in "nosing out all the sordid and seedy strands of nothingness that haunt our human condition."[31] Much the same could be said about this work, which, in its critical moment, is not simply interested in describing the proliferation of nothing, but is also engaged in delineating the loss in the spread of non-places, -things, -people, and -services. Bear in mind, however, that it is frequently acknowledged throughout the book that nothing also has many positive characteristics and consequences.

It is in ideas like these associated with Sartre, as well as Heidegger's on technology, and perhaps some others, that this book's conception of loss (amid monumental abundance) does have some affinities with existentialism, although in most respects its intellectual affinities lie elsewhere.

The ideas of loss and the void, closely associated with Sartre and the existentialists, are well-reflected in Ernest Hemingway's (1933) short story, "A Clean, Well-Lighted Place":

> Turning off the electric light he continued the conversation with himself . . . what did he fear? It was not fear or dread. It was a nothing that he knew too well. It was all a nothing and a man was nothing too. It was only that and light was all it needed and a certain cleanness and order. Some lived in it and never felt it but he knew it all was nada y pues nada y nada y pues nada. Our nada, who are in nada, nada be thy name thy kingdom nada thy will be nada in nada as it is nada. Give us this nada our daily nada and nada us our nada as we nada our nadas and nada us not into nada but deliver us from nada; pues nada.
>   Hail nothing, full of nothing, nothing is with thee.[32]

Hemingway here seems to be reflecting a number of themes associated with existentialism in general, and Sartre in particular, including the absence of God, the nothingness of existence, and the paradoxical fact that all we have is that existence.

By the way, it is worth remembering that for us, unlike others, nothingness is *in the form* and *not in the person* who is associated with it, at least not necessarily. That is, as is made abundantly clear, many people do *not* find their relationships with empty forms substantively empty; they often see them as quite full of substance. The emptiness is not in them, but in the form. No matter how empty the form, it can be defined as full and, as has been pointed out previously, in a curious way an empty form lends itself to being defined as full since it can be defined in so many different ways. Yet, most generally, it is undoubtedly a great struggle for a person to find substance in an empty form; it would be far easier in a form that is loaded with substance, that is something![33] Thus, if we cannot say that peoples' lives today are empty, we can at least say that because of the increase of largely empty forms, of nothing, it is harder for them to make their experiences and lives full, at least as far as their relationships to these forms are concerned.

It must seem strange to include Jerry Seinfeld in this elite company, but he has already attained that status in a volume, *Seinfeld and Philosophy: [A Book About Everything and Nothing]*, in which a number of philosophers seriously engage the famous television program from a number of different angles and perspectives.[34] Of special interest here, of course, is what the book says about nothing and the fact that *Seinfeld* was a show famously about just that. There are several interpretations of the meaning of nothing in *Seinfeld*, but I think the following gets at it best (in an essay from the above book that relates *Seinfeld* to the work of the famous philosopher, Ludwig Wittgenstein): "the commonplaces of contemporary life . . . the superficies of contemporary life . . . what goes unnoticed because of its familiarity. The show reorients its audience to the real foundations of contemporary life."[35] As laudable, and as sociologically interesting as such a sense of nothing is,[36] once again it is far from the way that term is used here.

Overall, then, a ransacking of the literature on nothing yields relatively little that relates directly to the way that concept is used here, although the negative side of nothing—the idea of loss—discussed in Chapter 7 is better informed by at least some of this work. Perhaps the reason that a review of this literature yields so little is because the focus in this book is a sociology of nothing, and sociologists have had little or nothing to say directly on this topic, likely because it seems too philosophical. It is hoped that this work, with its more sociological sense of nothing as forms (structures) involving centralized conception and control and lacking of distinctive substance, will lead to greater sociological interest in this topic.

Some Modern Methodological (Epistemological) Problems

There are various methodological problems associated with what has been undertaken in these pages. In the main, a very modern approach is employed here and there are difficulties involved with it from a modern perspective. One of these problems relates to whether it is possible (it is not!) to combine the placement of a given phenomenon (place, thing, person, or service) on each of the five continua employed here (see Chapter 2) in some way and thereby come up with a single something–nothing score for it. This is a modern problem not only because it involves mathematical or statistical analysis, but also because it seeks to reduce something quite complex and variegated to a single number.

One of the major sources of this problem is traceable to the complexities derived from the fact that any given phenomenon will certainly *not* fall in exactly the same place on each continuum. It is possible, even likely, that a phenomenon will stand toward one end of several continua and near the middle, or even the other end, of other continua. This does give us a much richer sense, one with many nuances, of what constitutes something and nothing, as well as a better feel for the character of any given phenomenon. However, it poses a series of methodological problems such as the difficulties involved in combining such diverse placements in order to come up with an overall sense of where a given phenomenon is to be positioned on the something–nothing continuum. For example, a ranking at the extreme end of one continuum (say unique–generic) might contribute to an overall score that obscures the fact that the phenomenon in question stands toward the opposite end on all the other continua.

A related problem involves the relative weight of each of the continua and, if they are weighted differently, how much each might contribute to some overall something–nothing score. The problem would be eased a bit if we could assume that each continuum is of equal importance and thereby a score on one would be given the same weight as the score on all the others. However, the difficulty is that there is no reason to assume that these continua are equally weighted, and it would be extremely difficult, to put it mildly, to come up with some system of weighting each of them. Furthermore, even if that could be accomplished (extremely unlikely), there is no reason to assume that the relative weighting of the continua for one phenomenon (say, chilies with walnut sauce) would be the same as that for another (say, muscle cars). For these and other reasons, the calculation of something–nothing scores is literally *impossible* and, in any case, *undesirable*. That is, a single score would conceal far more than it would reveal.

Rather, these continua, as well as the concepts that constitute their poles, should be viewed as "sensitizing" devices.[37] That is, they sensitize us to the several components of somethingness and nothingness and to the fact that a multitude of factors and judgments go into gaining a sense of where a given phenomenon stands on the overall something–nothing continuum. The number of subcontinua, and the possibility of very different placements on each of them, should be seen as offering the possibility of a much richer sense of any phenomenon under consideration and why it occupies the position that it does on the something–nothing continuum.

A modern point of view would not only lead us to want to quantify all of this and to create a single score, but it would also tend to accord considerable stability to such a score. However, it is clear that none of this is carved in stone. No phenomenon has a rigid and unchanging position on either the something–nothing continuum or on any of the subcontinua that make it up. Positions are constantly undergoing changes with the result that overall judgments about somethingness–nothingness may vary over time, as well as across geographic space. It is even possible for an entity that was at one time something to become nothing and, conversely, for nothing to become something. In terms of the latter, naturally beautiful sites that were at one time something are often transformed into nothing (or something approaching it) as a result of overdevelopment (for example, as discussed earlier in this book, the bay in Porto Cervo, Sardinia). Conversely, things once considered nothing can, over time, become something. One could imagine, for example, the Smithsonian creating a display devoted to the first McDonald's (it already has one on the Automat), perhaps at some point in the distant future when McDonald's has passed from the scene. Or, the cloned casino-hotels described earlier in terms of nothing might in the future achieve the status of something if they were to become lovingly maintained landmarks of an earlier era while the Las Vegas that surrounds them underwent dramatic changes.

Furthermore, there are often powerful efforts to transform nothing into something; to give nothing "soul," or at least the illusion of it. For example, in *Enchanting a Disenchanted World,* I discuss settings that are quite disenchanted (and therefore tend toward the nothing end of the continuum) but are nonetheless, or perhaps because of their lack of enchantment, deeply involved in trying to enchant themselves (to become something, or at least create the illusion of it; to give themselves soul).[38] Unfortunately, such efforts almost always fail, primarily because they are dominated by the inauthentic, the rationalized, and the disenchanted. Thus, contemporary Las Vegas, in spite of massive efforts to enchant itself in these ways, is a paradigm of nothingness. Indeed, what it has succeeded in doing is to transform itself from something surrounded by natural tourist attractions (the desert, startling formations of red rock) to nothing. Of course, it also demonstrates that nothingness pays; far more people are drawn to its outrageous nothingness than would be drawn to a Las Vegas in something approaching its pristine state or to Death Valley today, which is far closer to such a state than is contemporary Las Vegas.

The latter makes it clear that the reverse process also takes place—there are efforts to transform something into nothing. However, while the nothing to something route is undertaken consciously (if often misguidedly), the something to nothing road is usually undertaken unconsciously. It is rarely the case that people set out to destroy that which is something, but that is often the unintended consequence of seeking to create nothing. This is the classic problem created by developers, especially those who are allowed to operate in an unfettered way in areas characterized by something. Thus, for example, innumerable ocean beaches (something) are all but ruined by overdevelopment that permits high-rise hotels and condominiums, motels, housing communities, and shops and restaurants to edge their way down almost to the shore line. The same can be said of such developments near, or on, wetlands, lakes, mountains, and the like.

While the above are some key modern problems associated with the something–nothing continuum and the relevant subcontinua, the truly crucial methodological problems relate to the issues to be discussed in the following section(s).

Modern Concepts in a Postmodern Age

While a series of continua has been outlined above (especially in Chapter 2), the fact is that making the basic distinctions that lie at their base, as well as the most general distinction between something and nothing, poses great, and in some ways insurmountable, difficulties. Most of these difficulties have been pointed out and underscored by postmodernists. Indeed, postmodern social theory makes it difficult, to say the least, to operate with a modernist perspective such as the one being employed here (for example, one that is based on a series of binary oppositions, one that seeks to differentiate something from nothing and, worse yet, concerns itself with the loss of that which has distinctive substance).

Yet, as Zygmunt Bauman has pointed out (in yet another modernistic binary opposition), the basic choice today seems to be between a postmodern sociology and a (modern) sociology of postmodernity.[39] That is, we can either employ an irrational sociology, perhaps even one with the science fiction–like characteristics of at least some of Jean Baudrillard's work (especially the more recent texts[40]), or we can use a (modern) rational sociology in an effort to analyze the irrationality of postmodernity (assuming an association between it and the loss of somethingness). In this case, a postmodern sociology would eschew the wide range of conceptual tools developed in this book and deal with the issue of something–nothing in a far looser, perhaps even fictional manner. This stands in stark contrast to the more modern and rational approach employed in this book to analyze the irrationalities associated with the increase in nothingness.

In spite of his great sensitivity to postmodern social theory and the characteristics of the postmodern social world, Bauman opts to employ a sociology of postmodernity. He does so because the irrationality of a postmodern sociology would seem to militate against any kind of reasoned scholarly analysis. It is for much the same reason that this book follows the course charted by Bauman and does a sociology of postmodernity.

Thus, at least part of what has been presented here is a reasoned analysis of a fundamental irrationality of the contemporary social world, a world that for want of a better term can be described as postmodern. The basic irrationality analyzed in these pages is the increasing loss of something amid monumental abundance. Why is it that when so many different forms of something can be preserved, created, constructed, manufactured, or built, more often than not it is that which is substantively empty or contributes to a larger emptiness that comes into existence? And, why is it that when we have the possibility of filling our lives with something, we are increasingly opting for such empty forms?

Substantive answers to questions like these have been presented throughout this book. Here we must attend to the epistemological issues raised by adopting a modernistic approach to this subject (in the questions raised, and so on) given the postmodern critiques of such an approach. What might some of those issues be?

For one thing, even though they represent the opposite ends of a series of continua, each of the sets of characteristics developed here implies modernistic binary oppositions: something–nothing, unique–generic, and so on. One of the lessons of postmodern theory is that the propensity of modernists to make such polar distinctions tends to have dangerous intellectual and practical implications. The main danger lies in the fact that even though these distinctions seem to be made on "value-free" intellectual grounds,[41] there is often a proclivity to value one alternative over the other. This would seem to be true of this work where, in spite of my efforts to present the key terms in a dispassionate way, it is hard to avoid the view that something is generally to be preferred to nothing. Indeed, it appears that I place a high premium on something and devalue nothing, especially given the latter's association with the loss of that which is locally conceived and controlled and loaded with distinctive content. Furthermore, it is clear that I am concerned about the long-term historical trend away from something and in the direction of nothingness and that I fret over the decline of the former and the ascent of the latter. As was made clear in Chapter 1, my main worry is the negative consequences associated with the long-term trend toward empty forms and the tendency to emphasize, perhaps overemphasize, the positives associated with that development and to ignore the negatives, especially the loss, that are also linked to it.

Staying with ideas gleaned from Bauman's work, modern social theory and this work in particular are better described as having a *gardener* than a *gamekeeper* mentality and approach. That is, the implication would seem to be that it is not enough to be a good gamekeeper and simply oversee the smooth operation of the social world (even including the trend away from something and toward nothing). Rather, one must be a gardener and seek to sustain something as well as to prevent at least some forms of nothing (those with mostly negative characteristics and few redeeming qualities) from taking root. Furthermore, a logical derivative of this view would be that efforts must be made to eliminate such forms of nothingness that are able to develop roots and that threaten to undermine something.

Of course, the logical extremes of the gardener mentality involved the efforts of the Nazis to eliminate all Jews (and others) and those of Stalin and his henchmen to murder or exile everyone with even a remote possibility of posing a threat to his regime. This exemplifies the grave dangers associated with modern thinking. Since anything can be defined as problematic, a modern gardener approach legitimates efforts to "solve" such problems by, for example, eliminating minorities and threats to one's regime.

Clearly, it is impossible to align oneself with such a point of view and such a set of policies, but does that mean that one cannot make any value judgments? And then support actions designed to implement those judgments? We would certainly end up with a denuded and impotent sociology were we to answer both of those questions in the affirmative. Thus, while aware of the abuses, we must retain the modern ability to critique society and to propose policies that would deal with the sources of societal problems. Clearly, in light of recent history, and the postmodern critique, any such approach must learn from previous mistakes and proceed with great humility and respect for all humans and the way they choose to live their lives. Thus, we must acknowledge and respect the right of people to choose what has been described here as substantively empty. All we can do is describe the problems and dangers associated with such a choice (as well as the attractions of something) and hope that at least some heed the warnings.

A second lesson is that such binary oppositions are not only difficult but perhaps impossible to construct. The modern mind has tended to make clear-cut discriminations where no such simplistic distinctions are possible. For example, it is a daunting task, to put it mildly, to distinguish between that which is authentic and inauthentic. In a world in which virtually everything is a human product, or has been affected by human action, how does one clearly distinguish between authenticity and inauthenticity? At first glance, a natural site like Mt. Everest might be considered clearly authentic, but in fact it has been profoundly affected by pollution in general and more specifically by the now quite large number of people who have attempted to climb it. All sorts of debris, including human corpses, have been left behind in efforts to climb the mountain. In fact, climbers are endeavoring to clean up at least some of the mess as they undertake new efforts to climb the mountain.[42] There are even plans afoot to build a cyber café at base camp on the mountain.[43] Thus, even something as remote as Mt. Everest is no longer unequivocally authentic and if Mt. Everest cannot be considered authentic, then what can?

Mt. Everest and many other sites are natural localities that have been altered, largely inadvertently, by human action and made inauthentic, but in many other cases humans have set out quite consciously to create sites (and much else). How does one distinguish between an authentic and an inauthentic human creation? A classic work of art—say Rembrandt's *Night Watch* on display at the Rijksmuseum in Amsterdam—may seem to be clearly authentic since it was a singular artistic creation of one world-renowned artist. However, like all other works of great art, it is likely that it has been altered by pollution, wear and tear, efforts at restoration, and the sheer passage of time. Furthermore, *Night Watch* was vandalized and great efforts were made to restore it to its original state (of course, no matter how great the efforts, such attempts are doomed to failure). The result is that while it *may* have at one time been authentic (assuming, for example, that Rembrandt did the work and not his disciples), it is clearly no longer authentic, or at least not totally authentic.

On the other hand, few human creations would seem to be quite as inauthentic as the contemporary Las Vegas casino-hotel. The Paris casino-hotel is obviously a simulation of the city of Paris, France. There is even a simulated Arc de Triomphe exactly half the size of the authentic arch in the "real" Paris. However, it is certainly something real—a real casino-hotel, if not the real Paris, France—and to many visitors who will never have a chance to visit the latter, it may seem quite authentic.

While we might all agree, in spite of this discussion, that Rembrandt's *Night Watch* is authentic (or at least lies toward the authentic end of an authentic–inauthentic continuum) and any given casino-hotel is inauthentic (or lies at the inauthentic end of that continuum), this discussion illustrates the difficulties involved in making the kinds of choices that lie at the base of each of the continua outlined above as well as the overarching something–nothing continuum.

Also in the realm of the postmodern (and feminist) critique is the seeming "god's eye" perspective that pervades this discussion. It seems as if I, as the author, am able to make distinctions (as well as judgments) that most, if not all, others are unable to make. What gives me the right, or the ability, to make a set of distinctions that no one else seems capable of making? There is clearly an elitism associated with this self-aggrandizement, but there is an even more profound form of elitism associated with all of this. That is, since most people seem to prefer the nothing end of each of the continua discussed here (such as the Paris casino-hotel to Paris, France), there is an implied criticism of those choices and a clear preference for the something end of the continuum. It seems as if I know more than most people and that I am capable of making judgments—especially that they are increasingly choosing nothing over something *and* that that is a problematic choice—that most people are unable to make.

Thus, this analysis would seem to be subject to many of the same criticisms as those leveled at the Frankfurt School of social theory. The Frankfurt School was a group of neo-Marxian thinkers (for example, Max Horkheimer, Theodor Adorno, Herbert Marcuse) who were known, among other things, for their analyses and critiques of "mass" or popular culture (for example, the movies, radio programs). They came to be criticized for being elitists who were analyzing and judging the tastes of most people from their standpoint as elite intellectuals. There was no basis for the argument that elite tastes (for example, classical music) were any better than popular tastes (for example, jazz).

This points to at least two major differences between the approach taken here and that of the Frankfurt School. First, there is a set of objective criteria developed in Chapter 2 (as questionable as such a modern undertaking might be). Second, while there is certainly a critical thrust to this analysis, especially in Chapter 7 and the discussion of loss, the bulk of it is devoted to outlining what is meant by nothing and then describing the trend toward, and ultimately the globalization of, nothing.

Then there is the seeming objectivity of this analysis and the fact that it flies in the face of the fact that the something–nothing continuum and the subcontinua are based on a series of subjective judgments not only by this author but more importantly by people in general. Am I acting as an objective social scientist in distinguishing between something and nothing (as well as the other subcontinua)? Is my placement of Rembrandt's *Night Watch* and the Paris casino-hotel on that continuum objective? Is such objectivity possible? Or even desirable? Postmodernists, and other critics of the scientific model in the social sciences (for example, pragmatists), would answer negatively to all of these questions.

Salvaging a (Semi-) Modern Approach

Even though an awareness of these and other problems informs the way in which something–nothing and the related subcontinua are treated in this book, especially in the utilization of continua rather than simple dichotomies, modernism pervades this analysis and creates problems for us in light of the postmodern critique. However, while it is important to be sensitive and responsive to those postmodern critiques, it is my view that we must follow the lead of Jurgen Habermas and many others, and *not* give up on "modernity's unfinished project."[44] This decision has a variety of practical, political, and theoretical implications. In terms of our concerns here, it means that we retain the right to critique aspects of the contemporary world, to develop Archimedean points (base lines) in order to make those critiques, to suggest that we ought to be wary of at least some social trends (especially the loss associated with the trend away from something and toward nothingness), to root out those social trends with excessively negative consequences (especially those associated with the loss of that which is locally conceived and controlled and has distinctive substantive content), to nurture positive trends (for example, remaining instances of something), and to create new ones (for example, new types of something) wherever possible.

Furthermore, it is necessary to seek to salvage some vestige of the modern theoretical approach and its arsenal of concepts. And, as a matter of fact, this is far from the first such effort—several strands of social thought have sought to do just that. For example, a group of thinkers associated with what is known as French "post-postmodernism" has sought to rescue a sense of humanism from the postmodern (and poststructural) critique that much harm has been done in the name of humanism.[45] The best-known of the critics of humanism and its abuses is Michel Foucault.[46] In contrast, one representative of post-postmodernism writes of "a new defense of universal, rational norms in morals and politics, and especially a defense of human rights."[47] A similar defense of another idea closely linked to modernism—liberalism—emerged from the same intellectual milieu. Included under this heading would be support for such ideas as "human rights, constitutional government, representation, class, individualism."[48]

However, the movement to rescue modern concepts is far broader than that found in the work emanating from a small group of French intellectuals. Seidman and Alexander recently described a "new social theory."[49] One aspect of that "new theory" is its interdisciplinarity[50] and the resulting renewed interest in a series of modern ideas—"justice, democracy, equality, and authenticity"[51]—that has flowed into many different fields from work in political and moral philosophy. However, in light of the postmodern critique, and many others, these modern concepts have had to be modified and adapted to the new intellectual realities. Even though they have been altered, sometimes quite radically, they have been retained, thereby keeping alive modernity's unfinished project, at least in a conceptual and theoretical sense.

For example, in a major example of modern theorizing, John Rawls developed a famous general theory of justice in the 1960s.[52] However, within a decade that theory, which applied to all societies and all times, came to seem untenable. Thus, Michael Walzer sought to move away from such a general theory, but to retain a notion of justice, by arguing that there are spheres of justice (for example, the family, the economy) and standards of justice appropriate to each sphere.[53] Thus, there is no general standard of justice appropriate to society as a whole. Walzer retains a notion of justice, but within a narrower context.

Similarly, Alasdair MacIntyre rejected the idea of a universal theory of rationality, but instead suggested that rationality can be understood only within historically established traditions.[54] This, of course, means that there are multiple theories of rationality, but at least MacIntyre has *not* given up on the concept of rationality that goes to the very heart of modernity and modern thinking and theorizing (including the part of this work that deals with the notion of McDonaldization).

The objective here is to follow the direction charted by Walzer, MacIntyre, and other "new" social theorists and to seek to rescue our ability to talk about the distinction between not only something and nothing, but also the more specific distinctions used throughout this book.

This means that it is fully recognized here that what is considered to be something or nothing (as well as judgments that relate to the other distinctions and continua discussed in Chapter 2), as well as judgments about where any given phenomenon lies on that continuum and its subcontinua, vary from one group to another and one from one society to another. The same point applies to differences over time. Judgments of something–nothing, as well as all of the others, vary from one time to another. However, even though these considerations limit and temper our ability to discuss the issues of concern in this book, they do not prevent us from doing so. What this means, above all, is that we must adopt a stance of great humility toward doing this kind of analysis and making various judgments about the placement of phenomena on the something–nothing continuum in general and the other subcontinua in particular.

This means that the general position taken in this book, as well as the continua developed to allow us to adopt that position, is but one of many possible positions on, and modes of analysis of, the issues of concern here. For one thing, this means that other scholars can and do approach the issues of concern here in very different ways. More important, lay people analyze these topics in their own ways and adopt their own stances on these issues and those positions will differ from, and perhaps be diametrically opposed to, the positions and modes of analysis adopted here. Yet, those realities do not mean that it is impossible for a scholar to develop a general mode for analyzing the distinction between something–nothing (and related subcontinua) and to take a position on social changes related to it. As long as we recognize that such a scholarly approach is only *one* among many possible approaches, both scholarly and lay, we are on (reasonably) safe ground.

Furthermore, it is recognized that the kind of general analysis undertaken here will need to take into account analyses done, and the realities of, other times and places. Thus, this is very much an analysis done from within the context of the American scholarly community, especially that aspect of it concerned with globalization and consumption, in the early 21st century. It is clear that similar analyses undertaken by those associated with other scholarly communities and at other times and places would be quite different. Even more different, not only from the analysis presented here but also from each other, would be analyses done during the same time period by laypeople who reside in diverse communities such as a working-class area of Chicago, an upper-class area of Los Angeles, and a middle-class suburb of Atlanta. Furthermore, those done a century ago, or a century from now, in those areas, or by scholars with a variety of orientations, would also vary greatly from the one presented here.

In spite of a recognition of these and other limitations on the kind of modern study of a postmodern (at least in part) world undertaken here, our objective is to rescue our ability to use ideas like something and nothing, just as other scholars have sought to find ways of salvaging concepts like humanism, liberalism, justice, and rationality in a postmodern age.

A (General) Standpoint Theory

The general position to be adopted here, in light of the preceding discussion, is that despite the useful critiques of the postmodernists (and feminists) and the adaptations made by the new social theorists, we cannot give up on general concepts and the use of continua and the dichotomies that undergird them. Indeed, given the profusion of different theoretical positions—for example, what the feminists and others call *standpoint theories*—there is also a place for general theory *as long as it is recognized that in spite of its more general aspirations, it is acknowledged to be but one of many different possible theoretical and conceptual approaches.*

Indeed, a general theoretical approach offers a touchstone for the comparative analysis and study of other approaches adopted by other social thinkers and laypeople. It becomes a kind of ideal–typical theoretical position against which other positions can be measured. It is not necessarily more correct than these other positions, but its high level of generality allows it to function as a measuring rod for the many other available positions. This constitutes a modern approach, but it is one that takes into account many of the recent criticisms of such an approach. It is a general theoretical approach, but it recognizes the existence of many other approaches and does not accord itself supremacy over the others. If it has an exalted status, it is methodological rather than theoretical or substantive. It recognizes that it stems from a specific place in the social world and from a specific point in time. Other theories from other places and times are not only desirable, but necessary and inevitable. All of those theories can be measured and assessed against the kind of theoretical orientation being developed here. Does the general something–nothing continuum (or any of the subcontinua) work in other places and other times? If yes, does it work in the same way or differently? Would a specific phenomenon (say a housing community) be placed differently in other places and at other times?

While there are undoubtedly highly variable answers to each of these questions, they can be answered in general terms. First, it seems likely that the something–nothing continuum, or at least some version of it, would work, at least in a general way, at all times and in all places. Second, it is likely that it would work very differently at different times and in different places. Third, and most important, the placement of any specific phenomenon would vary enormously at different times and in different places. This can easily be demonstrated in terms of many of the examples used earlier to illustrate the subcontinua associated with something–nothing. Thus, the humble Kia or Neon automobile used in Chapter 2 to illustrate timelessness and therefore nothing (or at least one of its aspects) undoubtedly currently has a coterie of enthusiasts who regard it as something. Furthermore, it is highly unlikely, but not impossible, to imagine a time in the future that some group will come to define that car as something because it comes to be seen as making an important statement (for example, low-cost functionality) about the era in which it is created.

What all of this points to is the fact that in the real world something–nothing is, as was made clear earlier, a matter of social definitions. People can define *anything* as existing at the something or the nothing end of the continuum, or anywhere in between. Furthermore, those definitions are highly variable and changeable. The movie critic might define Alfred Hitchcock's original *Psycho* (1960) as something, but a subgroup of movie-goers might well prefer Gus Van Sant's 1998 much-maligned remake of that movie. Similarly, the Edsel automobile was almost universally deemed nothing when it was first introduced and, as a result, quickly failed. However, today there are enthusiasts who regard the Edsel as something, in part (and quite ironically) because it was such a massive failure.

While this variation resulting from differences in the definition of the situation is of great significance, it does not negate the importance of developing a general approach to something–nothing. In fact, it could be argued that this great variation makes such a general approach even more important. Without such a general approach, our ability to address such issues as the relationship between something and nothing would be compromised, perhaps fatally. A general approach may not be any better than the myriad other approaches out there, but it does perform the methodological function of allowing us to think about these issues and to compare and contrast the range of available orientations, *including* the general approach being proposed here.

While this is in line with the previously discussed efforts to salvage modern concepts, it differs from many of them in the sense that it retains a general sense of those concepts rather than attempting to delimit them, often quite radically. However, as pointed out above, this general orientation is retained not because it is better or more accurate than others, but because such a general position offers a methodological ground to *both* compare and contrast all other positions and with which to analyze the social world. In terms of the latter, of course, it must be borne in mind that it offers only one of myriad ways of analyzing that world.

Thus, what I want to argue here is that rather than contradicting standpoint theory, the perspective adopted here is consistent with it. That is, what I am arguing is that *one* standpoint is the kind of general perspective outlined here. Standpoint theorists have generally rejected this kind of perspective because of its aspiration to be *the* definitive perspective. However, if we begin by acknowledging that such a modern, general perspective is just one among many, and none is inherently superior to the other, I think we have responded to the concerns of standpoint theorists. Clearly, adopting a general perspective is no less, but no more, legitimate than adopting a perspective from any number of specific perspectives, especially those of various nonacademic and disadvantaged groups.

Much of this can be traced to Karl Marx's argument that it was the proletariat that was destined to gain a far more accurate picture of the nature of capitalism than the bourgeoisie. That is, in contemporary terms, the standpoint of the proletariat was inherently superior to that of the bourgeoisie. This was later transformed into the view that the perspectives of women in general, women associated with particular ethnic and racial minorities, and those of minorities in general were superior to those of members of the majority group and of scholars associated with it. Much of the logic for the latter was also in line with Marx's perspective. That is, Marx argued that the bourgeoisie could never attain an accurate picture of the system that encompassed them because they were too enmeshed, and too busy trying to succeed, in it. In contrast, the proletariat was the loser in the system and its position was growing worse over time. Eventually, it would lose all stake in the system and, in fact, many would fall through the floor of the system to become part of the reserve army of unemployed. Freed of virtually all stake in the system, the proletariat would be in a position to develop an unvarnished view of the way capitalism works. It is this kind of argument that stands behind many varieties of standpoint theory and points not only to the legitimacy of standpoint perspectives, but to their inherent superiority.

However, accepting standpoint theory, and even the more dubious view on its superiority, does not mean that one cannot accept the legitimacy of the kind of general theoretical perspective adopted here. We acknowledge that it is far from the only perspective available, and it may well not be the optimal point of view, but it *is* a legitimate viewpoint among the welter of possible perspectives.

Alternative Perspectives

Based on the discussion in the preceding section, there are basically four different ways of looking at the something–nothing continuum, as well as the various subcontinua discussed in Chapter 2.

First, they can be viewed as a set of objective factors used by the scholarly analyst to get at basic truths about the social world. Taken on its own, this would be an old-fashioned modern approach to the issues of concern here and difficult, if not impossible, to defend.

A second way of looking at the elements discussed in Chapter 2 is to view them as the objective factors ordinarily employed by people in general (not the author or the scholarly community) to distinguish, as dispassionately as possible, between something and nothing. In this perspective, people are seen as rational and this is in accord with the view of the actor in rational choice theory. This has the advantage of shifting the focus away from my judgments as the author of this book, or those of the scholarly community in general, and in the direction of the social world and the lay people whose ways of judging and dealing with something–nothing are what really matter. This also has the advantage of being part of Seidman and Alexander's "downward shift" in contemporary social theory.[55] Among other things, this means a shift down from the abstract concerns of social theorists to those of the people being theorized. However, this position remains vulnerable and questions can be raised about it that are similar to those raised about the first position described above. For example, is it possible to find such representative "ordinary people"? Who are these people to conclude that they, and only they, have divined the truly objective factors involved in making the distinctions of concern here? Are there any such things as truly objective factors? Are these the objective factors that people use? Are there others? Can anyone truly be objective about anything, including what it is that distinguishes something from nothing?

A third possibility is that these are the main factors that lay people ordinarily take into account *subjectively* in arriving at social definitions of what is something and nothing, and on the placement of phenomena on the relevant continuum and subcontinua. This acknowledges the fact that whether or not there are objective criteria by which one can make these distinctions, what really matters are peoples' subjective definitions of these criteria and the broader something–nothing continuum. However, in this case, it is argued that it is possible to identify the general factors involved in subjective definitions of something–nothing. That is, the criteria articulated above are, from this perspective, nothing more than broad areas in which people arrive at subjective definitions of something–nothing. While this position does emphasize subjectivity and moves away from an objective sense of the factors associated with something–nothing, it retains a somewhat modernist orientation (the objective domains in which subjective definitions are developed) and remains vulnerable, at least in part, to the kinds of criticisms outlined above (how do we know that these, and only these, domains are involved in those definitions?).

The final possibility is that neither these supposedly objective factors nor any others are involved in defining something–nothing; such judgments are *totally subjective*.[56] No one really knows much about how people go about making these judgments, or any others. A wide range of personal and more general factors is involved in *every* individual decision on something–nothing as well as the various factors involved in placing any given phenomenon on that continuum. Thus, it is not only impossible to identify any objective factors, but it is pointless to try because every decision is highly personal and subjective.

In order to write this book I remained agnostic on which of these four positions is most appropriate. (In fact, there are arguments to be made for each of them.) However, I did proceed *as if* the last position on total subjectivity was *not* the one to be adopted here. This permitted me to use the something–nothing continuum and the various subcontinua; they would have been irrelevant and unnecessary had the last position been adopted. In terms of the others, I leave it to the readers to mull over the possibilities and decide on the best way to use the tools developed here.

The introduction of subjectivity into this discussion leads, at the minimum, to a more nuanced grand narrative. In Chapter 1 it was argued that there is a long-term trend away from something and in the direction of nothing. However, it is likely that many in the past did not share this book's views on the something that predominated then, and many today do not share our perspective on the nothing that increasingly predominates now. That is, at least some in the past did not see much of substance in the something of the past and, more important, there are those today who do see a great deal of substance in that which is seen here as nothing. This leads to another grand narrative: People are increasingly seeing substance (something) in that which is seen here from an "objective" point of view as substance-less (nothing). To put it another way, *people are increasingly defining nothing as something*. Thus, we seem to live in a topsy-turvy world in which something is nothing and nothing is something. For example, many people today regard Venice, Italy, as nothing while it is the Venetian casino-hotel in Las Vegas that is seen by them as something.

Potential Criticisms

I can anticipate a number of criticisms of this analysis. The first is likely to be a charge of elitism. That is, it is likely that some critics will note that much of what is being described here as centrally conceived and controlled empty forms, and criticized for involving loss, are in fact among the most popular places, things, people, and services in the world. Virtually everyone seems to want these things and in great numbers and with great frequency. I am likely to be portrayed as an intellectual snob who is simply aghast at what the masses seem to want so desperately.

A second major criticism is that all of this is animated by a romantic vision of the past and a deep desire to turn back the clock and return to a more idyllic world where the forms of nothingness described in these pages did not exist, or at least not in such profusion.

I must admit that there is some truth to these criticisms. I am an intellectual, at least I have most of the characteristics people usually associate with that label (I am a professor, I have a PhD, I write "learned" books and articles, and so on). In addition, I was born and grew up in an era before the arrival of most of the forms of nothingness described in these pages had come into existence, let alone proliferated throughout the United States and eventually the world. Furthermore, I grew up in New York City in an era in which it, and most other great cities in the world, were dominated by something in its myriad forms. There is no question that these and other factors incline me to being both elitist and incurably romantic, nostalgic about the past, and desirous of a world more characterized by something than nothing.

In spite of the latter, I am not unmindful of the problems associated with the past, with those things that I am calling something, and with the many advantages that have come into being with the growth of nothing in its various forms. For example, small town America circa 1950 may have been characterized by many phenomena that stood toward the something end of the continuum, but there were innumerable problems in comparison to today's small towns dominated by nothing. For example, the local greasy spoon may have had home-cooked food, and offered much conviviality, but its standards of cleanliness were far lower than today's fast-food restaurant. Close personal relationships were more likely to exist, but they were apt to be fraught with more conflict than is found in today's fast-food restaurants where people are unlikely to have enough contact with one another to have even the possibility of conflict. More generally, the small American town in this era offered little in the way of diversity. Today, because of the arrival of Wal-Mart with its myriad products, small town America has far more available to it than ever before. In the food realm, the wide range of fast-food chains offering pizza, tacos, fajitas, lobster, "bloomin' onions," and so on give small town diners much more diversity in food than ever in their history.

One need not want a return to the past, indeed such a return is both impossible and undesirable, in order to be critical of the present and of future trends. A more appropriate basis for a critique of the present than a comparison to the past is a comparison to some sense of what the future could be, at least potentially, in this case a future that is rich, perhaps richer than ever before, in somethingness.

Rational Choice?

Another criticism, worthy of separate consideration, is that most people are rationally choosing the various forms of nothing described in this book. They are looking at the various alternatives, weighing the pros and cons, and in the main deciding that nothing is often preferable to what, here at least, is considered something. In effect, by opting for these things, people are defining that which is considered here to be nothing as something. This is not only a lay defense of the proliferation of nothing, but it also draws on one of the most powerful theories in the social sciences (especially economics, but also of growing importance in sociology): rational choice theory. If people are coldly and rationally assessing their alternatives and routinely choosing, say, Starbucks over local coffee or tea shops, who am I (or anyone else) to critique such a choice? To say that it does, or does not, involve loss?

There is certainly merit to the rational choice argument. Consumers do look at things like price and convenience and choose one alternative over others because it is lower in price or is more convenient. Thus, for example, ATMs do seem more rational than human cashiers, credit cards more rational than cash, and a pair of Gap jeans or khakis more rational than custom-made slacks. Furthermore, it could be argued that people are also rational about esthetic matters and, for example, choose a Whopper over a home-made hamburger because they think it tastes better. However, there are at least two reasons to question the rational choice perspective in this context (and many others).

First, most of the forms of nothing, because they tend to be mass-produced and distributed, are likely to be heavily advertised and marketed. Both advertising and marketing are usually oriented toward leading people to make choices based on non-rational, versus rational, considerations. Thus, while a few advertisements for the various forms of nothing might emphasize rational considerations like price advantage, most play on a variety of personal and emotional issues in order to lead the consumer in the direction of choosing a given product. Thus, for example, a recent ad campaign for Gap khakis shows young people happily swing-dancing, presumably aided by the fact that they are wearing those pants. The implication is that anyone who buys such pants will be (or at least feel) more youthful, more active, and dancing with attractive (and perhaps far younger) partners. To the degree that such ads are successful, people purchase Gap khakis, and many other things, for emotional and personal reasons, not rational reasons like price and convenience. It is likely that a very similar, perhaps even identical, no-name pair of khakis could be purchased more conveniently and at a lower price at the local K-Mart and that those slacks would have just about the same advantages as those available at the Gap (except for the label).

Second, the purveyors of nothing seek to gain an overwhelmingly power-ful position in the markets that they serve so that if one wants to use their products, one is hard-pressed to use anything but their brand or those of a limited number of other purveyors of nothingness. Thus, a rational choice on the part of the consumer becomes difficult, if not impossible, because there are often few alternatives to nothing. For example, if you want to use a credit card, your choice is pretty much between two almost identical brands—Visa and MasterCard (American Express and Diners Club are smaller players and, in any case are charge cards,[57] not credit cards). If you want to avoid the problems associated with credit cards (especially indebtedness) and use cash, you are likely to find it more difficult to use cash in some settings, especially when making expensive purchases. Furthermore, if you eschew credit cards, you are likely to experience difficulties in obtaining other types of credit (e.g., mortgage). Grantors of other types of credit now like to see a successful history of using credit cards and making timely payments on the sums due.

To take another example, if you want to eat lunch on the well-traveled main highway between Washington, D.C., and New York City, and you do not want to exit the road, you *must* eat in a fast-food restaurant. Travelers may rationally decide that the cholesterol, fat, and salt in fast food are too dangerous and that it is better to eat a healthy meal at a local restaurant. However, there are *no* local restaurants on that road and little that is healthy for sale in the chain restaurants. One's choice in this situation is dictated by structural realities and not by rational choice.

This gets at the broader point of this discussion of the national and global proliferation of nothing. That is, as nothing comes to dominate in more and more sectors and geographic regions, people have less and less choice of any kind, let alone rational choice. It is this that is the primary argument of sociologists against those, both in and out of the discipline, who adopt a rational choice perspective.

A supporter of the latter might argue that our traveler from Washington, D.C., to New York could pack a healthy lunch for the trip or venture off the highway and spend the time necessary to find a local restaurant offering healthy foods. However, these alternatives are much more difficult and awkward than simply choosing to accept structural realities and eat junk food. In this sense, it is rational to eat such food in fast-food restaurants. However, the rationality of this choice is dictated by the fact that nothing— the fast-food restaurants in this case—has, like a cancerous growth, virtually eliminated the healthier alternatives. In other words, it is rational within an increasingly narrow world that is being circumscribed by the forces that profit from nothing. Truly rational choices require some real alternatives, not endless copies of the same or similar things.

Are Consumers Judgmental Dopes?

The issue of rational choice is related to another critique that can be made of this analysis. That is, the implication seems to be that consumers are often judgmental dopes who are routinely choosing nothing over something. As we have seen, this kind of position has been associated with the Frankfurt School, among others, and has been roundly, and to some degree rightly, criticized by contemporary students of consumption.[58] There are several reasons why I do not think the analysis presented here is assailable on these grounds. First, the choice of nothing, at least in its primary meaning here, is usually the smart thing to do. That is, there are, as we have seen, many advantages associated with nothing, and that is one of the reasons why so many choose it so often. Second, with forms characterized by nothing (in the descriptive sense) progressively driving out something, it is harder and harder to find, let alone opt for, something. Thus, increasingly the problem is not with people's choices but with the range of options readily available to them. Finally, with forms of something progressively disappearing, younger generations have less and less contact and experience with them. Thus, the choice of what is described here as nothing is not a function of a lack of intelligence, but of a lack of experience. As time goes by, there will be increasingly fewer opportunities to choose something, with the result that nothing will be the increasingly most popular, if not the only, choice. What the last two points lead to is the conclusion that it is temporal and spatial (geographic) changes that are leading to the increasing propensity to choose nothing over something.

However, it is also the case that the implicit argument being made here is that if everyone gave as much time and thought to the issues discussed in this book as has the author, they too would be concerned about the long-term trend in the direction of nothing and the loss associated with it. They would perhaps make a greater effort to avoid at least those aspects of it that maximize loss and to make fewer choices that contribute to its spread. However, this has nothing to do with how smart anyone involved is, but rather about possessing the necessary information and a broad enough perspective to assess historical changes and contemporary realities. Having come to the end of this book, the reader now knows what I know. It is up to the reader, then, to decide whether there is any validity and utility to what is presented here and then to decide what, if anything, to do about the developments and problems discussed. While I would like to see the reader choose a particular course of action, I do not think that other choices are indications that those making them are judgmental dopes.

Notes

Chapter 1

1. See, for example, Stiglitz's attack on the economics of globalization, especially the policies of the International Monetary Fund (IMF); Stiglitz, J. E. (2002). *Globalization and its discontents.* New York: W.W. Norton.

2. In more formal academic terms, we might think of the *dialectic* between something and nothing as lying at the core of this analysis.

3. Barrow, J. D. (2000). *The book of nothing* (p. 1). New York: Pantheon Books.

4. As we will see, there are some forms of nothing that are locally conceived or controlled. While the reader should keep this caveat in mind throughout this book, it will not necessarily be repeated in future definitions of nothing.

5. The use of the terms *form* and *content* bring to mind the work of the philosopher Immanuel Kant and many neo-Kantians, especially within sociology, such as Georg Simmel. We will discuss their ideas in the Appendix, where it will be clear that they use the terms differently than they are employed here.

6. Ritzer, G. (1995). *Expressing America: A critique of the global credit card society.* Thousand Oaks, CA: Pine Forge Press; Manning, R. (2000). *Credit card nation.* New York: Basic Books.

7. There are such things as "personality" cards, whereby a card might identify the holder as, for example, an Elvis fan or indicate one's astrological sign. Of course, there is then little to distinguish among the large numbers of holders of each of these types of cards.

8. U.S. Bureau of the Census. (2001). *Statistical abstract of the United States, 2001* (p. 735). Washington, DC: U.S. Government Printing Office.

9. The idea of a grand narrative has been greatly criticized by postmodernists, but modernists continue to develop such theories of general historical developments. Furthermore, the postmodern critique is called into question by the fact that so many postmodernists (including and perhaps especially the ultimate postmodern social theorist Jean Baudrillard) in fact develop grand narratives of their own. That is not to say that there are not great problems with grand narratives and we will have occasion to discuss that issue, and its relevance to this book, in the Appendix. See Lyotard, J.-F. (1984). *The postmodern condition.* Minneapolis: University of Minnesota Press.

10. Appadurai, A. (1996). *Modernity at large: Cultural dimensions of globalization*. Minneapolis: University of Minnesota Press.

11. However, it should be borne in mind that medicine (and education) can be seen as arenas of consumption.

12. Walsh, R. (2003, January 16). Globalization's McBacklash. *Houston Press*. Retrieved from www.houstonpress.com.

13. As in the case of the caveat about the definition of nothing, there are some forms of something (see discussion of VW Beetle in Chapter 2) that are centrally conceived and controlled. Once again, while the reader should keep this caution in mind throughout this book, it will not necessarily be repeated in future definitions of something.

14. For a critique of dichotomous thinking, see Mudimbe-Boyi, E. (Ed.). (2002). *Beyond dichotomies: Histories, identities, cultures, and the challenge of globalization*. Albany: State University of New York Press.

15. Gottdiener makes this point, based on his discussion of airports, arguing that it is "wrong to create a dichotomy between place and placelessness because there are always elements of both in any milieu." See Gottdiener, M. (2000). *Life in the air* (p. 60). Lanham, MD: Rowman and Littlefield.

16. If the grand narrative being described here is from personal lines of credit (something) to credit cards (nothing), where does that leave money? When we recognize that most nations have different currencies, then money is something in contrast to the major credit card brands that are used in many different nations; in this comparison money is unique (something) and credit cards are generic (nothing). Once again, we can see the trend from something to nothing (the use of money declining and that of credit cards increasing) as we head toward the eventuality of a cashless society.

When we look at the euro and its recent (2001) arrival we see, yet again, a change from something (the money specific to many different European countries) to nothing (a currency common to all participating nations). The euro is more generic than national currencies and to make it even more generic, images specific to any given European nation have been removed from the faces of its bills. For a bit more on this, see Chapter 5.

17. The great German social theorist, Max Weber, praised rationalization in general, and the bureaucracy in particular, for greatly limiting such biases in decision making. See Weber, M. (1921/1968). *Economy and society* (3 vols.). Totowa, NJ: Bedminister Press.

18. This implies, of course, that there were other phases of globalization that did *not* have an association with nothing. Clearly, for example, mercantilism was a system with a global reach, but because, for one thing, it existed before an era of mass production, it was less likely to foster the global spread of nothing.

19. In the course of the book this grand narrative will be specified even further by, for example, making it clear that in many cases something is also increasing, but just not as rapidly as nothing.

20. Augé, M. (1995). *Non-places: Introduction to an anthropology of super-modernity*. London: Verso; see also, Morse, M. (1990). An ontology of everyday

distraction: The freeway, the mall and television. In P. Mellencamp (Ed.), *Logics of television: Essays in cultural criticism* (pp. 193–221). Bloomington: Indiana University Press; Relph, E. (1976). *Place and placelessness.* London: Pion.

21.   Augé, M. (1995). *Non-places: Introduction to an anthropology of super-modernity* (p. 79). London: Verso.

22.   Wilmington, Delaware, and its banks are described in Chapter 7 in terms that lead us to think of them as non-places.

23.   The notion of an "ideal type" is also derived from the work of Max Weber. For a good overview of constructive typologies, see McKinney, J. (1966). *Constructive typology and social theory.* New York: Appleton-Century-Crofts.

24.   Berger, P., & Luckmann, T. (1967). *The social construction of reality.* Garden City, NY: Anchor.

25.   For example, talking to one employee may reinforce a sense of nothing, while another employee may deal with us in a very human manner.

26.   Getting a handle on what is meant here by nothing (and something) is obviously not easy. Three additional ideas may help the reader get a better feel for this elusive concept. We can begin with the idea of an *empty manifold.* (I would like to thank Bob Antonio for suggesting these clarifications to me.) A manifold involves the centrally conceived and controlled repetition, perhaps over and over, of some phenomenon. Most, if not all, forms of nothing are composed of such a multitude of units and furthermore each of those units is largely or totally empty. A fast-food restaurant is a largely empty manifold in that its form can be repeated throughout the United States and the world, while the nature of its contents can vary greatly between chains, between parts of a country, or from nation to nation. Similarly, shopping centers can be seen as empty manifolds, with each highly similar iteration filled with variable content. The fast-food restaurant and the shopping mall are both non-places, and nothing, at least in the sense of empty manifolds, is relatively easy to see in such physical settings.

Other terms that relate to, and enhance our understanding of, nothing are *template* and *grid.* The latter concept communicates much the same idea as a (empty) manifold; that is, a series of parallel lines (like each of the ten-yard lines on a football field; a *grid*iron) repeated over and over with "nothing" between the lines. Thus, the endless repetition of a chain of fast-food restaurants can be seen as forming a kind of grid, as can their dispersion throughout a given geographic area. Indeed, fast-food chains such as McDonald's and Starbucks give careful study to the geographic placement of their settings and, in at least some places, set them up in a grid-like fashion.

The idea of a template, while related to that of a manifold and a grid, emphasizes something a bit different about nothing. Here we are talking about some sort of basic pattern or mold that is conceived and used centrally to create each new form. Since the same pattern is used over and over, each iteration of the form is more or less exactly the same as every other. Thus, all popular, branded commodities are clearly based on templates and in almost all cases each iteration is, for all intents and purposes, exactly like every other one (say, cans of Coca-Cola, each type of Nike athletic shoe, every Whopper, and so on). Certainly, non-places are created on the basis of templates, although they are now more variable in their construction (at least on the surface) and less obviously like every other non-place of a given type. In spite of these variations, a basic template undergirds the creation of every non-place such as a fast-food restaurant. And there are even templates used to train and constrain non-people and their offering of non-services (e.g., those created and used at McDonald's Hamburger University as well as by graduates of that university who come to own or manage a McDonald's restaurant).

Terms like (empty) manifold, grid, and template help us to get a better understanding of nothing. At the same time, naturally, they enhance our sense of something as that which is *not* a product of a manifold, is *not* created on the basis of a grid or in a grid-like manner, and is *not* based on a template used to churn out many nearly identical copies.

Closely related to the idea of nothing, and more specifically manifold, template, and grid, is the idea of simulations, most closely associated with the work of the French postmodernist, Jean Baudrillard. To Baudrillard, a *simulation* is a copy of a copy for which there is no original. It could be argued that *all* forms of nothing are also simulations. That is, it is originals that have distinctive content (and are something), but copies—simulations—are by definition lacking in such content; they are nothing! Further, it is precisely simulations that tend to be centrally created and controlled. Baudrillard's assertion that the world is being increasingly characterized and dominated by simulations is consistent with this book's grand narrative about the global proliferation of nothing. (See Baudrillard, J. [1983]. *Simulations*. New York: Semiotext[e].)

27. In a clever, satirical essay titled "Nothing: a Preliminary Account," Donald Barthelme endeavors to come up with a list of nothing, an effort that is doomed to failure since everything he iterates turns out *not* to be nothing. To Barthelme, nothing is the opposite of that which exists; it is characterized by "non-appearances, no-shows, incorrigible tardiness." However, that is not quite what we mean by nothing here. The nothing of concern throughout this book—the credit card, the fast-food restaurant, the casino-hotel—clearly exist; there is no question about their existence. The issue, again, for us is the existence of centrally conceived and controlled forms that are to a large degree devoid of substance. Here, nothing (although it never exists in a pure form) clearly exists, indeed it is an increasingly dominating existence, but it is an existence that is largely empty of distinctive content. See Barthelme, D. (1979). Nothing: A preliminary account. In *Guilty pleasures* (pp. 161–165). New York: Farrar Straus Giroux.

28. Barrow, J. D. (2000). *The book of nothing* (p. 10). New York: Pantheon Books.

29. Even though it was composed of blank pages, *The Nothing Book,* published in 1974, went through several editions. See Barrow, J. D. (2000). *The book of nothing* (p. 7). New York: Pantheon Books.

30. Lindley, D. (2002, September 8). Quaint's nice, but sprawl makes me weak at the knees. *Washington Post,* pp. A1, A4.

31. Lindley, D. (2002, September 8). Quaint's nice, but sprawl makes me weak at the knees. *Washington Post,* p. A1.

32. Lindley, D. (2002, September 8). Quaint's nice, but sprawl makes me weak at the knees. *Washington Post,* p. A1.

33. Lindley, D. (2002, September 8). Quaint's nice, but sprawl makes me weak at the knees. *Washington Post,* p. A4; italics added.

34. Lindley, D. (2002, September 8). Quaint's nice, but sprawl makes me weak at the knees. *Washington Post,* p. A4.

35. Lindley, D. (2002, September 8). Quaint's nice, but sprawl makes me weak at the knees. *Washington Post,* p. A4.

36. Lindley, D. (2002, September 8). Quaint's nice, but sprawl makes me weak at the knees. *Washington Post,* p. A4.

37. While, on occasion, they may have been purchased, often they are gifts from friends and family in the developed world, hand-me-downs, or cheap knock-offs of the originals.

38. Retrieved from www.nikewages.org/FAQs.html

39. Stiglitz, J. E. (2002). *Globalization and its discontents.* New York: W.W. Norton.

40. Glantz, A. (2003, February 26). Jordan's sweatshops: The carrot or the stick of US policy? *Corpwatch.*

Chapter 2

1. This idea is related to Relph's thinking on the "soulful" and the "soulless" in his work on places and spaces; see Relph, E. (1976). *Place and placelessness.* London: Pion; Crang, M. (1998). *Cultural geography.* London: Routledge. I have generally, but not always, shied away from using these terms because they are even more value-laden than nothing and something and even more difficult to translate into concrete sociological terms.

2. While I disagree with much else of his analysis (e.g., his opposition to agency), this is in accord with Stephan Fuchs's recent critique of essentialism, especially its preference for "static typologies and rigid classifications" and its "failure to allow for variation." See Fuchs, S. (2001). *Against essentialism: A theory of culture and society* (p. 14). Cambridge, MA: Harvard University Press.

3. Tonnies, F. (1940). *Fundamental concepts of sociology (Gemeinschaft und Gesellschaft).* New York: American Book.

4. McKinney, J. (1966). *Constructive typology and social theory* (p. 101). New York: Appleton-Century-Crofts.

5. However, as will be discussed in the Appendix, it is not simply a matter of somehow just adding these positions together to come up with an overall score, and therefore placement, on the something–nothing continuum.

6. For a critique of this kind of dichotomous thinking and an alternative, see Baldamus, W. (1976). *The structure of sociological inference.* New York: Barnes and Noble.

7. A caveat is needed here. These continua, taken individually and collectively, are not infallible in distinguishing something from nothing: there are anomalies. For example, as a general rule, they are better at distinguishing the man- (and woman-) made from that which is largely natural. Thus, while these continua work very well

on shopping malls, credit card loans, Gap jeans, Valentino gowns, and the like, they work less well on things like diamonds, pets, and lettuce. For example, most would consider diamonds (and other precious stones) to be something, and we would not quarrel with that view, but diamonds lie toward the nothing end of several of the continua employed above. While diamonds clearly stand toward the something end of the unique–generic (every diamond is unique, although it would take an expert to find most differences) and the enchanted–disenchanted (a diamond, especially one that is of high quality, is quite magical) continua, it could be argued that they are closer to the nothing end of the other continua since they lack local ties, they are time-less, and they are dehumanized. In spite of the fact that they stand toward the nothing end of more subcontinua than they do toward the something pole of others, the fact is that on the overarching something–nothing continuum, diamonds would stand toward the something end because of their distinctive substance. This includes not only the idiosyncratic characteristics of every stone, but also the specific events and people involved in the giving and receiving of them.

At one level, the case of a diamond simply illustrates the utility of the various tools developed here and the subtleties involved in analyzing any given phenomenon. At another level, it could be interpreted as revealing limitations in the use of these tools. It may well be that there are phenomena like diamonds that are not well analyzed with this conceptual arsenal. It could be that there is something quite unusual about diamonds (and a limited number of other phenomena) that makes them different from most other phenomena. Or, it could be that they reveal some weaknesses in the concepts and flaws in the basic argument. However, it is clear that, in the main, the tools developed here do a good, though imperfect, job of analyzing that which is of concern in this book. In an era where the faith in modernity in general, and modern science in particular, has been undermined, if not destroyed, that may be the best we can do.

Nonetheless, overall, and especially in terms of the focal interests of this book, these continua are useful in making the general distinctions that lie at the base of this work and, more generally, in helping us to understand better the general trend toward the increase of nothing.

8.   While it is obvious the other four subcontinua to be discussed below can be subsumed under the something–nothing continuum, that is not immediately obvious in this case. Unique–generic sounds very similar to, if not identical with, something–nothing. However, unique–generic is more specific than something–nothing. For example, unique (one-of-a-kind) literally refers to something singular (e.g., Rembrandt's *Night Watch*), but that which is something can be repeated (e.g., a particular style of vase preferred by a potter), perhaps even a number of times (although at some point we begin to move from something to nothing).

9.   Of course, it is true that even the most generic of products—say a Big Mac—has subtle differences. Any given Big Mac may have a bit more lettuce, a few less sesame seeds on the bun, and so on. Nonetheless, it is clear that each Big Mac is far better described as being generic than unique.

10.   By the way, to avoid the charge of elitism (more on this as we proceed), the chef can either be a professional in an expensive restaurant or someone who uses homegrown products with great skill to cook gourmet meals at home at low cost.

11.   Although many more of them are likely to lack distinction and to be unnatural chemical additives of one kind or another.

12.   Wilbur, T. (1993). *Top secret recipes: Creating kitchen clones of America's favorite brand-name foods.* New York: Plume.

13.   Pitzer, G. (2001). *Secret fast food recipes: The fast food cookbook.* Marysville, MI: Author.

14.   Few such lunches, however, could be considered gourmet.

15.   This continuum and the next one reflect the great interest these days in the social sciences in space and time.

16.   Although they may have complexity of another type derived from a multitude of inputs from many locales. For example, scholarly work often derives much of its complexity from the multitude of intellectual inputs and the idiosyncratic way in which a particular scholar puts them together. The currently popular fusion cuisine is another, more mundane, example of complexity stemming from a variety of ingredients and recipes from many different parts of the world.

17.   Interestingly, Oaxaca recently voted to ban one of the major examples of nothing—McDonald's. See "McDonald's, rechazado por el munipio de Oaxaca, Mexico." Retrieved December 12, 2002, from www.clarin.com/diario/hoy/t-488322.htm

18.   Retrieved from www.manos-de-oaxaca.com/jr_frmst.htm

19.   Retrieved from www.manos-de-oaxaca.com/intro.htm

20.   Thorstein Veblen pokes fun at the preference for handmade products and the kind of devaluation of mass-produced products found here. See Veblen, T. (1884/1994). *The theory of the leisure class.* New York: Penguin Books.

21.   Although the mixing might well produce a unique clay.

22.   Hunt, M. C. (2000, January 12). Beyond burritos: US cooks starting to appreciate bright flavors of authentic Mexican cooking. *San Diego Union-Tribune,* p. 1ff (FOOD).

23.   Retrieved from www.manos-de-oaxaca.com/intro.htm.

24.   Although it is true that it could be tied to the time period since the introduction of mass production and the Industrial Revolution. However, mass production is applied to an enormous range of products and has little to do with pottery per se. The real point is that mass-produced products in general, and pottery in particular, cannot easily be tied to any particular time period; they are more likely to seem time-less in the sense in which this term is defined below.

25.   Sometimes, they can reflect a place as well as a time period. One example is the "lowrider" car associated with Chicano subcultures in the United States circa 1950, but now attracting attention in other parts of the world. See Johnstone, F. (2002, August 10). Lowriding: The lowdown. *The Daily Telegraph,* p. 16.

26.   Campisano, J. (1995). *American muscle cars.* Metro Books.

27.   Other automobiles that lie toward the something end of the continuum reflect other eras of American history. Examples include the Stutz Bearcat (first produced in 1914), which reflects the exuberance and hubris of the United States about to emerge as a true world power in WWI, and the Jeep, whose enduring appeal is traceable to the mobility and triumph, through the mass manufacture of war matériel, of the United States in WWII.

28. Of course, there are other, much more conscious reasons for defining muscle cars as something, not the least of which is their powerful engines.

29. Retrieved from www.bbc.co.uk/motoring/tcts_hall_of_fame/beetle.shtml

30. Retrieved from www.geocities.com/thenewtbird/

31. Retrieved from www.fordvehicles.com/cars/thunderbird/index.asp?bhcp=1

32. Retrieved from www.canadiandriver.com/articles/bv/convertible.htm

33. And this is not just a price issue: The original (and to a lesser extent the contemporary) Volkswagen was quite inexpensive.

34. Jacobs, G., & Klebahn, P. A. (1999). *Bug tales: The 99 most hilarious, outrageous and touching tributes ever compiled about the car that became a cultural icon.* Oval Window.

35. Patton, P. (2002). *Bug: The strange mutations of the world's most famous automobile.* New York: Simon and Schuster; Kiley, D. (2001). *Getting the Bugs out: The rise, fall and comeback of Volkswagen in America.* New York: Wiley; Ludvigsen, K. & Hirst, I. (2000). *Battle for the Beetle.* Cambridge, MA: Bentley; Nelson, W. H. (1998). *Small wonder: The amazing story of the Volkswagen Beetle.* Cambridge, MA: Bentley.

36. Of course, mass manufacturing is not, in itself, the source of the difference because muscle cars and Volkswagens are mass manufactured as well.

37. Patton, P. (2002). *Bug: The strange mutations of the world's most famous automobile.* New York: Simon and Schuster.

38. Iacocca, L., & Novak, W. (1986). *Iacocca: An autobiography.* New York: Bantam Books.

39. Of course, these are just tendencies. For a discussion of humanized relations in a non-place, the mall, see Lewis, G. H. (1990). Community through exclusion: The creation of social worlds in an American shopping mall. *Journal of Popular Culture, 24,* 121–136.

40. We will have much more to say about the Internet, and its relationship to nothing, in Chapter 6.

41. The University of Phoenix also offers more traditional classes in various locations.

42. Esquivel, L. (1992). *Like water for chocolate* (pp. 10–11). New York: Doubleday.

43. Esquivel, L. (1992). *Like water for chocolate* (p. 39). New York: Doubleday.

44. And muscle cars have fans throughout the world.

Chapter 3

1. Crang, M. (1998). *Cultural geography.* London: Routledge; Foote, K. E., Hugill, P. S., Mathewson, K., & Smith, J. (1994). *Rereading cultural geography.* Austin: University of Texas Press.

2. Relph, E. (1976). *Place and placelessness.* London: Pion; see also Jacobson, D. (2002). *Place and belonging in America.* Baltimore, MD: Johns Hopkins

University Press; Feld, S., and Basso, K. H. (Eds.), (1996). *Senses of place*. Santa Fe, NM: School of American Research Press.

   3. Relph, E. (1976). *Place and placelessness* (p. 141). London: Pion.

   4. Relph, E. (1976). *Place and placelessness* (p. 143). London: Pion.

   5. Augé argues that places and non-places are intertwined today and the possibility of being a non-place is never far these days from any place. Augé, M. (1995). *Non-places: Introduction to an anthropology of supermodernity*. London: Verso.

   6. Augé, M. (1995). *Non-places: Introduction to an anthropology of supermodernity* (p. 34). London: Verso.

   7. Augé, M. (1995). *Non-places: Introduction to an anthropology of supermodernity* (p. 78). London: Verso.

   8. Castells, M. (1996). *The rise of the network society*. Malden, MA: Blackwell.

   9. One problem with Castells's conceptualization is that it tends to conflate space (non-place) and place.

   10. Ironically, because it was the first of its kind, Levittown appears to have developed, at least in some ways, into something.

   11. Exceptions are those communities—Disney's Celebration in Florida is the best example—that are purposely designed to simulate communities of a bygone era. However, as simulations, these communities cannot be considered unique; they are better seen as copies and as generic and therefore closer to the nothing, rather than the something, pole.

   12. Kuntsler, J. H. (1994). *The geography of nowhere: The rise and decline of America's man-made landscape*. New York: Touchstone Books. Kuntsler gets at his idea of place in a later book; see Kuntsler, J. H. (1996). *Home from nowhere: Remaking our everyday world for the twenty-first century*. New York: Simon and Schuster. For an interesting view of nowhere (in this case those who live full-time in motor homes and often park them in Wal-Mart parking lots when they are on the road), see *This is Nowhere* (Missoula, MT: High Plains Film, 2002).

   13. An interesting example of a non-place is described in Diller, E., & Scofido, R. (2002). *Blur: The making of nothing*. New York: Harry N. Abrams. Diller and Scofido are architects who designed a structure for Swiss Expo 02 that, through the use of jets of water, was designed to appear to be a blur, nothing, in Lake Neuchatel. It was not only designed to appear to be a blur from a distance, but there was nothing inside and the structure performed no function other than allowing visitors to experience the blur.

   14. Hurley, A. (2001). *Diners, bowling alleys and trailer parks*. New York: Basic Books; Jones, S. (2002, April 8). Back to basics: Silver Diner retreats from growth to focus on food and service. *Washington Post*, pp. E1, E12. Another example, this time in Great Britain, is the fish and chips shop; see Walton, J. K. (1992). *Fish and chips and the British working class, 1870–1940*. Leicester, U.K.: Leicester University Press.

   15. Schlosser, E. (2000). *Fast food nation*. Boston: Houghton Mifflin.

   16. Oldenburg, R. (1989/1997). *The great good place*. New York: Marlowe; Oldenburg, R., ed. (2001). *Celebrating the third place*. New York: Marlowe.

17. Oldenburg, R. (1989/1997). *The great good place* (p. 18). New York: Marlowe.

18. Oldenburg, R. (1989/1997). *The great good place* (p. xvii). New York: Marlowe.

19. Oldenburg, R. (1989/1997). *The great good place* (p. 16). New York: Marlowe.

20. May, R. A. B. (2001). *Talking at Trena's: Everyday conversation at an African American tavern* (p. 25). New York: New York University Press.

21. May, R. A. B. (2001). *Talking at Trena's: Everyday conversation at an African American tavern* (p. 19). New York: New York University Press.

22. Neighborhood restaurants come to be "homes away from home." (1996). *Nation's Restaurant News, 30*(33), p. 66.

23. Watson, J. (1997). Transnationalism, localization, and fast foods in East Asia. In J. Watson (ed.), *Golden arches east: McDonald's in East Asia* (p. 6). Stanford, CA: Stanford University Press.

24. Watson, J. (1997). McDonald's in Hong Kong: Consumerism, dietary change, and the rise of children's culture. In J. Watson (ed.), *Golden arches east: McDonald's in East Asia* (pp. 77–109). Stanford, CA: Stanford University Press.

25. Ritzer, G. (2000). *The McDonaldization of society*. Thousand Oaks, CA: Sage; Ritzer, G. (1998). *The McDonaldization thesis*. London: Sage; Ritzer, G., ed. (2002). *McDonaldization: The reader*. Thousand Oaks, CA: Pine Forge Press.

26. An apparent exception is the children's play areas associated with many fast-food restaurants. They do enhance the quality of the experience for children (and their parents who can get a brief respite while the children play), but the major reason they are there is as a magnet to children and their parents; fast-food restaurants, especially McDonald's, could not survive without the business of children and those who must accompany them. In addition, they serve to segregate the children in the play area and out of the way of adult diners who may want to avoid children.

27. Hurley, A. (1997). From hash house to family restaurant: The transformation of the diner and post-World War II consumer culture. *Journal of American History, 83*, pp. 1282–1308; Hurley, A. (2001). *Diners, bowling alleys and trailer parks*. New York: Basic Books.

28. The movie *Diner* (1982) is a nostalgic look at the role that one diner played in the lives of young people in Baltimore in the late 1950s.

29. McDonald's recently announced that it was closing more than 100 restaurants and scaling back its plans for new outlets.

30. McDonald's may have reached its peak, at least for the moment, but other American (e.g., Starbucks) and foreign (e.g., Pret A Manger—owned in part by McDonald's) chains are more than compensating for McDonald's recent decline.

31. An obvious attempt to associate itself with a paradigmatic great good place.

32. Applebee's, "America's favorite neighbor," reopens its doors just blocks away from ground zero. (2002, July 22). *Business Wire*.

33. Jones, S. (2002, April 8). Back to basics: Silver Diner retreats from growth to focus on food and service. *Washington Post*, p. E12; italics added.

34. An exception might be a chain like Applebee's, but its efforts to adapt to the local environment seem more like simulations than authentic efforts to be local. Acting local, when it is a result of corporate dictates, is less convincing than those efforts that stem from truly being embedded in the local.

35. Kokopellis are replicas of ancient images of a humpbacked flute player. For more on this see, Chapter 5 as well as Malotki, E. (2000). *Kokopelli: The making of an icon*. Lincoln: University of Nebraska Press.

36. Interestingly, there is an Atlanta restaurant by that name, a simulation based on a simulation found in a book and a movie.

37. One exception to this is Johnny Rockets, which seeks to re-create the 1940s hamburger and malt shop, down to the soda jerk outfits. However, the name communicates something very modern, perhaps to compensate for the chain's orientation to the past. The very contemporary name and the old-fashioned orientation tend to cancel each other out leaving one with a sense of time-lessness.

38. Jones, S. (2002, April 8). Back to basics: Silver Diner retreats from growth to focus on food and service. *Washington Post*, p. E1.

39. Interestingly, instead of seeking to appear time-less, there is a not-insignificant number of McDonaldized settings that seek to simulate those of a particular time period. Good examples abound in Las Vegas, including the Excalibur Hotel-Casino that simulates England of the 11th century and New York, New York that conjures up an image of pre-1950 New York City. We already mentioned the Applebee's chain that presents itself as an old-fashioned neighborhood restaurant. Then there are English pub chains (Inn Partnership, Scottish and Newcastle) that seek to export this phenomenon with deep roots in English history to many places around the world. All of these are, of course, simulations and there is an enormous difference between a setting that emerges from a particular time (and place) and one that simulates a time period (and a place).

40. Jones, S. (2002, April 8). Back to basics: Silver Diner retreats from growth to focus on food and service. *Washington Post*, p. E12.

41. Jones, S. (2002, April 8). Back to basics: Silver Diner retreats from growth to focus on food and service. *Washington Post*, p. E12.

42. Ritzer, G. (1999). *Enchanting a disenchanted word: Revolutionizing the means of consumption*. Thousand Oaks, CA: Pine Forge Press; Ritzer, G. (2000). *The McDonaldization of society*. Thousand Oaks, CA: Sage.

43. Petrini, C. (2001). *Slow food*. Chelsea, VT: Chelsea Green; Kummer, C. (2002). *The pleasures of slow food: Celebrating authentic traditions, flavors, and recipes*. San Francisco: Chronicle Books; Miele, M., & Murdoch, J. (2002). Slow food. In G. Ritzer (Ed.), *McDonaldization: The reader* (pp. 250–254). Thousand Oaks, CA: Pine Forge Press.

44. Although they could simply purchase, say, 100 grams of sliced Culatella ham and eat that, perhaps in a sandwich, as quickly as a Big Mac. This reminds us of the fact that the problem is not fast food, but the kind of fast food sold by the chains and the way it is consumed.

45. McCracken, G. (1988). *Culture and consumption: New approaches to the symbolic character of consumer goods and activities*. Bloomington: Indiana University Press.

46. Schlosser, E. (2000). *Fast food nation*. Boston: Hughton Mifflin.

47. Ritzer, G. (2002). Revolutionizing the world of consumption: A review essay on three popular books. *Journal of Consumer Culture, 2*, pp. 103–118.

48. Schlosser, E. (2000). *Fast food nation* (p. 171). Boston: Houghton Mifflin.

49. The study of things, bringing things into social analysis, has been popularized by actor-network theory. See Law, J., & Hassard, J., (Eds). (1999). *Actor network theory and after*. Oxford: Blackwell.

50. Following and extending Marx and neo-Marxian theorists, it could be argued that both workers and consumers are *alienated* from non-things like Big Macs.

51. Goffman, E. (1959). *Presentation of self in everyday life*. Garden City, NY: Anchor Books; Ducharme, L., & Fine, G. A. (1995). The construction of non-personhood and demonization: Commemorating the traitorous reputation of Benedict Arnold. *Social Forces, 73*, pp. 1309–1331; Davis, F. (1959). The cabdriver and his fare: Facets of a fleeting relationship. *American Journal of Sociology, 65*, pp. 158–165.

52. Disney's worlds have been subjected to innumerable analyses. See, for example, Fjellman, S. (1992). *Vinyl leaves: Walt Disney World and America*. Boulder, CO: Westview; Bryman, A. (1995). *Disney and his worlds*. London: Routledge.

53. Oldenburg, R., (Ed.). (2001). *Celebrating the third place*. New York: Marlowe.

54. May, R. A. B. (2001). *Talking at Trena's: Everyday conversation at an African American tavern* (p. 14). New York: New York University Press.

55. Appadurai, A. (1996). *Modernity at large: Cultural dimensions of globalization*. Minneapolis: University of Minnesota Press.

56. Carlson, J. (2001, December 15). In a bar named after a mead hall, bartender talks to many. *Associated Press*.

57. Schutz, A. (1931/1967). *The phenomenology of the social world*. Evanston, IL: Northwestern University Press.

58. On the other hand, Disney, his movies, his characters, and his worlds have all become cultural icons.

59. Interestingly, there is now a cruise ship on which people are able to purchase very expensive condominiums and live in them full-time as they circumnavigate the globe, perhaps over and over.

60. Nelson, J. (2001). On mass distribution: A case study of chain stores in the restaurant industry. *Journal of Consumer Culture, 1*, pp. 119–138.

61. Klein, N. (2000). *No logo: Taking aim at the brand name bullies*. Toronto: Vintage Canada.

62. The search for origins is another modern idea that has fallen victim to the critiques of such new social theorists as the postmodernists.

63. Although, as we have seen, some mass-produced automobiles (muscle cars, the VW Beetle) come to be defined by some people as things. Even the Model-T Fords that survive today would likely now be considered things by aficionados.

64. Goldman, S. L., Nagel, R. N., & Preiss, K. (1995). *Agile competitors and virtual organizations: Strategies for enriching the customer*. New York: Van Nostrand Reinhold.

65. Pine, J. (1993). *Mass customization: The new frontier in business competition*. Cambridge, MA: Harvard Business School Press.

66. It has also led to an increase in things, although the increase in things was minuscule in comparison to the increase in non-things.

Chapter 4

1. Among the theorists who have addressed the issue of globalization are Bauman, Z. (1998). *Globalization: The human consequences*. New York: Columbia University Press; Beck, U. (2000). *What is globalization?* Cambridge: Polity; Giddens, A. (2000). *Runaway world: How globalization is reshaping our lives*. New York: Routledge; Kellner, D. (2002). Theorizing globalization. *Sociological Theory, 20,* pp. 285–305; Urry, J. (2003). *Global complexity*. London: Polity. We will deal with some of the other important contributions to this literature in the next several pages.

2. As we will see, the meaning of this concept is not unambiguous. An effort will be made to sort this out in the ensuing discussion.

3. Rostow, W. W. (1960). *The stages of economic growth: A non-communist manifesto*. Cambridge, U.K.: Cambridge University Press; Tiryakian, E. A. (1992). Pathways to metatheory: Rethinking the presuppositions of macrosociology. In G. Ritzer (Ed.), *Metatheorizing* (pp. 69–87). Beverly Hills, CA: Sage. The opposition to modernization theory plays a particularly central role in the work of Appadurai. See Appadurai, A. (1996). *Modernity at large: Cultural dimensions of globalization*. Minneapolis: University of Minnesota Press.

4. This line of work was inaugurated by the publication of Wallerstein, I. (1974). *The modern world-system*. New York: Academic Press.

5. See, for example, Frank, A. G. (1967). *Capitalism and underdevelopment in Latin America*. New York: Monthly Review Press.

6. Appadurai, A. (1996). *Modernity at large: Cultural dimensions of globalization*. Minneapolis: University of Minnesota Press.

7. Lechner, Frank. (forthcoming). Globalization. In George Ritzer (Ed.), *Encyclopedia of Social Theory*. Thousand Oaks, CA: Sage.

8. For an excellent overview, see Antonio, R. J., & Bonanno, A. (2000). A new global capitalism? From "Americanism" and "Fordism" to "Americanization-Globalization." *American Studies 41,* pp. 33–77; see also, Lechner F., & Boli, J. (Eds.). (1999). *The globalization reader*. Malden, MA: Blackwell.

9. J. N. Rosenau. (1990). *Turbulence in world politics: A theory of change and continuity*. Princeton, NJ: Princeton University Press.

10. Hirst, P., & Thompson, G. (1996). *Globalization in question: The international economy and the possibilities of governance*. Cambridge, U.K. Polity.

11. Hamilton, R., Savitch, H., & Stewart, M. (Eds.). (2002). *Globalism and democracy: Challenge and change in Europe and North America*. New York: Palgrave.

12. Hobsbawm, E. (1997). The future of the state. In C. Hewitt de Alcantara (Ed.), *Social futures, global visions*. Oxford, U.K.: Blackwell; Meyer, J., Boli, J.,

Thomas, G., & Ramirez, F. (1998). World society and the nation state. *American Journal of Sociology, 103,* pp. 144–181.

13. Sassen, S. (1991). *The global city.* Princeton, NJ: Princeton University Press; Sassen, S. (2000). The global city: Strategic site/new frontier. *American Studies, 41* (2/3), pp. 79–95.

14. DePalma, D. A. (2002). *Business without borders: A strategic guide to global marketing.* New York: John Wiley; Stegner, M. (2002). *Globalism: The new market ideology.* Lanham, MD: Rowman and Littlefield.

15. Hornborg, A. (forthcoming). *The power of the machine: Global inequalities of economy, technology, and environment.* Walnut Creek, CA: AltaMira Press.

16. Yunker, J. (2002). *Beyond borders: Web globalization strategies.* Indianapolis, IN: New Riders; Porter, D. (Ed.). (1997). *Internet culture.* London: Routledge.

17. Drori, G. (forthcoming). The global digital divide. In G. Ritzer (Ed.), *Handbook of international social problems.* Thousand Oaks, CA: Sage.

18. Beyer, P. (1994). *Religion and globalization.* London: Sage.

19. Maguire, J. (1999). *Global sport: Identities, societies, civilizations.* Cambridge, U.K.: Polity Press.

20. Seago, A. (2000). "Where hamburgers sizzle on an open grill night and day"(?): Global pop music and Americanization in the year 2000. *American Studies 41* (2/3), pp. 119–136.

21. Bhalla, S. S. (2002). *Imagine there's no country: Poverty inequality and growth in the era of globalization.* Washington, DC: Institute for International Economics.

22. Castells, M. (1998). *End of millenium.* Malden, MA: Blackwell.

23. Altman, D. (2001). *Global sex.* Chicago: University of Chicago Press.

24. Farr, K. (forthcoming). *The international sex trade.* New York: Worth.

25. Scruton, R. (2002). *The West and the rest: Globalization and the terrorist threat.* Wilmington, DE: Intercollegiate Studies Institute.

26. Elliott, L. (1998). *The global politics of the environment.* London: Macmillan.

27. Singer, P. (2002). *One world: The ethics of globalization.* New Haven, CT: Yale University Press.

28. Robertson, R. (2001). Globalization theory 2000+: Major problematics. In G. Ritzer & B. Smart (Eds.), *Handbook of social theory* (pp. 458–471). London: Sage.

29. Robertson, R. (2001). Globalization theory 2000+: Major problematics. In G. Ritzer & B. Smart (Eds.), *Handbook of social theory* (p. 462). London: Sage.

30. Robertson, R. (2001). Globalization theory 2000+: Major problematics. In G. Ritzer & B. Smart (Eds.), *Handbook of social theory* (p. 461). London: Sage.

31. They deal with when globalization began, whether the nation state is being undermined by globalization, and the relationship of the latter to modernity. These are all important issues, but they will not concern us here largely because of a desire to keep this book focused and because no book can cover everything. Furthermore, other observers would surely contest Robertson's list of central issues and come up with very different lists.

32. Robertson, R. (1994). Globalisation or glocalisation? *Journal of International Communication 1*, pp. 33–52.

33. Appadurai says that he is strongly predisposed "toward the idea that globalization is not the story of cultural homogenization." See Appadurai, A. (1996). *Modernity at large: Cultural dimensions of globalization* (p. 11). Minneapolis: University of Minnesota Press. See also Berger, P., & Huntington, S. (Eds.). (2002). *Many globalizations: Cultural diversity in the contemporary world.* Oxford: Oxford University Press.

34. Robertson, R. (2001). Globalization theory 2000+: Major problematics. In G. Ritzer & B. Smart (Eds.), *Handbook of social theory* (pp. 458–471). London: Sage. Glocalization is at the heart of Robertson's own approach, but it is central to that of many others. The most notable are Appadurai's views on the "Indianization of cricket" and that the "new global cultural economy has to be seen as a complex, overlapping, disjunctive order" (see Appadurai, A. [1996]). *Modernity at large: Cultural dimensions of globalization* [pp. 32, 95]. Minneapolis: University of Minnesota Press.) While John Tomlinson uses other terms, he sees glocalization as "friendly" to his own orientation (see Tomlinson, J. [1999]. *Globalization and culture.* Chicago: University of Chicago Press).

35. I feel apologetic about adding yet another neologism, especially such an ungainly one, to a field already rife with jargon. However, the existence and popularity of the concept of glocalization requires the creation of the parallel notion of grobalization in order to emphasize that which the former concept ignores or downplays.

36. I am combining a number of different entities under this heading (nations, corporations, a wide range of organizations, and so on), but it should be clear that there are profound differences among them including the degree to which, and the ways in which, they seek to grobalize. I feel the same way about "grobalization" as Charles Peirce did about the creation of the concept of "pragmaticism" to distinguish it from the way "pragmatism" had come to be used by others (especially William James). Peirce felt that "pragmaticism" was "ugly enough to be safe from kidnappers". Cited in Halton, E. (forthcoming). Pragmatism. In G. Ritzer (Ed.), *Encyclopedia of Social Theory.* Thousand Oaks, CA: Sage.

37. We have previously discussed the elements of McDonaldization. Here we discuss it as a process that is sweeping across the globe as a centrally important grobalization process.

38. States further the interests of capitalist organizations, but also further their own interests, some of which are separable from the capitalist system.

39. Ritzer, G. (1999). *Enchanting a disenchanted world: Revolutionizing the means of consumption.* Thousand Oaks, CA: Pine Forge Press.

40. Best, S., & Kellner, D. (1997). *The postmodern turn.* New York: Guilford; Ritzer, G. (1997). *Postmodern social theory.* New York: McGraw-Hill. For an explicit effort to link globalization and postmodern social theory, see Featherstone, M. (1995). *Undoing culture: Globalization, postmodernism and identity.* London: Sage.

41. Kuisel, R. F. (1993). *Seducing the French: The dilemma of Americanization.* Berkeley: University of California Press; Ritzer, G. (1995).

Expressing America: A critique of the global credit card society. Thousand Oaks, CA: Pine Forge Press.

42. Giddens, A. (1990). *The consequences of modernity.* Stanford, CA: Stanford University Press.

43. Hannerz, U. (1990). Cosmopolitans and locals in world culture. In M. Featherstone (Ed.), *Global culture: Nationalism, globalization and modernity* (pp. 237–252). London: Sage.

44. Canclini, N. G. (1995). *Hybrid cultures: Strategies for entering and leaving modernity* (pp. 45–68). Minneapolis: University of Minneapolis Press; Pieterse, J. N. (1995). Globalization as hybridization. In M. Featherstone, S. Lash, & R. Robertson (Eds.), *Global modernities* (pp. 45–68). London: Sage.

45. Stiglitz, J. E. (2002). *Globalization and its discontents* (p. 34). New York: W.W. Norton.

46. Meyer, J., Boli, J. W., Thomas, G. M., & Ramirez, F. (1997). World society and the nation-state. *American Journal of Sociology 103,* pp. 144–181.

47. Barber's view of McWorld is not restricted to politics; he sees many other domains following the model of McWorld; Barber, B. (1995). *Jihad vs. McWorld.* New York: Times Books.

48. More broadly, there are those who focus not only on politics but on the global influence of a multiplicity of institutions. For example, few if any countries can afford the American system of health and medical care, but most have at least been influenced by it to some degree. While the grobalization of aspects of the U.S. health care system has led to some degree of homogeneity, glocalization resulting from the interpenetration of that system with folk remedies and systems has led to increases in heterogeneity.

49. See, for example, Cowen, T. (2002). *Creative destruction: How globalization is changing the world's cultures.* Princeton, NJ: Princeton University Press.

50. Watson, J. (Ed.). (1997). *Golden arches east: McDonald's in East Asia.* Stanford, CA: Stanford University Press.

51. Watson, J. (Ed.). (1997). *Golden arches east: McDonald's in East Asia* (p. 6). Stanford, CA: Stanford University Press.

52. Canclini, N. G. (1995). *Hybrid cultures: Strategies for entering and leaving modernity.* Minneapolis: University of Minneapolis Press; Pieterse, J. N. (1995). Globalization as hybridization. In M. Featherstone, S. Lash, & R. Robertson (Eds.), *Global modernities* (pp. 45–68). London: Sage.

53. Hannerz, U. (1992). *Cultural complexity: Studies in the social organization of meaning.* New York: Columbia University Press.

54. Zwingle, E. (2000). A world together. In K. Sjursen (Ed.), *Globalization* (pp. 153–164). New York: H.W. Wilson.

55. See, for example, Kuisel, R. (1993). *Seducing the French: The dilemma of Americanization.* Berkeley: University of California Press.

56. See, for example, Hayes, D., & Wynyard, R. (Eds.). (2002). *The McDonaldization of higher education.* Westport, CT: Bergin and Garvey; see also a number of the essays in Ritzer, G. (Ed.). (2002). *McDonaldization: The reader.* Thousand Oaks, CA: Pine Forge Press.

57. Appadurai is a strong representative of this position; see Appadurai, A. (1996). *Modernity at large: Cultural dimensions of globalization*. Minneapolis: University of Minnesota Press.

58. Although everyone recognizes that grobalization and more generally globalization play themselves out differently in various local and national contexts. See Mudimbe-Boyi, E. (Ed.). (2002). *Beyond dichotomies: Histories, identities cultures, and the challenge of globalization*. Albany: State University of New York Press.

59. Other examples are imperialism and (neo-) colonialism.

60. As we will see, this is no easy matter. For example, Disney is a capitalistic organization, its origins clearly lie in the United States, and it is highly McDonaldized.

61. Marx, K. (1867/1967). *Capital: A critique of political economy* (Vol. 1). New York: International.

62. This is part of what Marx called *the general law of capitalist accumulation*.

63. We could have easily added another section here on technology, which can be seen as a grobalizing force in its own right. However, it is also closely linked to capitalism, Americanization, and McDonaldization (non-human technology is, of course, one element of this process).

64. This is what Kellner calls "techno-capitalism." See Kellner, D. (1989). *Critical theory, Marxism and modernity*. Baltimore, MD: Johns Hopkins University Press. On the role of technology in globalization, see Hornborg, A. (forthcoming). *The power of the machine: Global inequalities of economy, technology, and environment*. Walnut Creek, CA: AltaMira Press.

65. Wood, E. M., & Foster, J. B. (Eds.). (1997). *In defense of history: Marxism and the postmodern agenda* (p. 67). New York: Monthly Review Press.

66. Burawoy, M. (1990). Marxism as science: Historical challenges and theoretical growth. *American Sociological Review 55*, pp. 775–793.

67. Implied, at times, in Marx's work, and more explicit in the work of some neo Marxists, is the idea that it is the economy that is of ultimate importance in society, and everything else (politics, religion, and so on) is merely "superstructure" that is erected on that all-important economic base. It should be clear why this is often associated with *economic determinism*, an idea that is anathema to most non-Marxists and even neo-Marxists.

68. Although the United States has supported many authoritarian regimes when it is in its interest to do so.

69. Dicke, T. S. (1992). *Franchising in America: The development of a business method, 1840–1980*. Chapel Hill: University of North Carolina Press.

70. Ritzer, G. (2000). *The McDonaldization of society*. Thousand Oaks, CA: Pine Forge Press.

71. Weber, M. (1921/1968). *Economy and society* (3 vols.). Totowa, NJ: Bedminster Press.

72. Weber, M. (1927/1981). *General economic history*. New Brunswick, NJ: Transaction Books.

73. Hayes, D., & Wynyard, R. (Eds.). (2002). *The McDonaldization of higher education*. Westport, CT: Bergin and Garvey.

74. Turner, B. (1999). McCitizens: Risk, coolness and irony in contemporary politics. In B. Smart (Ed.), *Resisting McDonaldization* (pp. 83–100). London: Sage; Beilharz, P. (1999). McFascism: Reading Ritzer, Bauman and the Holocaust. In B. Smart (Ed.), *Resisting McDonaldization* (pp. 222–233). London: Sage.

75. Drane, J. (2001). *The McDonaldization of the church*. London: Darton, Longman and Todd.

76. Robinson, M. B. (2002). McDonaldization of America's police, courts, and corrections. In G. Ritzer (Ed.), *McDonaldization: The reader* (pp. 77–90). Thousand Oaks, CA: Pine Forge Press.

77. Robertson, R. (2001). Globalization theory 2000+: Major problematics. In G. Ritzer & B. Smart (Eds.), *Handbook of social theory* (p. 464). London: Sage. See also Appadurai, A. (1996). *Modernity at large: Cultural dimensions of globalization* (p. 29). Minneapolis: University of Minnesota Press; Beck, U. (2000). *What is globalization?* (p. 49). Cambridge, U.K.: Polity; Watson, J. (Ed). (1997). *Golden arches east: McDonald's in East Asia* (p. 35). Stanford, CA: Stanford University Press.

78. Ritzer, G. (1998). *The McDonaldization thesis* (pp. 174–183). London: Sage.

79. While McDonald's is not likely to go out of business any time soon, it does find itself in an already overcrowded, saturated market in which profits are being driven down by increasingly intense price competition. This problem is likely to be exacerbated as foreign competitors increasingly enter the American market. However, even if McDonald's were to disappear, the process of McDonaldization would continue apace, although we might need a new label for it. For more on this, see below.

80. Williams, F. (1962). *The American invasion*. New York: Crown Williams.

81. Murden, T., & Miller, P. (2002, April 28). Coke beats Irn-Bru to be top of the pops. *Sunday Times*.

82. Kael, P. (1985). Why are movies so bad? or, The numbers. In P. Kael (Ed.), *State of the art* (pp. 8–20). New York: E.P. Dutton.

83. Said, E. (1978). *Orientalism*. New York: Pantheon.

84. Ritzer, G. (1999). *Enchanting a disenchanted world: Revolutionizing the means of consumption*. Thousand Oaks, CA: Pine Forge Press.

85. By the way, almost all of the new means of consumption can be placed toward the non-place end of the place–non-place continuum.

86. The inclusion of McDonald's as one of the new means of consumption and as an example of Americanization makes it clear once again that Americanization and McDonaldization cannot be clearly and unequivocally distinguished from one another.

87. Scally, D. (2002, December 5). Coffee drinkers not swallowing Starbucks line. *Irish Times*, p. 14.

88. It is worth remembering that it was not too long ago that the United States was the world leader in production. In many ways, consumption has replaced production as the focus of the American economy and it has become the nation's prime export to the rest of world. It is interesting to ponder the implications of what it means to have gone from the world leader in the production of steel to, say, the world leader in the exportation of fast-food restaurants and shopping malls.

89. De Graaf, J., Wann, D., & Naylor, T. H. (2001). *Affluenza: The all-consuming epidemic*. San Francisco: Berrett-Koehler.

90. This, of course, is closely linked to the "epidemic" of obesity sweeping the nation.

91. Chung, C. J. et al. (2001). *Harvard Design School guide to shopping*. Koln: Taschen.

92. Actually, in an increasing number of cases, "American" products sporting "American" brand names (Nike products, for example) are manufactured elsewhere and exported around the world. These are still considered American products in this context because their origins are in the United States, they are usually still thought of as American, and the bulk of the profits still flows back to the United States.

93. Cited in Kuisel, R. (1993). *Seducing the French: The dilemma of Americanization* (p. 230). Berkeley: University of California Press. In this case, Americanization yields what Appadurai calls "soft" cultural forms that are relatively easy to transform, but Americanization also produces "hard" cultural forms that are more difficult to change. See Appadurai, A. (1996). *Modernity at large: Cultural dimensions of globalization* (p. 90). Minneapolis: University of Minnesota Press.

94. And, given their American roots, McDonaldized systems have many of these characteristics as well.

95. Ohnuki-Tierney, E. (1997). McDonald's in Japan: Changing manners and etiquette. In J. Watson (Ed.), *Golden arches east: McDonald's in East Asia* (pp. 161–182). Stanford, CA: Stanford University Press.

96. As usual, artificial distinctions are being made here.

97. For a discussion of this from the perspective of the interests of this book, see Ritzer, G. (2002). September 11, 2001: Mass murder and its roots in American consumer culture. In G. Ritzer (Ed.), *McDonaldization: The reader* (pp. 213–221). Thousand Oaks, CA: Pine Forge Press.

98. Bove, J., & DuFour, F. (2001). *The world is not for sale: Farmers against junk food*. London: Verso; Morse, D. (2002). Striking the golden arches: French farmers protest McD's globalization. In G. Ritzer (Ed.), *McDonaldization: The reader* (pp. 245–249). Thousand Oaks, CA: Pine Forge Press.

99. Although in some cases, such as the Japanese Boy Scout and McDonald's mentioned above, that linkage is lost.

100. Keller, B. (1990, September 12). Of famous arches, Beeg Meks and rubles. *New York Times,* section 1, pp. 1, 12; Wedge of Americana: In Moscow, Pizza Hut opens two restaurants (1990, September 12). *Washington Post,* p. B10.

101. Kincheloe, J. L. (2002). *The sign of the burger: McDonald's and the culture of power*. Philadelphia: Temple University Press.

102. Ross, S. (2002, December 4). Survey says: Foreigners like U.S. culture but not policies. Associated Press; Retrieved from www.boston.com/dailynews/338/wash/Survey_says_Foreigners_like_U_:.shtml

103. For an alternate view, see James, H. (2001). *The end of globalization*. Cambridge, MA: Harvard University Press.

104. Derber, C. (2002). *People before profit: The new globalization in an age of terror, big money, and economic crisis* (p. 15). New York: St. Martin's Press.

105. Thus, for example, in international fine art sales, Great Britain is poised to supplant the United States as the world leader. See Brewster, D. (2002, September 20). US loses ground to Britain in global art sales. *Financial Times,* p. 23.

106. Goodman, D. (forthcoming). The contradictions of consumer culture. In G. Ritzer (Ed.), *Handbook of international social problems.* Thousand Oaks, CA: Sage.

107. Bak, S. (1997). McDonald's in Seoul: Food choices, identity, and nationalism. In J. Watson (Ed.), *Golden arches east: McDonald's in East Asia* (pp. 136–160). Stanford, CA: Stanford University Press.

108. Money, R. B., & Colton, D. (2000). Global advertising. *Journal of World Business 35,* 189–205.

109. Robertson, R. (1995). Glocalization: Time–space and homogeneity–heterogeneity. In M. Featherstone, S. Lash, & R. Robertson (Eds.), *Global modernities* (pp. 25–44). London: Sage.

110. Schutte, H., & Ciarlante, D. (1998). *Consumer behavior in Asia.* New York: New York University Press.

111. Terrio, S. (1996). Crafting *grand cru* chocolates in contemporary France. *American Anthropologist, 98,* 67–79.

112. Beng-Huat, C. (2000). Consuming Asians: Ideas and Asians. In C. Beng-Huat (Ed.), *Consumption in Asia. Lifestyles and identities* (pp. 1–34). New York: Routledge.

Chapter 5

1. And there is not an *elective affinity* between grobalization and something and glocalization and nothing.

2. Indeed, it is difficult to accept the view that there are *any* such relationships in the social world.

3. Howe, R. H. (1978). Max Weber's elective affinities: Sociology within the bounds of pure reason. *American Journal of Sociology, 84,* pp. 366–385.

4. An interesting example of the trend toward nothingness is the increasing use of audio guides and rented tape players at such shows and at museums more generally.

5. Delacoma, W. (2002, October 26). Silk Road, CSO explore the East. *Chicago Sun-Times,* p. 20.

6. I would like to thank Professor Daina Iglitis for suggesting that I deal with this issue.

7. Disney and Hong Kong: Government breaks ground on first theme park in China. (2003, January 12). *PR Newswire.*

8. However, new, eclectic cuisines and cookery do involve the combination of the most unlikely of foods. Nonetheless, such combinations are unlikely to be attractive to a large, global population of consumers, or at least one as large and global as that for, say, Coca-Cola.

9. An apparent exception is the uproar over "Coca-Colonization" in France after World War II, but that quickly died out and today Coca-Cola is only one of

many non-things widely accepted in France. See, for example, Kuisel, R. (1993). *Seducing the French: The dilemma of Americanization.* Berkeley: University of California Press.

10.   Pavitt, J. (2001, July 9). Branded: A brief history of brands: 1. Coca Cola. *Guardian,* p. 4.

11.   Bickerton, I., & Jones, A. (2002, April 25). Heineken plans to grow with a new generation at the helm. *Financial Times,* p. 30.

12.   Mathiesen, C. (2002, March 4). Foster's no longer just about beer. *The Times.*

13.   Daykin, T. (2002, October 7). Point Brewery uncaps root beer. *Milwaukee Journal Sentinel,* p. 2D.

14.   Survey-Pharmaceuticals. (2001, April 30). *Financial Times,* p. 1.

15.   Abate, T. (2002, June 10). Biotrends. *San Francisco Chronicle,* p. E1.

16.   Wahab, S., & Cooper, C. (Eds.). (2001). *Tourism in the age of globalisation.* London: Routledge.

17.   Tam, K., Dissanayake, W., & Yip, T. S. (2002). *Sights of contestation: Localism, globalism and cultural production in Asia and the Pacific.* Hong Kong: Chinese University Press.

18.   Wellington, E. (2002, November 7). From shady beginnings, knockoffs rise to respectability and big profit. *Pittsburgh Post-Gazette,* p. D2.

19.   In fact, there are strong regional differences in the United States in the nature, style, and taste of Chinese food (for example, rice is served free with meals in the East, but in Seattle one must pay extra for rice), even among particular styles of Chinese cooking (Cantonese, Hunan, Szechuan, and so on).

20.   Interestingly, in spite of a number of efforts, there is no large, highly successful chain of Chinese restaurants. Tight structural models do not seem to be able to compete with loose structural models in this domain and others.

21.   Indeed, the services of relatively new shipping businesses that make this possible—FedEx, DHL, and so on—themselves take on the character of the grobalization of nothing.

22.   Appadurai, A. (1996). *Modernity at large: Cultural dimensions of globalization.* Minneapolis: University of Minnesota Press.

23.   Of course, returning to the grobalization of something, programs produced by PBS, and more importantly BBC, are shown around the world. However, their global presence pales in comparison to that of sitcoms and soaps.

24.   Interestingly, one reason given to support the euro was the nothingness resulting from the Americanization of Europe: a case of creating nothing to defend against nothing. See, Hutton, W. (1999, September 26). A pox on euro sceptics. *The Observer,* p. 30.

25.   Of course, one could envision a time when the euro could become something to future residents of a more united Europe.

26.   There are real national landmarks from European countries on one side of euro coins.

27.   Chains and franchises can be thought of as technoscapes.

28.   Ferri, J. (1996, October 27). Clubs help new arrivals to U.S. hold on to heritage. *Tampa Tribune,* p. 35.

29. In order to be widely accepted, these ideas are watered down and denuded so that they are often little more than pale imitations of the ideas that lay at their source.

30. However, as pointed out in Chapter 2, some mass-produced objects (e.g. muscle cars, VW Beetles) can be considered something.

31. Malotki, E. (2000). *Kokopelli: The making of an icon.* Lincoln: University of Nebraska Press; retrieved from www.acaciart.com/stories/archive 10.html

32. Of course, some may be produced as local crafts.

33. Retrieved from www.giftogive.com/doll.htm

34. Korchagina, V. (2002, September 11). Souvenir makers ride a wave of American pride. *Moscow Times.*

Chapter 6

1. I would like to thank Nicholas Wilson for his input into this chapter. While still an undergraduate, Nick has offered a level of help and assistance on this chapter, and on the book as a whole, that is the equal of what one could expect from a professional colleague.

2. As we will soon see, there are important exceptions to this.

3. Of course, there are many areas of the world with little or no access to the Internet in general and these large-scale consumption sites in particular. Further, those who do not understand English also lack such access.

4. Turkle, S. (1997). *Life on the screen: Identity in the age of the Internet.* New York: Touchstone Books.

5. Miller, S. A. (2002, October 27). Internet: A gateway to new universe. *Milwaukee Sentinel Journal,* p. 1Eff.

6. Smith, M. A., & Kollock, P. (Eds.). (1998). *Communities in cyberspace.* London: Routledge.

7. Miller, S. A. (2002, October 27). Internet: A gateway to new universe. *Milwaukee Sentinel Journal,* p. 1Eff.

8. D'Innocenzio, A. (2002, November 28). Retailers use e-mail to target customers. *Toronto Star,* p. M6.

9. Krim, J. (2003, March 13). Spam's cost to business escalates. *Washington Post,* p. A1.

10. An exception to this is www.homesickgourmet.com. This Web site does not sell anything, but simply serves as an information clearinghouse for those in search of hard-to-find foods from all over the world. Hunt, M. C. (2001, November 28). Homesick gourmet: Order a taste of a favorite place for culinary comfort. *San Diego Union-Tribune,* p. E1.

11. Jerney, J. (2001, January 30). Will peer-to-peer be the "next big thing." *Daily Yomiuri,* p. 9.

12. Cha, A. E. (2002, December 20). File swappers eluding pursuers: Unlike Napster, Kazaa's global nature defies legal attacks. *Washington Post,* pp. A1, A8, A9.

13.   There are some centralized rules on what can and cannot be sold—I recently heard that previously worn women's panties cannot be sold on eBay—but they are not very extensive.

14.   Although traditional malls, and the shops in them, have sought to become more flexible; see Reidy, C. (2002, October 22). Filene's will test smaller, more flexible suburb store. *Boston Globe,* p. C1.

15.   One broad type of restriction is the nature of the ending of an address—.com, .org, .gov, .edu, and so on. However, even within each of those broadly restricted categories, a great quantity and diversity of content is available.

16.   Levy, S. (2002, December 16). The world according to Google. *Newsweek,* pp. 46–51.

17.   Walker, L. (2002, December 15). Google turns its gaze to online shopping. *Washington Post,* p. H7.

18.   This seems to contradict the preceding point about Internet sites not being able to respond immediately and therefore requiring greater prior conceptualization and preset methods of control. However, this is a different point. On the one hand, because no humans are on duty, Internet sites are not as adaptable as brick-and-mortar malls. On the other hand, because they are immaterial, Internet malls can be altered dramatically literally overnight (although this might require much preplanning), while traditional malls are very difficult and time-consuming to alter because of their materiality.

19.   Chung, C. J., et al. (2001). *Harvard Design School guide to shopping.* Koln: Taschen.

20.   Ritzer, G. (2001). Ensnared in the E-Net: The future belongs to the immaterial means of consumption. In G. Ritzer (Ed.), *Explorations in the sociology of consumption: Fast food restaurants, credit cards and casinos* (pp.145–159). London: Sage.

21.   Retrieved from www.adbusters.org/home/

22.   Although, as we have seen, that content can change, sometimes quickly and dramatically.

23.   See www.bsos.umd.edu/socy/ritzer/

24.   However, as we will soon see, it is largely composed of quite generic products.

25.   Kuntsler, J. H. (1994). *The geography of nowhere: The rise and decline of America's man-made landscape.* New York: Touchstone Books.

26.   As I have pointed out elsewhere, this is basic to many rationalized (McDonaldized) settings; see Ritzer, G. (2000). *The McDonaldization of society.* Thousand Oaks, CA: Pine Forge Press.

27.   Perhaps I shouldn't have been surprised since Southwest is known for this kind of thing and has become very successful (while many other airlines have faltered) because of it. However, it is also the case that it has succeeded because it has cut costs by bringing many non-services (no assigned seating and passengers required to jostle in line in order to get a good seat) to the airline industry.

28.   Walker, L. (2002, December 15). Google turns its gaze to online shopping. *Washington Post,* p. H7.

29.   Lindstedt, S. (1998, July 14). Taylors seeks unique employees. *Buffalo News,* p. 3D.

30.   Ritzer, G. (1999). *Enchanting a disenchanted world: Revolutionizing the means of consumption*. Thousand Oaks, CA: Pine Forge Press.

31.   Although, as we have seen, the nature of globalization is such that it is difficult to think of the local anymore, at least in the sense that it is unaffected by the grobal. That is, all, or virtually all, of the local may now be glocal. Thus, even local car dealers are affected by global processes.

Chapter 7

1.   Nelson, J. L. (2001). On mass distribution: A case study of chain stores in the restaurant industry. *Journal of Consumer Culture, 1,* pp. 119–138.

2.   Fast-food restaurants predate McDonald's, but they really came of age with the founding of that chain.

3.   Of course, the increase in population plays a central role in this.

4.   For some contemporary examples that still resemble the old-fashioned greasy-spoon, see Oldenburg, R. (Ed.). (2001). *Celebrating the third place.* New York: Marlowe.

5.   Diehl, L. B., & Hardart, M. (2002). *The Automat: The history, recipes, and allure of Horn & Hardart's masterpiece.* New York: Clarkson N. Potter.

6.   Schumpeter, J. (1950). *Capitalism, socialism and democracy* (3rd ed.). New York: Harper and Brothers.

7.   Jones, S. (2002, April 8). Back to basics: Silver Diner retreats from growth to focus on food and service. *Washington Post,* pp. E1, E12.

8.   Klier, J. D., & Lambroza, S. (Eds.). (1992). *Pogroms: Anti-Jewish violence in modern Russian history.* Cambridge, U.K.: Cambridge University Press.

9.   We will discuss below the fact that in actuality this may be more a perception than a reality; nothing is certainly not always inexpensive.

10.   This is made possible by the fact that those who do not pay their bills in full, who regularly carry a balance, pay high fees and, in effect, support those who pay their bills in full each month.

11.   Gofton, L. (1995). Convenience and the moral status of consumer practices. In D. W. Marshall (Ed.), *Food choice and the consumer* (pp. 52–181). London: Blackie Academic and Professional.

12.   This is consistent with many defenses of consumption. See, for example, Twitchell, J. (1999). *Lead us into temptation: The triumph of materialism.* New York: Columbia University Press; also Lipovetsky, G. (1994). *The empire of fashion: Dressing modern democracy.* Princeton: Princeton University Press.

13.   As was pointed out above, there are exceptions.

14.   Leland, J. (2002, December 1). How the disposable couch conquered America. *New York Times,* Section 6, p. 86.

15.   Chung, C. J., et al. (2001). *Harvard Design School guide to shopping* (p. 135). Koln: Taschen.

16.   However, once again it is important to point out that since something is not necessarily desirable (for example, a pogrom is something according to our

definition), the loss of it is not necessarily to be regretted (it might even be welcomed). However, regrettable or not, it still represents a loss.

17. Stuever, H. (2002, June 16). Just one word: Plastic. *Washington Post Magazine*, p. 27; italics added.

18. Stuever, J. (2002, June 16). Just one word: Plastic. *Washington Post Magazine*, p. 18; italics added.

19. Stuever, H. (2002, June 16). Just one word: Plastic. *Washington Post Magazine*, p. 28; italics added.

20. The implication is that Gucci is something and it is distinguished from the various forms of nothingness. However, given the definition employed in this book, Gucci would be considered nothing. As we will see, there is a continuum from nothing to something and while Gucci may be seen as being closer to the something end of the continuum than the other brands discussed here, it is still better thought of as nothing.

21. Or, more recently, an off-track betting site.

22. Sandoval, G., & La Canfora, J. (2003, March 13). Jagr: Gambling was a mistake. *Washington Post*, pp. D1, D6.

23. This is also true in the world of credit cards. See Ritzer, G. (1995). *Expressing America: A critique of the global credit card society*. Thousand Oaks, CA: Pine Forge Press; Klein, L. (1999). *It's in the cards: Consumer credit and the American experience*. Westport, CT: Praeger; Manning, R. (2000). *Credit card nation: The consequences of America's addiction to debt*. New York: Basic Books.

24. Gergen, K. (2000). *The saturated self*. New York: Basic Books.

25. As discussed above, there are, of course, satisfactions associated with consumption on the Internet.

26. Thomas, W. I., & Thomas, D. S. (1928). *The child in America: Behavior problems and programs*. New York: Knopf.

27. This argument has some similarities to that of Walter Benjamin and his view that while technological change leads to various advances, it is also associated with the loss of "aura." See Benjamin, W. (1968). The Work of Art in the Age of Mechanical Reproduction. In *Illuminations* (pp. 217–242). New York: Schocken.

28. Kummer, C. (2002). *The pleasures of slow food* (p. 23). San Francisco: Chronicle Books.

29. Boas, M., & Chain, S. (1976). *Big Mac: The unauthorized story of McDonald's* (p. 117). New York: E.P. Dutton.

30. Diehl, L. B., & Hardart, M. (2002). *The Automat: The history, recipes, and allure of Horn & Hardart's masterpiece*. New York: Clarkson N. Potter.

31. Chung, C. J., et al. (2001). *Harvard Design School guide to shopping*. Koln: Taschen.

32. Jakle, J. A., & Wilson, D. (1992). *Derelict landscapes*. Savage, MD: Rowman and Littlefield.

33. In addition, little or nothing needs to be extracted from these empty forms because there is so little there to remove.

34. In contrast, designer clothes are likely to be discarded when they begin to show wear.

35. Even in the United States, it derives meaning from its association with that place and time.

36. Another interpretation is that its global popularity stems from the fact that its emptiness makes for the possibility of transforming it into something. However, the fact that this occurs so rarely casts doubt on this interpretation.

37. Browne, J. (1973). *The used car game: A sociology of the bargain.* Lexington, MA: Lexington Books.

38. But not exclusively. There are certainly many forms of something—a home-made soup or stew, a hand-knitted ski cap, homemade ice cream—that are inexpensive, indeed far less costly than comparable store-bought products.

39. For example, Wood points out that elite cookery is subject to standardization. See Wood, R. C. (1995). *The sociology of the meal* (p. 97). Edinburgh: Edinburgh University Press.

40. Fake villages that derive their name from Grigori Aleksandrovich Potemkin, who had them built on an elaborate scale for Catherine the Great when she visited the Ukraine and the Crimea.

41. Why we're so fat. (2002, October 21). *Business Week,* pp. 112–114.

42. Bad money drives out good money. See Raymond de Roover. (1949). *Gresham on Foreign Exchange.* Cambridge, U.K.: Harvard University Press.

43. Chung, C. J., et al. (2001). *Harvard Design School guide to shopping.* Koln: Taschen.

44. Small towns might be a different matter. Forms of something are likely to be well ensconced in such settings, and they are protected by the fact that the small population base may make the towns unattractive and unprofitable to various forms of nothing (fast-food restaurants, ATMs). I would like to thank Mike Ryan, who grew up in such a town, for pointing this out to me.

Chapter 8

1. Leiby, R. (2003, March 17). You want falafel with that? *Washington Post,* p. C1.

2. Grobalization tends to involve what Hansen calls "delocalization," or the deforming effects of the grobal on the local. See Hansen, C. E. (2002). *The culture of strangers: Globalization, localization and the phenomenon of exchange.* Lanham, MD: University Press of America. See also Stiglitz, J. E. (2002). *Globalization and its discontents.* New York: W.W. Norton.

3. For example, in the realm of the military, American weaponry is far more sophisticated than that of any other nation in the world; see Loeb, V. (2002, December 15). Burst of brilliance. *Washington Post Magazine,* pp. 6ff.

4. Loeb, V. (2002, December 15). Burst of brilliance. *Washington Post Magazine,* pp. 6ff.

5. Stiglitz, J. E. (2002). *Globalization and its discontents.* New York: W.W. Norton.

6. Faiola, A. (2002, August 6). Despair in once-proud Argentina. *Washington Post*, pp. A1, A9.

7. Ritzer, G. (1988). Problems, scandals and the possibility of 'TextbookGate': An author's view. *Teaching Sociology, 16,* pp. 373–380.

8. One example in sociology is Giddens, A., & Duneier, M. (2003). *Introduction to sociology* (4th ed). New York: W.W. Norton.

9. Robinson, M. B. (2002). McDonaldization of America's police, courts, and corrections. In G. Ritzer (Ed.), *McDonaldization: The reader* (pp. 77–90). Thousand Oaks, CA: Pine Forge Press.

10. Robinson, M. B. (2002). McDonaldization of America's police, courts, and corrections. In G. Ritzer (Ed.), *McDonaldization: The reader* (pp. 77–90). Thousand Oaks, CA: Pine Forge Press.

11. Drane, J. (2001). *The McDonaldization of the church*. London: Darton, Longman and Todd.

12. Turner, B. (1999). McCitizens: Risk, coolness and irony in contemporary politics. In B. Smart (Ed.), *Resisting McDonaldization* (pp. 83–100). London: Sage.

13. Barber, B. (1995). *Jihad vs. McWorld*. New York: Times Books.

14. Koehn, N. F. (2001). *Brand new: How entrepreneurs earned consumers' trust from Wedgwood to Dell* (p. 5). Boston: Harvard Business School Press.

15. The importance of emotions to brands is reflected in the fact that there are two books published about this issue with the same titled *Emotional Branding*. See Travis, D. (2000). *Emotional branding: How successful brands gain the irrational edge*. Roseville, CA: Prima Venture; Gobe, M. (2001). *Emotional branding: The new paradigm for connecting brands to people*. New York: Allworth Press.

16. I'd like to thank Todd Stillman for reminding me of this, and much else that appears in this book.

17. Trout, J. (2001). *Big brands, big trouble: Lessons learned the hard way* (pp. 6–7). New York: John Wiley; italics added.

18 By the way, this makes it clear that this critique of nothing, and non-things in particular, is not to suggest that the solution involves some sort of return to an era before mass manufacturing. Clearly, our large and complex world cannot survive without mass production. However, must it dominate all sectors of our lives? Isn't there a place and a role for something in the contemporary world?

19. Although Nike played a key role in "branding" Michael Jordan once he became a spokesperson for the company. However, Jordan had long since acquired a brand among basketball fans who appreciated his unique and extraordinary abilities.

20. Baran, P., & Sweezy, P. (1966). *Monopoly capital: An essay on the American economic and social order*. New York: Monthly Review Press.

21. Grimston, J. (2003, January 19). British Muslims find things go better with Mecca. *Sunday Times*, p. 12.

22. For more on this, see the Appendix.

23. Kummer, C. (2002). *The pleasures of slow food* (p. 26). San Francisco: Chronicle Books.

24. Kummer, C. (2002). *The pleasures of slow food* (p. 23). San Francisco: Chronicle Books.

25. Kummer, C. (2002). *The pleasures of slow food* (p. 23). San Francisco: Chronicle Books.

26. Kummer, C. (2002). *The pleasures of slow food* (p. 25). San Francisco: Chronicle Books.

27. Kummer, C. (2002). *The pleasures of slow food* (p. 25). San Francisco: Chronicle Books.

Appendix

1. Heath, P. L. (1967). Nothing. In P. Edwards (Ed.), *The encyclopedia of philosophy* (Vol. 5, p. 524). New York: Macmillan and Free Press.

2. Barrow, J. D. (2000). *The book of nothing* (p. 84). New York: Books Pantheon.

3. Barrow, J. D. (2000). *The book of nothing* (p. 84). New York: Pantheon Books.

4. Barrow, J. D. (2000). *The book of nothing* (p. 89). New York: Pantheon Books.

5. Kant, I. (2001). *Basic writings of Kant* (p. 43). New York: Modern Library.

6. Kant, I. (2001). *Basic writings of Kant* (p. 43). New York: Modern Library.

7. Houlgate, S. (1998). *The Hegel reader* (p. 188). Oxford, U.K.: Blackwell.

8. There is a dialectic in Simmel's work as well, but that aspect is of little relevance to us here.

9. Levine, D. (1971). Introduction. In D. Levine (Ed.), *Georg Simmel: On individuality and social forms* (p. xxxii). Chicago: University of Chicago Press.

10. This also obviously limits the utility of the work of Kant and Hegel.

11. Although, as is clear in Sartre's critique, this is less true of Heidegger than Sartre.

12. Heidegger, M. (1927/1996). *Being and time.* Albany: SUNY Press; Heidegger, M. (1977). *Basic writings.* New York: Harper and Row.

13. Barrett, W. (1958). *Irrational man: A study in existential philosophy* (p. 195). Westport, CT: Greenwood.

14. Heidegger, M. (1977). *Basic writings* (p. 109). New York: Harper and Row.

15. Polt, R. (1999). *Heidegger: An introduction* (p. 124). Ithaca, NY: Cornell University Press.

16. Barrett, W. (1958). *Irrational man: A study in existential philosophy* (p. 202). Westport, CT: Greenwood.

17. Polt, R. (1999). *Heidegger: An introduction* (p. 124). Ithaca, NY: Cornell University Press.

18. Heidegger, M. (1977). *Basic writings* (pp. 108, 110). New York: Harper and Row.

19. Sartre, J.-P. (1943/1958). *Being and nothingness: An essay on phenomenological ontology* (p. 21). London: Methuen.

20. Sartre, J.-P. (1943/1958). *Being and nothingness: An essay on phenomenological ontology* (p. 24). London: Methuen.

21. Heidegger, M. (1977). *Basic writings* (p. 106). New York: Harper and Row.

22. Michael Novak also offers a positive perspective on nothingness. See Novak, M. (1970/1988). *The experience of nothingness.* New Brunswick, NJ: Transaction.

23. Barrett, W. (1958). *Irrational man: A study in existential philosophy* (pp. 54, 55, 86). Westport, CT: Greenwood.

24. Barrett, W. (1958). *Irrational man: A study in existential philosophy* (p. 55). Westport, CT: Greenwood.

25. Barrett, W. (1958). *Irrational man: A study in existential philosophy* (p. 251). Westport, CT: Greenwood.

26. Barrett, W. (1958). *Irrational man: A study in existential philosophy* (p. 218). Westport, CT: Greenwood.

27. Heidegger, M. (1977). The question concerning technology. In M. Heidegger (Ed.), *Basic writings* (pp. 283–317). New York: Harper and Row.

28. Polt, R. (1999). *Heidegger: An introduction* (pp. 172–173). Ithaca, NY: Cornell University Press.

29. Weinstein, D., & Weinstein, M. A. (1999). McDonaldization enframed. In B. Smart (Ed.), *Resisting McDonaldization* (pp. 57–69). London: Sage.

30. Barrett, W. (1958). *Irrational man: A study in existential philosophy* (p. 218). Westport, CT: Greenwood.

31. Barrett, W. (1958). *Irrational man: A study in existential philosophy* (p. 220). Westport, CT: Greenwood.

32. Barrett, W. (1958). *Irrational man: A study in existential philosophy* (p. 251). Westport, CT: Greenwood.

33. Although, again, that which is loaded with substance offers much that can put off people who may not be comfortable with part or all of it.

34. Irwin, W. (Ed.). (2000). *Seinfeld and philosophy: [A book about everything and nothing].* Chicago/La Salle, IL: Open Court.

35. Jolley, K. D. (2000). Wittgenstein and *Seinfeld* on the commonplace. In W. Irwin (Ed.), *Seinfeld and philosophy: [A book about everything and nothing]* (p. 115). Chicago/La Salle, IL: Open Court.

36. Many varieties of contemporary micro-sociology (ethnomethodology, existential sociology, symbolic interactionism, and so on) are concerned with just this domain.

37. Blumer, H. (1954/1969). What is wrong with social theory? In H. Blumer (Ed.), *Symbolic interaction perspective and method* (p. 141). Englewood Cliffs, NJ: Prentice Hall.

38. Ritzer, G. (1999). *Enchanting a disenchanted world: Revolutionizing the means of consumption.* Thousand Oaks, CA: Pine Forge Press.

39. Bauman, Z. (1992). *Intimations of postmodernity.* London: Routledge.

40. Baudrillard, J. (1990/1993). *The transparency of evil: Essays on extreme phenomena.* London: Verso.

41. Of course, the postmodernists, as well as has many others, reject the whole idea of a value-free science.

42. Krakauer, J. (1997). *Into thin air*. New York: Anchor.

43. Retrieved from http://news.bbc.co.uk/2/hi/south_asia/2766087.stm

44. Habermas, J. (1987). *The philosophical discourse of modernity: Twelve lectures*. Cambridge: MIT Press.

45. Ritzer, G. (1997). *Postmodern social theory*. New York: McGraw-Hill.

46. Foucault, M. (1975/1979). *Discipline and punish: The birth of the prison*. New York: Vintage.

47. Lilla, M. (1994). The legitimacy of the Liberal Age. In M. Lilla (Ed.), *New French thought: Political philosophy* (p. 20). Princeton, NJ: Princeton University Press.

48. Lilla, M. (1994). The legitimacy of the Liberal Age. In M. Lilla (Ed.), *New French thought: Political philosophy* (p. 16). Princeton, NJ: Princeton University Press.

49. Seidman, S., & Alexander, J. C. (Eds.). (2001). *The new social theory reader*. London: Routledge.

50. Another is what Seidman and Alexander call the "downward shift." This work, which shies away from grand abstractions and concentrates on concrete examples—primarily from the realm of consumption—is an example of such a shift.

51. Seidman, S., & Alexander, J. (2001). Introduction. In S. Seidman & J. C. Alexander (Eds.), *The new social theory reader* (p. 3). London: Routledge.

52. Rawls, J. (1999). *A theory of justice* (Rev. ed.). Cambridge, MA: Belknap.

53. Walzer, M. (1983). *Spheres of justice: A defense of pluralism and equality*. New York: Basic Books.

54. McIntyre, A. (1988). *Whose justice? Which rationality?* Notre Dame, IN: Notre Dame University Press.

55. Seidman, S., & Alexander, J. (2001). Introduction. In S. Seidman & J. C. Alexander (Eds.), *The new social theory reader* (p. 3). London: Routledge.

56. Logically, there is another possibility: People do not concern themselves in any way with something–nothing.

57. This means that you are expected to pay your bill in full each month; these companies do not extend credit and earn their money mainly from annual fees to consumers and higher charges to sellers.

58. See, for example, Miller, D. (2001). The poverty of morality. *Journal of Consumer Culture, 1*, pp. 225–243.

Index

About the Author

George Ritzer is Distinguished University Professor at the University of Maryland, where he has also been a Distinguished Scholar-Teacher and won a Teaching Excellence Award. He has also won a Distinguished Contributions to Teaching Award from the American Sociological Association. Among his many books from Pine Forge Press are *The McDonaldization of Society* (2000, new edition forthcoming) and *McDonaldization: The Reader* (2002).